The Civil War Memoirs of a Virginia Cavalryman

The Civil War Memoirs of a Virginia Cavalryman

Lt. Robert T. Hubard, Jr.

EDITED BY THOMAS P. NANZIG

THE UNIVERSITY OF ALABAMA PRESS
Tuscaloosa

The University of Alabama Press
Tuscaloosa, Alabama 35487-0380
uapress.ua.edu

Hardcover edition published 2007.
Paperback edition published 2016.
eBook edition published 2010.

Inquiries about reproducing material from this work should be addressed to the University of Alabama Press.

Typeface: Minion

Manufactured in the United States of America
Cover image: *The Rebel Raid into Pennsylvania—Stuart's Cavalry on their Way to the Potomac*, sketched near Poolesville, Maryland, by Mr. A. R. Waud; from *Harper's Weekly*, November 1, 1862
Cover design: Erin Kirk New

∞

The paper on which this book is printed meets the minimum requirements of American National Standard for Information Science–Permanence of Paper for Printed Library Materials, ANSI Z39.48-1984.

Paperback ISBN: 978-0-8173-5878-5
eBook ISBN: 978-0-8173-8198-1

A previous edition of this book has been catalogued by the Library of Congress as follows:
Library of Congress Cataloging-in-Publication Data
Hubard, Robert Thruston, 1839–1921.
The Civil War memoirs of a Virginia cavalryman : Lt. Robert T. Hubard, Jr. / edited by Thomas P. Nanzig.
p. cm.
Includes bibliographical references and index.
ISBN-13: 978-0-8173-1530-6 (cloth : alk. paper)
ISBN-10: 0-8173-1530-6
1. Hubard, Robert Thruston, 1839–1921. 2. Confederate States of America. Army. Virginia Cavalry Regiment, 3rd. 3. United States—History—Civil War, 1861–1865—Cavalry operations. 4. Virginia—History—Civil War, 1861–1865—Personal narratives. 5. United States—History—Civil War, 1861–1865—Personal narratives, Confederate. 6. Virginia—History—Civil War, 1861–1865—Regimental histories. 7. United States—History—Civil War, 1861–1865—Regimental histories. 8. Soldiers—Virginia—Biography. I. Nanzig, Thomas P.   II. Title.
E581.63rd .H83 2006
973.7′455092—dc22
[B]
2006014147

In memory of John E. Divine,
historian, author, teacher, friend

Spur on! spur on! We love the flashing
Of blades that struggle to be free,
'Tis for our sunny South they're clashing;
For Household, God and Liberty.
                    —William W. Blackford, CSA, "The Cavalier's Glee"

Contents

Illustrations

Maps

Preface

[Robert is] a very gallant fellow and a young man of superior parts. I wish very much that he could get into some favorable position—some place where he could make his mark. He says that placing implicit trust in a "Merciful God" he is determined to do boldly and manfully whatever falls his lot. This sounds like the true metal, and I know full well I am not deceived.

—William B. Hubard to James L. Hubard, 1 August 1861

Such was the description penned by one brother of another during the American Civil War. Like so many other young Virginians of the era, Robert Thruston Hubard, Jr., was bound to do his duty as he understood the priorities of ancestors: God, family, state, and nation. But adherence to his religious beliefs, his kin, and his Commonwealth of Virginia left no room in Hubard for duty to the Federal government of 1861. As a trooper in a Virginia cavalry regiment, Hubard supported the sovereignty of his state and the dream of a Southern confederacy. Penned in 1865–1866, Hubard's war memoir traces the adventures of this young, well-educated, idealistic Virginian through four years of service as a cavalryman in General J. E. B. Stuart's command.

Robert Hubard was not born to the rugged life of a warrior. His early years were marked by privilege and paternalism. He was born on 9 March 1839, at Rosny, a Hubard plantation in Buckingham County, Virginia, and the roots of his family tree were anchored deep in Virginia's past. His father's family traced their Virginia ancestry through George Washington's Continental army and to the early years of the colony. His mother, Susan Pocahontas Bolling, went the Hubard claim one better as a seventh-generation descendant of John Rolfe and the Algonquian "princess," Pocahontas.[1]

Moreover, Hubard was born into one of the commonwealth's most successful nineteenth-century planter families. After marrying in 1834, Robert T. Hubard, Sr., and Susan Bolling raised six sons (James, William, Robert, Jr., Edmund, Francis, and Bolling) and one daughter (Louisa) at the Rosny plantation. Susan delivered their eighth child, Philip, in Oc-

tober 1849, but she died within several weeks of his birth, on 17 November 1849. Robert, Sr., thrust into the role of widower-father to eight children under the age of fifteen years, remained at Rosny until 1853, when
he moved his family to Chellowe, a property in his wife's family that he
had purchased in 1842.

From Chellowe Robert, Sr., manipulated his agricultural pursuits and
financial accounts so adeptly that his annual gross income in the 1850s
was more than $20,000. According to the 1860 census records and plan-
tation account books, the Hubard estates were valued at more than
$300,000. Altogether, Robert Hubard owned two farms in Buckingham
County, Rosny and Chellowe, as well as three parcels of farmland in Nelson County, 180 slaves at the several plantations, and numerous investments in railroad, city, and bank stocks and bonds. According to one historian, "In 1860, Robert T. Hubard, Sr., had achieved a degree of success
uncommon among Virginia planters of that period: he was financially
solvent."[2]

As well as tending to his agricultural and financial interests, Hubard saw to it that each of his children received appropriate educational
and vocational opportunities. James and William were sent to colleges
as they came of age, and then they returned to Buckingham County
to pursue lives as planters. Robert, Jr., was tutored through his early
years and then sent with younger brother Edmund to attend Episcopal
High School in Alexandria in 1855. Robert finished his college prepara-
tory courses at the Brookland School near Waynesboro in 1857 and then
earned a degree at Hampden-Sydney College in nearby Prince Edward
County, where he delivered the class valedictory address in 1859. Returning home for the summer, he tutored his younger siblings until enrolling
at the University of Virginia law school in the autumn of 1860. Hubard
had all but completed his first year of law studies in April 1861, when the
crisis at Fort Sumter erupted into war.

Robert Hubard's memoir begins with his final days of law school in
Charlottesville. His departure from the university immediately after the
outbreak of hostilities found him accompanying his father to Richmond
to view the Virginia secession convention. Within days, father and son
returned home to Buckingham County, from which place Robert, Jr.,
left in May 1861 for neighboring Cumberland County to enlist in that
county's mounted militia unit, the Light Dragoons. The Cumberland
detachment was destined to become Company G, 3rd Virginia Cavalry.

Although he was eventually called on to serve as the regimental adjutant, Robert Hubard's war service was as rugged as that of any trooper. He fought in his full share of battles, narrowly escaped capture on several occasions, and suffered several of the illnesses and infirmities so prevalent among cavalry troopers of the Civil War. Untouched until the last week of the war, Hubard was spared the pain of surrender at Appomattox Court House only because he was struck down by a bullet at the Battle of Five Forks on 1 April 1865.

Hubard's memoir is straightforward narrative with occasional re-created lines of dialogue. Although it is doubtful that Hubard was able to retain his regimental papers after being assisted from the Five Forks battlefield, he probably used the letters he sent home from the field as his primary source material. He was also able to call on his recollections as the regimental adjutant in order to weave a remarkable four-year tapestry of Fitz Lee's Virginia Cavalry Brigade and its campaign history.

Concentrating primarily on the actions of his own unit, Robert Hubard recorded observations regarding locations, numbers of troops engaged, and subsequent casualties that were, more often than not, very close to the mark. Moreover, Robert Hubard's memoir serves as a window into the world of a young man with dreams, romances, and military aspirations.

His view of military life and its attendant glories was swiftly brought to heel by a long, hot ride to Richmond and subsequent hours on a dusty drill field. Hubard's unit was sent from Richmond to Yorktown for additional training under a young but rising Confederate officer, Major John Bell Hood. Service near Yorktown in the summer of 1861 found Hubard standing dreary hours at picket posts. Although trained by West Point graduates Hood and Colonel Robert Johnston at Yorktown, Hubard experienced a war that was more hit-and-run warfare than the noble combat he had envisioned. Occasional forays from Yorktown toward Fort Monroe and less-frequent ambush-style skirmishes marked Hubard's term of service on the Peninsula. Indeed, the men in the unit did not engage in any significant cavalry action until more than a year after their enlistment.

After the 3rd Virginia Cavalry was added to General J. E. B. (Jeb) Stuart's command in May 1862, Hubard saw plenty of combat and the losses attendant to hard campaigning. But unique to this memoir is that he also bore witness to a gradual decay from within the ranks of his Confederate comrades. According to Hubard, the election of officers in April 1862 "was a disgraceful piece of demagogism that . . . did more than all other things combined to bring about our final defeat. Not only did the men as a general rule select in preference the most amiable men who would indulge them most . . . but ever after during the war officers feared another re-organization and never dared enforce discipline." As a result of this lack of discipline, Hubard later observed that "men would purposely neglect their horses to break them down and get these [remount] details so that the indifferent soldiers and worthless men, for they were synonymous, were nearly always home or on the road and the good men had all the fighting to do and all the hard drudgery of military life. Yet this would be the case anyway where the *discipline* could not be enforced as was the case with the Confederate soldiers." Clearly, what Robert Hubard saw in his four years made a signal impression on a young man who had gone to fight a patriot's war, only to find that not everyone served with the same patriotic zeal.

His view of the home front as documented in his surviving war letters shows an active antebellum social life, including the natural concerns of a young man bent on winning a young lady as his life mate. Robert's wartime efforts at long-distance romance, however, were destined for disappointment, but not without young Hubard resolving to learn from his bittersweet experiences. Corresponding with his sister-in-law after a dispiriting romantic rebuff, Hubard took the patriotic high ground as he dealt with his disappointment: "This is no time for a man to indulge in personal griefs. I shall, therefore, strive to forget myself in the great struggle and devote my whole time and thoughts to the duties I owe the country. After the war I cannot believe I will be regarded so stupid or worthless as to be unable to find someone worthy of one who will be willing to love and accept my hand."

Romances not excepted, most strongly felt was Robert Hubard's desire to rise to a position of company-level leadership. Although he achieved a modicum of success in being appointed to a lieutenancy as the regimental adjutant, it is clear that Robert Hubard had aspired to greater rank and responsibility. Older brother James, a Virginia Military Institute graduate (1855) and an antebellum militia colonel, was appointed lieutenant colonel of the 44th Virginia Infantry at the outbreak of war. What better role model could there be for Robert? In point of fact, it was

Robert, not James, who turned out to be the natural warrior. James was voted out of office in the May 1862 reorganization of the Confederate armies. After being appointed a major in the cavalry six months later, James resigned, allegedly for health reasons. He finished the war as a drafted private in the 4th Virginia Cavalry. According to a documentary study of the Hubard family, "James' inability to adjust to military life might well have resulted from the knowledge that he could never live up to the high standards of personal and public conduct which his father set for him. His brother Robert came closer to fitting the particular idealized image of a gentleman soldier his father created."[3]

But Robert's desire to exercise his leadership talents was, for the most part, a bittersweet experience. His early letters and subsequent reflections reveal the disappointment he felt in being passed over in several regimental elections. Citing the "electioneering" of one successful candidate and asserting that another competitor "used arguments and persuasions which I scorned to use against him," Hubard found the world of regimental politics less gentlemanly than the style to which he had undoubtedly become accustomed at his father's knee. In one 1863 missive to his father, young Robert observed, "You seem, as usual, inclined rather to discourage any attempt on my part to obtain promotion. In all kindness and reverence, I would like to ask if it had not occurred to you that your sons are too little inclined naturally to rely on themselves and push themselves, and do we not need a spur to encourage our ambition rather than a bit to curb it." It appears that Robert was raised according to the old Virginia ways; a gentleman waited to be recognized as a leader and was then rewarded with appropriate responsibility and rank. A gentleman did not crassly promote himself or bargain for votes. General Robert E. Lee expressed this traditional sentiment in a letter regarding another cavalryman's disappointment: "All personal feelings and aspirations should be subordinated to the great end of rendering all the service in every man's power to the common cause. The man who is actuated by this principle will, I think, find in the end, ample compensation for any disappointment of his personal wishes and aspirations, in the consciousness of duty faithfully performed, and it will generally happen that it is the most certain road to honorable advancement."[4]

As he became more familiar with the democratic ways of his new military world, Hubard adapted to it. His sister-in-law Isaetta Randolph Hubard, with whom he carried on an active correspondence throughout the war, was a niece of George Wythe Randolph, Confederate secretary of war. He also corresponded regularly with his uncle, Edmund W. Hubard, who, at fifty-five years of age, was a respected veteran of the 1840s Virginia congressional delegation. Too old to serve and with sons too young to enlist, Edmund exhibited much interest in the martial welfare of his Hubard nephews.[5] On several occasions the nephews called on him for advice and intercession with Confederate bureaucrats. As Robert learned more about the worlds of the military and politics, he went so far as to write a letter of petition to Confederate senator Robert M. T. Hunter in December 1864. Hubard asked for equal treatment of adjutants on the promotion ladder. Although his logic was sound on the issue, the end of the war four months later effectively ended debate over his dreams of martial advancement.

Hubard's recollections also serve to document the life of his regiment. Although there has been a great deal written about Stuart's cavalry, including published diaries, memoirs, biographies, war narratives, and unit histories, the spotlight has tended to shine more brightly on some regiments than on others. Among those units that served from first to last but with little documentation until recent years was the 3rd Virginia Cavalry. Raised on the Peninsula and in several Southside counties, the 3rd Virginia spent its first year patrolling the trails and thickets between Williamsburg and Fort Monroe in companies and squadrons. Rarely did the entire regiment ride together during their peninsular service. As well, the unit lacked the charismatic leadership of a Jeb Stuart, the name recognition of Robert E. Lee's nephew, Fitz Lee, or the prestige of the wealthy South Carolina planter Wade Hampton. Not until the regimental elections of April 1862 and the coincidental arrival at Yorktown of Stuart's cavalry brigade did the 3rd Virginia begin to show potential as a combat unit.

Under Stuart's command and placed in Fitz Lee's all-Virginia Brigade, the 3rd Virginia initially took only a limited part in the cavalry division's campaigns. Neither Stuart nor Lee knew much about the 3rd Virginia, so they acted cautiously in their use of the regiment. The only 3rd Virginia representatives on Stuart's first "Ride around McClellan" in June 1862 were two New Kent County troopers who served as guides. During the Seven Days' campaign (25 June–1 July 1862), the regiment saw little action, serving primarily as cavalry reserve.

Following the Seven Days' campaign, Stuart's entire cavalry division was sent to Hanover County for routine duty and additional training. Here the 3rd Virginia finally became an integral part of Fitz Lee's brigade, which already numbered the 1st, 4th, 5th, and 9th Virginia regiments in its ranks. A raid on a Federal wagon train near Fredericksburg on 4 August 1862 gave the 3rd Virginia its first real chance to shine. Splitting the Federal supply column in two, the 3rd Virginia pursued fleeing teamsters in two directions and claimed a dozen wagons and seventy prisoners. Service in the Sharpsburg (Antietam) campaign in September cost the regiment in officer casualties as well as in troopers but gave the men a sense of what campaigning under Stuart's and Lee's leadership meant.

The 3rd Virginia Cavalry participated in the actions that followed the return of the Confederate army to Virginia soil. They rode in the Chambersburg raid of October 1862 and then in a series of sharp clashes near Mountsville and Upperville and finally screened General Thomas J. "Stonewall" Jackson's right flank at Fredericksburg in December 1862.

Winter found the infantry and artillery in permanent camps but not so Stuart's cavalry. Riding a raid under Fitz Lee's command, the 3rd Virginia saw service in the snowy Hartwood Church affair of February 1863 and suffered its heaviest losses of the war in turning back the Federal raid at Kelly's Ford on 17 March 1863.

The Chancellorsville, Gettysburg, and Bristoe Station campaigns of 1863 tested the endurance of the men as much as it tested their martial skills. But for brief interludes of hard fighting at Todd's Tavern (Chancellorsville) in May and Aldie in June and several running fights with Federal cavalry in October, long days and longer nights spent in the saddle were as hard on the troopers as was the combat. At the end of the year and following a brief expedition into West Virginia, Stuart allowed many of his regiments, the 3rd Virginia among them, to disband temporarily in order to find forage for their horses.

Springtime saw General Ulysses S. Grant's 1864 Overland campaign begin with savage, dismounted cavalry fighting in the Wilderness and at Spotsylvania Court House. Battles and skirmishes followed one after the other: Chilesburg, Beaver Dam Station, Mitchell's Shop, and Yellow Tavern. The loss of Jeb Stuart to a mortal wound at Yellow Tavern notwithstanding, the cavalry war continued unabated at Meadow Bridge, Fort Kennon, Haw's Shop, Cold Harbor, Trevilian Station, Samaria Church, and Reams' Station.

The Federal siege of Petersburg limited the role of the cavalry corps to such an extent that General Robert E. Lee sent much of his mounted force, including the 3rd Virginia, to the Shenandoah Valley in September 1864 to supplement General Jubal A. Early's Army of the Valley. Riding under the cavalry guidons of Generals Fitz Lee and Thomas L. Rosser, the 3rd Virginia endured a checkered campaign of minor victories at Weyer's Cave, Waynesboro, Edinburg, and Mt. Jackson, only to be offset by bitter defeats at Front Royal, Tom's Brook, and Cedar Creek. The end of the campaign in the Shenandoah Valley found the 3rd Virginians exhausted. An ill-advised December raid into West Virginia all but finished the effectiveness of the regiment. Many of the regiment's horses were shoeless, and all the men were starving. One veteran believed the unit was capable of rebellion because rations and supplies were in such short supply.[6]

Midway through February 1865, the regiment was moved to Richmond, where conditions for men and beasts improved markedly. The 3rd Virginia watched the James River west of Richmond during March as Federal general Philip H. Sheridan hovered with his cavalry divisions near Charlottesville. As Sheridan descended the James to join the Army of the Potomac near Petersburg, the 3rd Virginia scouted the Federal columns and sent reports to the Confederate high command. With the opening of the spring campaign in late March, the 3rd Virginia was sent with Fitz Lee's cavalry corps to Dinwiddie County to assist General George E. Pickett's infantry force. At Dinwiddie Court House on 31 March and Five Forks on 1 April, the Confederates severely tested the Federal forces but were eventually defeated by Sheridan's troops. The fall of the Confederate position at Five Forks led to the evacuation of both Petersburg and Richmond on 2 April 1865.

Accompanying General Robert E. Lee's retreating forces were the diminishing ranks of the 3rd Virginia Cavalry. Although part of the regiment was from the James River Peninsula, more than half of the men hailed from counties on or near the route of the retreat. Records do not indicate how many 3rd Virginians fell out of ranks and returned to their homes in those last hours, but the temptation to do so must have been great. As Federal horsemen soon realized, however, the Southern cavalry was still a potent force. They fought several holding actions along the route to Appomattox Court House, and they defeated and captured several Federal infantry and cavalry units, including some at Painesville on 5 April, High Bridge on 6 April, and Farmville on 7 April.

At Appomattox Court House on the morning of 9 April, the Confederate cavalry corps broke through the encircling Federal troops and rode westward to Lynchburg. Thus the few remaining troopers of the 3rd Virginia escaped the surrender of Robert E. Lee's Army of Northern Virginia. A few of the horsemen rode south to join Joseph E. Johnston's Confederate army in North Carolina, only to surrender to William T. Sherman on 26 April. As for the rest, they turned their mounts toward their homes, tired of war but confident they had done their duty for Virginia and the Confederacy.

Douglas S. Freeman, in his prefatory assessment of another Virginia cavalryman, wrote, "He will be read and respected as a citizen-soldier of honest mind, exceptional intelligence and just judgment, a 'gentleman unafraid.'"[7] The same may be said of Robert Hubard, to whom all credit is due for this remembrance of war, as fine a documentary record of the 3rd Virginia Cavalry as the troopers of the old regiment could have envisioned.

Acknowledgments

The first time I threaded a filmed copy of Robert Hubard's handwritten manuscript onto a library microfilm reader, I realized that this young Virginian's memoirs were very special. Hubard's colorful and engaging descriptions of his war years in the 3rd Virginia Cavalry, a unit very familiar to me from earlier regimental research, were both enlightening and entertaining.

My wife, Barbara, who had already endured two similar projects, was as excited as I was to ride once again with the 3rd Virginia Cavalry. She shared in all of the travel and in much of the research necessary to bring this delightful project to a successful conclusion. In addition, she was my comfort and strength whenever I stumbled or grew faint in pursuit of Hubard's story. I could not have finished this book without her love and support.

If I could not have finished this book without Barbara's support, I know I could not have begun without the able assistance of my nephew and proud University of Virginia alumnus, Ryan Rosebush. With little more to go on than a brief telephone description of the Hubard papers, Ryan wasted little time in visiting the Alderman Library Special Collections Department and representing my interests in the Hubard papers to the staff. He did more than simply gather information, however. Ryan, with his ready smile and quick wit, created a positive foundation on which I was able to build a productive long-distance relationship with the Special Collections staff.

William Stebbins Hubard of Roanoke, Virginia, made available to me a virtual treasure chest of Hubard genealogical information that I could not have found as quickly or as accurately. Curiously, we found in our first telephone conversation that we are fellow alums of the College of William and Mary and that he was born and raised in the Thornton house, a historic Farmville, Virginia, home directly across the street from the Longwood College administrative offices that I occupied in the 1980s.

Margery (Gerry) Crowther of Palmyra, Virginia, was both gracious and generous in her willingness to share her love of Hubard history with us. Gerry's late husband, John Bell Henneman, Jr., was a descendant of Marion Hubard, eldest daughter of Robert and Sallie Hubard. Gerry welcomed Barbara and me into her home during a research visit to Virginia and then guided us on a tour of Chellowe, the Hubard family cemetery, and Indian Gap, a Hubard-Henneman property adjacent to Chellowe.

This work was made more complete by the outstanding maps of the battles and raids in which Robert Hubard and the 3rd Virginia Cavalry participated. All credit for these maps goes to Fred Olsen, an exceptional graphic artist, friend, and neighbor in Ann Arbor.

To my mother-in-law, Kay Sturm, my continuing thanks for supporting my Civil War habit through her generous contributions to my library. The notes to this memoir are much the clearer as a result of receiving many valuable reference volumes since beginning this project.

In addition, my sincere thanks to the following individuals and institutions who made gathering material for this project such a pleasure: the librarians and staff of the Alderman Library, University of Virginia, especially Regina Rush of the Special Collections Department; Millie Atkins at UMI-ProQuest (Ann Arbor, Michigan); David Feinberg at the Library of Virginia; the late Richard Couture at Longwood College (Farmville, Virginia); Jilla Biza, librarian, and Lance Burghardt, photographer, at St. Joseph Mercy Hospital (Ann Arbor, Michigan); Pat Golden at the Williamsburg (Virginia) Regional Library; Chris Calkins (Petersburg National Battlefield Park, Virginia); Don Pfanz (Fredericksburg National Military Park, Virginia); Ed Longacre (Newport News, Virginia); Bob Trout (Myersville, Pennsylvania); Eric Wittenberg (Columbus, Ohio); Ned Armstrong, Betty Austin, and John and Marion Davis (Colonial Heights, Virginia); Lucy and Nabil Dubraque (Manassas, Virginia); Kenneth Fisher (Del Rio, Texas); Tina Holt (Midlothian, Virginia); Amelia Hough (Sumter, South Carolina); Bert Murch and Pam

Newhouse (Ann Arbor, Michigan); and Douglas Powell (Halifax, Virginia).

The staff of the University of Alabama Press made the design, production, and publication of this book a real pleasure. On a more personal note, copyeditor Kathy Swain was a delight as she reviewed my manuscript. Her intense scrutiny, her gentle corrections, and her good humor throughout the review process were very, very much appreciated.

Finally, my thanks to Harold Howard, who encouraged my interest in the 3rd Virginia Cavalry when he invited me to write the unit's history for his splendid Virginia Regimental History Series. His trust, patience, and support have not been forgotten.

Editor's Note

The ledger book into which Robert T. Hubard, Jr., entered his Civil War experiences contained somewhat more text than appears in this edited account. Hubard was interested not only in relating his own service actions and those of his regiment but also in documenting other military campaigns that affected the course of the war. Although Hubard's accounts of such campaigns as Vicksburg, Chickamauga, and Chattanooga are accurate, for example, they were, at best, secondhand reiterations of immediate postwar histories and, at worst, simple recitations of newspaper accounts. Moreover, they do not lend any information of interest to his own first-person account of the war in Virginia or shed any new light on the campaigns he mentions. Consequently, I have chosen to delete those passages in this edition.

Although most of Bob Hubard's campaign and battlefield reminiscences are eyewitness accounts of his own experiences, he is careful to note those campaigns in which he did not participate due to illness. Understandably, he has attempted to fill these voids with facts that were probably provided by his comrades as well as by accounts written in his commanders' battle reports on his return to duty.

A few paragraphs containing background information on Hubard's regimental officers and cavalry commanders have been relocated within the text for the sake of clarity.

Capitalizations, sentences, and paragraphs were somewhat irregularly determined in Civil War–era compositions, even among college graduates such as Hubard. Corrections have been made for the sake of clarity in the case of improper capitalizations. Lengthy sentences and paragraphs have been modified by creating multiple sentences and paragraphs wherever a distinct division of thought occurs.

Hubard's spelling was, for the most part, correct, with occasional interesting British usages such as "ardour," "sabre," and "defence." In order to retain a bit of the flavor for the document as Hubard wrote it, misspellings of easily recognized words (for example, "gayly" for "gaily") and some proper names (for example, "Custar" for Custer) have been left uncorrected. Note, too, that throughout his memoir, Hubard refers to his home as "Chellow" even though descendants, locals, the current owners, and most publications spell it "Chellowe."

Brackets have been used throughout the document to clarify names and phrases and to insert omitted or corrected dates.

Several of the officers' portraits (Hood, Phillips, and McClellan) are of men who rose to higher rank with other units later in the war. All three have been listed at the highest ranks that were reached by each man during his term of service with the 3rd Virginia Cavalry. In addition, General Roger A. Pryor, who rose to the rank of general early in the war, lost his brigade due to political-military issues. He subsequently joined the 3rd Virginia Cavalry, Company E, as a private but carried his general officer's title out of military tradition and courtesy.

Introduction

The following record of events, so far as they were connected with the personal experiences of the writer, does not claim completeness (even as to that experience) for, begun (as it is) on the 21st of July 1865, much that is now forgotten is necessarily omitted, and there are doubtless some inaccuracies as to dates, etc. But in reference to direct operations and positive historical statements there will be, it is confidently believed, few grounds for doubt in the mind of any one who may hereafter read this record. Certain it is that the aim and conscientious desire of the writer is to present a simple and truthful narrative of facts, which shall display "malice toward none, charity toward all" (Lincoln's last message).

No one single cause can satisfactorily account for the most determined, costly, exhaustive, and desolating war of modern times. It is conceded on all sides that of the three million of men called into the field by the Federal government at least five hundred thousand perished whilst the South, which had altogether perhaps one million of troops must have lost 250,000 at least by death. The war cost the Federal government about three billion dollars and the South about two billion dollars,[1] one million of horses and mules in the Federal service and probably three hundred thousand by the South whilst the devastation of the Southern States by the invading armies is almost without parallel. General Sheridan, U.S.A., destroyed in a single campaign (September 1864) in the Valley of Virginia four hundred mills and two thousand large barns containing an immense supply of flour and wheat.[2]

Every speaker and every writer both north and south of "Mason's and Dixon's Line" has his own theory of the war! Excuse me, then, generous reader, if I have mine also, and ask you to give it your consideration. It is this—there were a number of secondary or incidental causes of the War, all depending upon and springing out of one great fundamental, first cause—a cause inherent in the Constitution of the United States—which grew with the growth and strengthened with the strength of the government to which the government gave birth.

A zealous republicanism combined with speculative visions of universal liberty and equality produced that strange anomaly in the science of government—a complex sovereignty (if I may so speak). The United States government certainly enjoys most of those supreme rights which are usually regarded as the attributes of sovereignty. Yet it is equally certain that the original thirteen States retained each of them to itself many of the necessary attributes of Sovereignty—among them the control of the question of citizenship and power over the lives of their citizens, under the laws of treason.

This unfortunate cause of a diversity of opinions soon began to produce its effects. Formidable opposing parties were formed, one claiming "liberal construction" of the Constitution whereby the Sovereignty of the States would appear to have been merged in that of the General Government which would be consequently sovereign to all intents and purposes. The other a "strict construction" of the instrument, whereby the sovereignty of the States would be unimpaired and the General Government be regarded as "a mere agent of the States" with powers "limited and defined."

Slavery early being abolished in the New England and Middle States, they having become in a great measure manufacturing and commercial, first the former and afterwards the latter, were prompted by inclination and interest alike, to prefer "a strong central government." Adopting "Abolition of Slavery" as the war-cry of the Consolidation party in order to win over the ignorant and fanatical masses and to conceal from the people their design of violating the Constitution and reducing the States to the condition of provinces whilst the power of the Federal government should become absolute, its authority supreme. This party eventually succeeded, not only in New England and the Middle States, but also in Western States, whose interests were in almost direct conflict with the former, and whose people, had they been enlightened and free from fanaticism about slavery, would have been the allies and earnest supporters of the Slave States.

As the encroachment of the Federal government would not operate any immediate and apparent injury to the people of the free States, they submitted to them almost without resistance. For, whilst the States'-rights party of those states battled manfully for its existence, it became weaker and weaker, until it was overthrown and driven from places of "honor and trust" in nearly every one of them.

The case was far different in the Slave States. Not only did their better knowledge of the philosophy of government teach them that the doctrine of state sovereignty was true; and that the liberty, peace, and happiness of the American people would be best promoted by its universal recognition and rigid maintenance; but the threats, menaces, and violence of the Abolition party forewarned the South that she was to be the *first victim* of the Federal usurpation; that the property of three million dollars in four million of slaves was to be destroyed completely, and further that, as far as possible, she was to be regarded, and made dependent upon the mercy of the North. Feeling that to give up State Sovereignty was to give up everything that was dear, the South resolved to maintain it "at all hazards."

The Presidential election of 1860 resulted in the triumph of "the North," and the complete supremacy of the United States government within the Union;—the defeat of "the South" and necessity for its submission within the Union, or an effort at Independence out of it. Hence, a long, protracted, often varied political conflict culminated in the horrible four years' war just closed.

Having pressed their view so far as to drive the Southern States into secession, the Republican Party could not for a moment entertain the thought of losing forever the great source of all Northern wealth and power. Anxious as they had been to make us subject to the behests of the Northern majority so that they might use, or abuse, us according to their pleasure, and apparent interest. They valued us too highly to let us go without an effort to retain us *by violence.* For compromise and conciliation were out of the question since they were resolved on *requiring*—not *requesting*—us to yield to their opinion and wishes. Having once firmly resolved to adhere to their views of consolidation and as firmly resolved not to lose the Southern States the door to conference and reconciliation was closed, and the issue—"Independence or Subjugation," was finally drawn.

It was an immense stake. The South felt that, with the loss of Liberty, it might lose everything. The North felt that with the loss of the Slave States political and financial ruin would befall them. Whilst the sober, intelligent section of the latter section realized this finally, the mad multitude, the wild, raving fanatics, the "red Republican Radicals," neither regarded, nor understood, their interests. Like infuriated beasts, they were wildly rushing headlong under the impulsion of the vilest passions, of the human *heart*; inflamed to the highest degree by the vile, false and incendiary speeches, plays and books, with which their section was flooded.

"The leaders" will understand the nature of these classes, and how to manage each. The first were appealed to, to uphold the honor of the "Old Flag," to preserve the "Union of our Fathers" to "know no North no South no East no West" but "the Union one and inseparable." The second were told there was an "irrepressible conflict between free-labor and slave labor" the states must be either "all free or all slave states." "Slavery should not be tolerated in the Land of Liberty." "Universal freedom in the Great Republic," "Equal Laws and Equal Rights," etc., were their mottoes.[3] Thus by a different kind of appeal to each separate class, a heterogeneous population was made one powerful homogeneous mass, all equally bent on making the Southern States submit unconditionally to the power of the Federal Government;—a power which was to make "the abolition of slavery" the first exercise of its usurped authority.

Even the *most liberal* constructions ever put upon the Constitution were strict as compared with President Lincoln's interpretation of that instrument. Measures which the Constitution expressly declared should *not* be adopted were by him adopted. And, for his authority, he pointed to the article conferring upon the President and Congress the "war making power" of the Country. Where he could not find even a shadow of support in this article, he pleaded "military necessity" and appealed to Congress to legalize his acts and relieve him of the *perjury* of which he himself thought he was probably guilty.

Year 1
1861

1
"Three Cheers for the Southern Flag!"

The State of Virginia, having been eminently conservative, did not at once follow the lead of the impulsive State of South Carolina; but chose rather to first exhaust every means of settling the difficulties which had arisen and restoring harmony. At the election of members to the State Convention, the Union candidates—generally representing their opponents as "unconditional secessionists" and themselves as *not adverse* to such a measure after exhausting all honorable means of restoring good feeling, succeeded in carrying a large majority of the counties.[1]

On the 12th of April, 1861, General [Pierre G. T.] Beauregard, commanding at Charleston, opened on Fort Sumter at 4 a.m.. Edmund Ruffin, Sr., of Virginia., fired the first gun.[2] On the 14th this stronghold surrendered. On the same day the President of the United States called out by proclamation the militia of "the loyal states" to the number of 75,000; and in the same proclamation, called upon all persons in arms against the United States to disperse, and return to their homes within twenty days.

Virginia could no longer remain inactive. She had to fight somebody and, choosing rather to fight the Yankees who had been making war upon the South for thirty years, than her sister slave states, between whom and herself there had always been perfect cordiality and sympathy, she passed an Ordinance of Secession from the United States on the 17th of April, 1861.[3] Immediately the whole state became a great military camp. Colonel Robert E. Lee, having resigned his commission in the U.S. Army, was appointed by the Virginia Convention General-in-Chief of the Virginia forces; and Governor John Letcher was directed to place at his disposal the entire volunteer force which had already quite an efficient company organization and now numbered ten or fifteen thousand men.

I was myself at the Virginia University studying law. The day after the President's proclamation appeared [April 16] I was early aroused by loud hollering and the desultory firing of pistols and guns. Hurriedly pulling on my clothes I rushed out and beheld, with satisfaction and delight, the Southern flag ("Stars and bars") floating from the top of the University whilst the rays of morning sun were playing beautifully upon its ample folds. The excited students stood in groups on the Lawn, waving their hats and cheering lustily. Soon Jacherie, the janitor, was seen on top of the Rotunda approaching the flag staff.

"Touch that flag," cried the students, "and your body, pierced with bullets, shall be hurled lifeless to the ground."

"Not I," said he. "You boys have been kind to me. Virginia has treated me well and I'll stand by her forever! Three cheers for the Southern flag!!"

This response touched their hearts and brought forth tremendous applause.

Soon after the Chairman of the Faculty, Dr. [Socrates] Maupin, appeared on the steps of the Rotunda and briefly addressed the students. He said, "The University of Virginia was not a political, not a sectional institution, that it was strictly and emphatically a *literary* institution; and that, having been so regarded, its session was now being attended by young men from almost every state in the Union. That on this account it was greatly to be regretted that some had allowed their enthusiasm to carry them so far and that he hoped that on further reflection, they would perceive that it would be far better to leave the whole matter of secession to the legislative bodies." He hoped that for the sake of harmony among themselves, for the sake of the reputation of the University, etc., those who hoisted the flag would go voluntarily and haul it down. After the excitement had somewhat subsided this advice was taken.[4]

The University was now wild with excitement. Studying was impossible, at least with an excitable body like me. Numbers of students were withdrawing and going home. I left Wednesday morning [April 17], met my father in Richmond, and remained there till Saturday [April 20]. Thursday [April 18], while returning from the Armory, I heard a Negro boy exclaim: "Um! Dey gwine down South to Dixie sartin"; and looking up, saw the "Confederate flag" adopted by the Confederate Congress at Montgomery waving over the Capitol of Virginia.[5]

Commissions were sent a few days after to Montgomery and the preliminary arrangements were made for the admission of Virginia into the Confederation, while the question of secession was submitted to the people for their ratification. The vote was about one hundred and twenty thousand for and about twenty thousand against the measure. The latter vote was cast almost exclusively in North West Virginia.

I had lost no time in joining the army but did so two days after reaching home, entering the "Cumberland Light Dragoons" as a private. This was a splendid troop of horse about seventy strong, of excellent material, and officers as follows: Captain Henry Johnson, 1st Lieutenant Thomas F. Willson, 2nd Lieutenant William A. Perkins, Jr., 2nd Lieutenant Benjamin W. Allen, all of Cumberland County.[6]

We drilled some few days at Cumberland Court House and tendered our services to the Governor. We had very showy uniforms, silver-mounted helmets, with long flowing [horse] hair, dark blue-cloth frock coats with two rows of silver buttons, elaborate trimmings of white cord across the breast [and] between the buttons and silver mounted epaulets on the shoulders and dark blue pants with white cord on the outside seam. We were armed with splendid sabres and Colt "Navy six-shooters." Our undress suit consisted of dark blue cap, blouse and pants of same color.

Ere long, the joyful tidings came that the Governor had ordered us to report forthwith to Colonel R[obert] H. Chilton commanding Camp of Instruction at Ashland.[7] On the 14th day of May, 1861, after several farewell speeches had been made and a formal leave taken, we commenced our march from Cumberland Court House leaving many a weeping, sorrowful, yet brave and patriotic mother and wife and sister behind us.

We were halted at Dr. Henderson's, two miles down the road, to partake of a sumptuous dinner provided by the neighborhood people, and again at Dr. Robinson's to enjoy a large tub of mint julep, kindly provided by that gentleman.

We halted for the night at Powhatan Court House where we were told that "the officers would have rooms in the hotel and the men might make themselves comfortable on the *court green*." Having over-exerted myself cleaning my horse down after a very warm ride I was suffering from an excruciating headache. And not fancying a loll on the grass so well, I, with some difficulty, procured a mean feather bed in a poorly ventilated and intensely hot garret where I slept but little and perspired a great deal.

Next morning, after feeding and getting breakfast, we set out for Richmond. Crossing the Mayo's bridge about 4 p.m., we turned to the left on a small island where a large bowl of mint julep, prepared by Thomas Deane, Esq., awaited us. Soon after, we were refreshed with a very substantial dinner at the hands of the same gentleman. At night we occupied, as barracks, a carriage house opposite Metropolitan Hall, Franklin Street.

The next evening, about sunset, we arrived at Ashland and were put in the lower floor of the pavilion attached to the race-course there. A long picket rope extended along the center of the course served for us to fasten our horses to. Our quarters were extremely filthy and we were tired and hungry. Our friends of the Amelia Troop, Captain [Samuel S.] Weisiger, invited us to sup with them.[8] But for that, we should have nothing to eat.

Next day our messes were formed, eight to a mess, and one camp kettle, one "spider [skillet or frying pan with attached legs]," and one skillet was issued to each mess. We then drew the rations for the day: one-and-an-eighth pound flour, one pound beef, one ounce coffee, two ounces sugar.

We were now regularly mustered into the service of the State of Virginia for twelve months from the 14th of May, 1861. A detail for camp guard was made, the guard mounted, and kept up in strict conformity with the U.S. Army regulations adopted by the Confederate Government.

The second day we had ascertained all the "calls of the day." The bugle was sounded regularly at the appointed hour and everything went on like clock-work: reveille at daybreak, stable call, sick call, breakfast call, guard mounting, drill call, 12 noon roll-call, orderly call, dinner call, drill call, retreat, tattoo, taps. At the last call every light had to be instantly extinguished.

Our drills were on horseback in a large field one mile from camp from 10 to 12 noon and from 3 to 5 p.m. We found this rather serious sport as the dust was suffocating, the weather being extremely dry. Frequently while exercising we could scarcely see the men immediately in our front.

Among the companies with us at Ashland were the Prince Edward, Captain J[ohn] T. Thornton; Mecklenburg, Captain T[homas] F. Goode; King and Queen, Captain Wm. H. F. Lee. The first two were in [the] regiment afterward. Colonel Chilton was appointed Assistant Adjutant General for General R. E. Lee and he was succeeded by Major Charles Field.[9]

President Davis arrived in Richmond on the 29th of May and from this day it became the capital of the Confederacy. On the tenth (10) June, Colonel J[ohn] B. Magruder was attacked at Bethel Church on the York Peninsula, by four thousand men of Major General Butler's command under Brigadier General [Ebenezer W.] Pierce. His own force consisted of the 1st North Carolina Infantry under Colonel Daniel H. Hill, afterward a distinguished lieutenant general, 15th Virginia Infantry, T[homas] P. August, a Georgia battalion of infantry, and a four-gun battery, Richmond howitzers, under Major George W. Randolph. After a severe fight of three or four hours, the enemy was repulsed with loss and returned to Fortress Monroe.[10]

At one time a flanking column under Major [Theodore] Winthrop of Massachusetts was well-nigh successful, but the major, while acting most gallantly, was shot and killed and his column repulsed. I afterwards went to the spot, a fallen log from which he fell.[11]

On the 1st day of July, the Cumberland and Mecklenburg troops started to the Peninsula under Captain Goode. On the evening of the 3rd July, we arrived at Williamsburg. Remaining there on the 4th, we marched to Yorktown on the 5th and went into camp within one hundred yards of the shaft which marks the spot where General George Washington received the sword of Lord Cornwallis.

On the 7th we marched seven miles down the Hampton Road and went into camp at the little village of Cockletown. We had no drilling now and our life seemed about to become quite monotonous. We had blankets and some clothing issued us here. We packed up our fine uniforms and sent them home from Ashland.

On the 11th, Major John B. Hood, who had been assigned to the command of the cavalry companies on the Peninsula and who afterwards became a general, called for 120 men to go on a scout to be selected by volunteering.[12] I was among the number.

We started about sunset and marched till about 11 o'clock at night and, having entered a thicket of pine wood, were ordered to dismount and sleep with bridles in our hands and not to speak out of a whisper. As we were in five miles of a strong Federal garrison, Newport's News Point, and a half-a-mile of the road, leading thence to Fort Monroe, it may well be imagined that we slept but little.

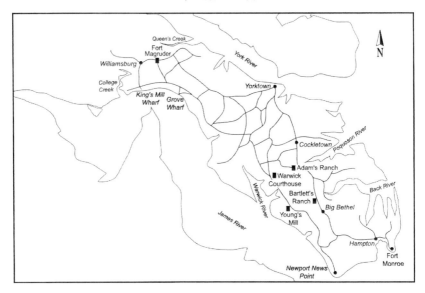

1. Southeastern Virginia Peninsula, 1862

Our party was nearly all armed with carbines and during the night a gun went off accidentally. Every man sprang to his feet at once and all thought a fight was imminent.

Next morning after daybreak we moved onward until we found that about one hundred men of the New York State Infantry had started up the road toward Bethel.[13] When we came into this road, they had already passed above us. We came up with them about 12 noon. They were in ambush awaiting our approach.

Major Hood dismounted about fifty men and charged them from their positions into the wood where the remaining seventy of us charged them on horseback, routing them completely. We killed five or six, wounded four, and brought off eleven prisoners. Our only loss was one or two horses killed and one was slightly wounded.

A few days after, we went on another scout but had no fight. Soon after we were electrified by the news of the Battle of "Bull Run" [Blackburn's Ford] on the 18th and the "Manassas" plains on the 21st July.

In the month of August we moved to Adams farm, about seven miles south of Bethel. Here our captain [Henry Johnson], who had declared in his speech at Cumberland Court House, that we would "either return as conquerors or never return atall" [sic], found his health growing so extremely delicate that he could not discharge his duties to his satisfaction, resigned and went home. 2nd Lieutenant Perkins was chosen captain by ballot. Whereupon Lieutenant Willson, feeling his honor wounded, resigned his commission. He was a dashing officer, but a man of very little capacity.

Private James D. Isbell was chosen 1st Lieutenant. I was verdant enough to allow myself to be run by one or two warm friends, but as I had not been long a member of the company and was not well known, I received only nine or ten votes out of about 50 cast. Private Charles R. Palmore was chosen Junior 1st Lieutenant, Allen having become the 2nd Lieutenant.[14]

General Magruder was fond of keeping his pickets well out, so we picketed in about eight miles of Newport's News and Fort Monroe at least twenty from Yorktown.

During August our regiment was formed. Major Hood became colonel of the 4th Texas Infantry. Lt. Robert Johnson [Johnston], U.S.A., of Richmond, was appointed our colonel.[15] The companies comprising the regiment were Old Dominion (Elizabeth City), Captain Jefferson Phillips; New Kent, Captain T[elemachus] Taylor; Charles City, Captain Robert Douthat; Dinwiddie, Captain [William A.] Adams; Mecklenburg, Captain [Thomas F.] Goode; 1st Halifax, Captain [Thomas H.] Owen; 2nd Halifax, Captain William Collins; Nottaway, Captain John Jones; Prince Edward, Captain John T. Thornton; and Cumberland, Captain Perkins.[16] In the order in which they *now stand,* they were afterwards designated by the letters "B," "F," "D," "I," "A," "C," "H," "E," "K," "G," respectively.

I believe that I omitted to state that Captain Goode of Company A was made lieutenant colonel and Captain Phillips, Company B, major of our regiment. Lieutenant [William H.] Jones became captain of Company A and Lieutenant [William R.] Vaughan of Company B, both by election of the members.[17]

Our regiments were composed of ten companies. Each company had (1) captain, (1) 1st lieutenant, (1) 2nd lieutenant, (1) junior 2nd lieutenant, (1) orderly, or 1st, sergeant, (4) sergeants, and (4) corporals. Cavalry companies had 75 privates, infantry, 56, and artillery, 120. But these numbers often did not indicate the exact number as the law was not strictly complied with. Each regiment had one colonel, lieutenant-colonel, major, adjutant, quartermaster, commissary, surgeon, assistant surgeon, and chaplain. They also had, from among the enlisted men, one sergeant major, one quartermaster sergeant, one commissary sergeant, one ordnance sergeant, one color sergeant, and one hospital steward.

We got very reasonable quantities of forage most of the time. But during September we went several times three or four miles from camp and cut down green corn with our sabres for the horses. This was very warm work. Having water courses on both sides of us we got many delicacies from our homes while the country abounded in delicious sweet potatoes, oysters, crabs, and fish. We also enjoyed the salt water baths extremely.

In October we moved to Nash's farm on the line of works from Young's mill to Bethel. The country was very flat and wet. There were numbers of bogs and fens and marshes and swamps. Frogs and musquitoes abounded in great numbers and filled the air with their noise. Numbers of men had been sick with chills and some with measles. But the October frost dispelled the former.

Correspondence, 1861

Camp near Cockleton
Wednesday, Aug. 14th, 1861
My Dear Sister,[1]

Having learnt where you were only yesterday, I have not written to you hitherto but once since I saw you. I directed that letter to Richmond and suppose it never reached you.

Since I saw you we have had one little skirmish in which we killed or took prisoners thirty of thirty-three which we have at last ascertained from their confessions. I had but little share in the fight save in frightening them by the charge. I took no prisoner and had but one shot which was at long range with a carbine whose lower sight was out.[2]

Hitherto we have changed our encampment almost every week. Sometimes we have encamped around the dwellings of wealthy farmers now absent and partaken of their meats and vegetables, at others in piney old fields abounding in ticks, etc.

Once or twice a week it comes to my turn to go off on pickett duty and then I frequently have a pleasant time of it, some of the posts being very desirable. For instance, yesterday I was at a post which is in the lower part of the lawn adjoining and in the rear of the dwelling of Mr. Young. His grounds are divided by four terraces; on the first is his yard proper and his flower garden, the 2nd, 3rd, and 4th extend in order down toward the shore of the James River. They have fine turf on them and abound in shade trees. This place is twelve miles above Newport's News and commands a fine view of the James River and also of the Warwick which flows into the James just above the house. Mr. Young has two sisters-in-law, one about 20 and the other 17, both said to be pretty and gay. Wouldn't it have been nice if they had been there and helped to chase away the weary hours with their sweet society? But the very circumstance that placed me there caused their absence.

I reflected much upon the differences between the dirty, humble Private Hubard standing in that beautiful but deserted yard surrounded by the beautiful scenery of the place, feeling most keenly the want of society and the absence of those fair creatures whose figures were wont to appear in fairy beauty upon the lovely green and the same youth, such as he used to be, arrayed in costly raiment as free as the birds of the air, vain as a peacock, dancing around among the girls and paying any devotions with all the ardor of my nature; or walking leisurely along the lawn with the fair Miss Bettie; or gentle Mary Greene, whispering into her innocent and confiding ears such soft words of admiration and fond affection as young and innocent girls delight to hear; girls who anticipate with a thrill of joy the happy day when they shall find those who are worthy of their love, and proud to have it.

The two pictures were *so* different. But times are altered now; and we must not wonder nor grieve at such change of our own circumstance when we remember how the whole course of our country's high career is suddenly altered and how the tide of our affairs no longer flowing in its smooth and peaceful way, now moved to and fro so distressingly. Eating hard crackers and strong bacon, occasionally drinking muddy water, being looked down upon by conceited officers, all these may be borne as disadvantages and inconveniences; ills that at present we should rather bear than flee from. Interruption of studies and business generally, even absence from home, can be borne with an effort. But to be shut off, entirely excluded from the society of the fair sex so long, requires me to summon all my powers of endurance to bear. My life seems to be a blank. There seems to be a vast vacancy in the world I now inhabit. The birds may sing gayly, the flowers diffuse their fragrances through the air, soft breezes fan the cheek and all nature assumes her most attractive shape. These I enjoy very much, but they bring not perfect contentment. There is still a consciousness that something is wanting to perfect the beauty of the scene and sound the keynote which delights the ear. They are the lovely form and gentle voice of woman. I would give all my pay for a few hours in the society of any one of certain ladies I know. All things human have an end, so I have the consolation of knowing that the war will not last forever and that I shall not be always a soldier.

They are making an effort at home to get up a company for one. If it succeeds, I shall have a few weeks holiday, I hope.

I have not written to "The Col." [James Hubard], your better half, yet. I did not know his post office. But I shall be always happy to hear from you and him also, either directly or from you, if he hasn't time to write. Give my love to him when you write and to Dr. and Mrs. Randolph and "Robert Randolph, Esq."[3]

I am quite well, in fine spirits and if I could only see a gay young lady this evening should be ready for a flirtation.

With kindest wishes for your wellfare, I am your affectionate brother,

Robert T. Hubard, Jr.

⁓

Camp Phillips, near Yorktown
Sunday, September 29th, '61
My Dear Brother [James],

I was sorry to learn by a letter from home received last night that you, after having been subjected to a plurality of evils in the way of sickness are now sick with jaundice at Dr. Randolph's. I fear you have been imprudent in eating and drinking and exposing yourself. It is true I have not had to make any forced marches as you have done, yet I have often been subjected to many hardships such as sleeping out on the ground, cold rainy nights, and in an open field holding my horse by the bridle, etc. Still, I have never been sick a day. In this great region for agues and for jaundice while many of our men have had them, I have been perfectly well. I have the life of a private to lead, you the more comfortable one of a Lt. Col., yet your health is bad and mine is good. I think the reason I have escaped is my great particularity with myself. I am very sorry your health is so indifferent at present. I hope that when you get well, though, you may, by prudence, continue in good health without further sickness. That carefulness will preserve your health, I have no doubt.

I was feeling great anxiety about you and I had heard your regiment had gone to join Floyd who is expected to have a fight with the odds against him.[4] While I feel no concern about going into a battle myself, I must confess I feel uneasy at the idea of your going into one though I should trust in God's mercy to shield you from danger. And certain it is that those whom he determines to protect will not be hurt though five hundred men should shoot at one man. It is a refreshing and delightful thought, that his ministering angels are present on every field to watch over and preserve those whom he wills to save while others around them fall riddled with balls. I hope it may be his good pleasure to restore peace speedily and conduct us both safely to Chellow again.

I have written two letters to sister Isa. and one to you at Monterey. I suppose none of them ever reached you as I have not heard of them. You seem as averse to writing as ever. I hope, however, you may have leisure to write to me now and give me some account of your adventures.

I ran for 1st Lieutenant of the troop lately but came out badly. The reason was satisfactory to me, however. It was not personal unpopularity, but the fact that being second choice of the majority of the best men in the troop and being deprived of the votes of the young and thoughtless by Elijah Grigg's running and electioneering, I got a small vote; whilst had he not run I should have gotten his votes and probably beaten Mr. Isbell who was elected. On the other hand, if Mr. Isbell had not run, I am confident I should have beaten Mr. Grigg. I think Elijah would not have been elected under any circumstances because he is not a man of sufficient intelligence and character.[5] I have never stood higher in these respects with any men than with this troop. And by two short speeches, one before the election, the other after the first ballot when I withdrew, pleased the company so much that had Allen resigned the 2nd Lieutenancy as it was expected he would do, I should have been elected almost without opposition. He had urged Willson to resign (the 1st Lt.) because Perkins was elected captain. W[illson] did so, now Allen has a private (Isbell) elected over him, gets only 7 votes himself, is dropped on 1st ballot, yet *he holds on.*

Perkins place is to be filled. There were so many candidates (and for other reasons), I did not run for it. 1st [ballot] Towles ran and got 5 votes, J. P. Woodson—10, Dr. Blanton—12, Jeffries—19, G. H. Matthews, Jr.—26.

2nd [ballot] Blanton—18, Jeffries—19, Matthews—26

3rd [ballot] Jeffries—30, Matthews—30.[6]

I think Matthews will be elected tomorrow. I see no chance now of getting any position atall, and am tolerably well contented where I am. I would, of course, prefer an office could I get it in a gentlemanly, independent way—otherwise not.

Scaling ladders are arriving in considerable numbers and I think Newport's News is to be attacked soon. We have twelve thousand men down here, five thousand on the sick and furlough lists. General Magruder makes the cavalry go out and cut down fields of corn with thin sabres. It surpasses anything since the attack on the windmill by Don Quixote. Since the arrival of four companies [of] Georgia cavalry making fifteen companies and one thousand men, our duties as pickets are not quite so onerous.[7] Yet we go out about twice in ten days owing to the hypocracy of men pretending to be sick, having sick horses, etc.

Our troop now have long, double-barrelled guns and, being better officered than heretofore, I hope will be more efficient than ever before.

Can't you make up a match between [brother] William and Miss Lelia Skipwith? I hear she is in Albemarle. She is a fine specimen of the genuine lady and I should be happy to hail her as sister.[8]

Present my kindest regards to your wife and all of Dr. Randolph's family and believe me to be a war sympathizer with you in your sickness and

Your Affectionate Brother, Robert T. Hubard, Jr.

Camp Phillips
Wednesday, October 9th, 1861
My Dear Brother,

I received quite an interesting letter from you on the day I last wrote to you, which was about a week ago. A letter from home came about the same time. All were about as well as usual there.

We are having a dull time here. It is a cloudy, rainy day and everything wears a gloomy aspect. General orders have been issued establishing a line of defense from the mouth of the Poquoson River, the west bank, a point known as Ship's Point, across to "land's end" on the west bank of the Warwick River at its mouth. Wherever this line crosses the public roads strong field works have been erected, while the other portions of the line traverse dense pine forests and impassable marshes of miles in extent. A telegraph connecting with that from Richmond to Yorktown stretches from the latter point to Ship's Point then across to Young's Mill on the Warwick road three miles east of the Court House, one of the principle of the field works. From the latter place to Harrod's Mill, another of these works on the Yorktown & Hampton road, three miles west of halfway House (put down on the state map), a road one hundred feet wide is to be cut through the woods. Major (now Lieutenant Colonel, I hear) Goode is to have four companies cavalry near land's end, Colonel Johns[t]on five companies near Young's Mill, Cobb's cavalry at Cockletown, and two companies at Bethel.[9] So we are to be dispersed soon. Our company will go with the Colonel, I hear.

My impression is that Magruder will first make this line of defense as strong as possible and then advance further by degrees. I have not a very high opinion of the General. I think he would make a fine officer of engineers but is incompetent for the command of a department. His policy is the most vacilating in the world, plainly indicating a want of decision and firmness.[10]

The 40-gun steam frigate, "Merrimac," taken at Norfolk, you remember, has been razed and its masts cut away so as to make it a bomb proof gun boat with shelving roof. It will be ready in a few weeks and it is confidently believed that with the aid of "Patrick Henry" [gunboat] it will be able to clear the James River of the blockade. I learn that two fine iron-bound steam frigates, built for our service, have run the blockade with British colors and reached Savannah and New Orleans, respectively, with arms and other munitions of war.[11] There are six or seven ordered, I believe, at high prices and it is said they will be able to break the blockade and play sad havoc with the rotten Lincoln ships.

Two deserters who came in last week brought in some news. The last said they had fifteen thousand men at their different works on the peninsula and intend making an advance soon. But we don't believe the latter part of the statement.

As soon as we reach our new encampment, which will be next week at furthest, we will commence the heavy job of building winter quarters. I hope by the first of November we will be through with the work and comfortably fixed.

At present I am enjoying life quite much. I live in very aristocratic style. I have a servant to attend to my horse, bring water and clean my shoes in the morning and a like interest in a cook who has charge of all culinary affairs.

While in camp, I spend my time reading and writing in my tent, an excellent one. I look forward to the hardships of winter, standing on picket on cold January nights in the snow and rain, etc. with no great satisfaction but I shall trust in the protection of the same power which has given me such good health and security hitherto. Once through the winter we shall have nothing to apprehend from the weather.

I entirely approve of your idea of trying to get a transfer instead of resigning your commission. For I think the latter would be injudicious unless you expect to retire from the service for the war. Once out of office you would find it difficult to get in again now.

The election for 3rd lieutenant is still going on, Matthews and Jeffries having tied. A new election was ordered. They tied again and were then dropped. Dr. Palmore, S. Booker, [Henry B.] McClellan (Perkins' teacher) ran.[12] Palmore—29, Booker—13, McClellan—7. Today the vote is between Palmore & Booker but there is so much party spirit neither will be elected, wanting a majority of the whole troop, and perhaps Colonel Johnston will have to appoint one.

I am sorry to impose so dull a letter upon you but really the times are quite dull here just now. I hope to hear of your speedy return to good health. I see your regiment were engaged in the fight in the northwest a few days since.[13]

Write whenever you can and you shall receive an answer. Give my love to your wife and the rest of Dr. Randolph's family. I have been rather unwell for several days but am nearly well now.

Your Affectionate Brother, Robert T. Hubard, Jr.

~

3rd Cavalry Camp, Nash's Farm
Thursday, November 14th, 1861
My Dear Brother,

A letter from sister Isa some weeks ago informed me of your intention to write me a long and interesting letter in a day or so. Hitherto I have been in an interesting state of expectancy on the subject. I will not wait for it longer but write to you.

As companion for Robert Page, I was detailed to go to Upper Brandon with him, he being sick, week before last. I stayed four days and improved the opportunity of cultivating my acquaintance with the Lower Brandon family.[14] I found them all very hospitable and enjoyed their society very much. Miss Belle was looking better than I ever saw her.

I returned to camp and a few days after [brother] Edmund came down. I took him about the peninsula and showed him our works of defence. He went to Yorktown with me Monday; thence to Grove Wharf and took the boat Tuesday morning.

Saturday Magruder moved about three thousand men including the cavalry and about eighty wagons to Bethel in order to gather corn beyond our lines in Back River toward Hampton. Monday M[orton] D. Blanton of our troop was acting as an advanced guard with three others near Hampton when a Yankee stepped forward and, taking Morton Blanton to be an officer, fired on him.[15] The ball took effect within two inches of the heart but passed around and came out five inches from its entrance in the back. Thinking himself mortally wounded, he leveled his carbine and was in the act of firing when a volley was discharged at him from the woods in his front. One ball struck the tube of his gun, discharging it and jarring his arm powerfully, another passed through his belt holster at his right side. He and his companions then galloped off. Some artillery was soon run down and unlimbered and fired into the woods dispersing the Yankees but it is not known whether any were killed.

Yesterday Leigh Blanton and [Thomas] French of Cumberland were on picket to protect our cavalry from surprise, the latter being in ambush near Newport's News.[16] Presently they saw about three hundred infantry and knowing that such a body of men were out and seeing white bands on their hats, rode up in front of the line and in ten steps of it and saluted the officers.[17] An Old Dominion [Company B] trooper was there acting as guide for the infantry who had been on picket with French repeatedly. They were asked, "Who are you?"

"Cumberland Troopers," was the reply.

"Troopers—Hell," said the guide, "Shoot them."

The officers commanded, "Fire," and the whole line blazed away. Our fellows were compelled to run the gauntlet of half the line, there being no other escape. One had his reins cut and shawl pierced in several places. Blanton was severely wounded, two balls passing through his right leg, one in the calf, the other in the thigh near the joint. Their escape was miraculous, the conduct of the infantry infamous. The guide and officer commanding should be shot. But nothing will be done, I suppose. What adds to the outrage, Col. [Thomas R. R.] Cobb (whose men they were), Major Bagley, and captain and private were off a little way at the time. The Colonel's clothes were riddled by the discharge, the Major killed, captain shot in the hand, and private mortally wounded.[18]

To have shot at two Yankees so close and completely in their power would have disgraced the Georgians but when our men told who they were *and were distinctly heard* and had white bands on besides, it was outrageous.

I am staying [in] camp, having lent another my horse to keep Edmund company while here. There will be no fight I expect.

There is no news further save that four thousand Yankees have landed on Eastern Shore.

In haste, Your Affectionate Brother,
Robert T. Hubard, Jr.

P.S. I am quite well. Write soon.

~

Cavalry Camp, Young's Mill
Monday, Dec. 30th, 1861
My Dear Brother,

I have desired to write to you for some time but could not learn your post office till today. By a letter from home a few days since I learn that you have gone on to join your regiment and are probably on the top of Allegheny mountains by this time. I am much gratified to find that your health is good enough to justify this return and hope with prudence and nursing it will continue good. I have not heard from Dr. Randolph's lately but I hope they are all well there, especially your excellent lady.

Elijah Grigg received a letter from his brother Ned a few days ago. It was written before you reached the regiment. In a letter some time since, he complimented you in the highest manner and said you were universally popular in the 44th [Virginia].

We went down nearly to Newport's News with General [Lafayette] McLaws, who had about 1800 men, on the 24th. The advanced guard of the troopers under command of Colonel Cummings [John B. Cumming], 20th Georgia, saw the Yankees drawn out in a few hundred yards of the fort. I, among others, had the pleasure of brandishing my sabre at them at a distance of about eight hundred yards. The subject of our movement was to prevent reinforcements going toward Hampton to operate against Colonel [John A.] Winston of the 8th Alabama who expected to attack a body of Yankees there. There was no fighting that day.

A duel in the 5th Louisiana a few days since resulted most fatally. The firing was simultaneous, both parties were shot in the groin and died in a few hours. It is the only instance I ever knew of both parties being shot in the same place at the first fire. A day or two after another duel in the same regiment resulted in the death of one party.[19]

General Magruder has signed a recommendation to Honorable J[udah] P. Benjamin to send us home this winter.[20] Lieutenant Colonel Goode and Captain J. T. Thornton were sent to Richmond as a committee. We heard yesterday that Benjamin had approved the measure and we would go in about ten days. I think there is some probability that we will go up soon though I do not regard it as certain by any means, yet.

A member of our company, a very ordinary man, has, by his sycophancy, gotten a 2nd lieutenancy in the Confederate Army on the recommendation of Colonel Johnston and Major General J. B. Magruder.[21]

We have had excellent weather in consequence of which we have suffered but little from cold. We have had some good whiskey in camp this Christmas and thereby had the pleasure of partaking of nice egg nogs several times.

There is no prospect of a general fight here soon, I think and the peninsula is barren of news. I am quite well and hope you are also. Give my best to sister Isa. Your Affectionate Brother,

Robert T. Hubard, Jr.

Year 2
1862

2
"The Rapid Decline of Martial Spirit"

On the Peninsula we had not been idle during the fall and winter. Besides a tolerably strong line of advances works from a point on the York River via Bethel to Young's mill and thence to James River, Yorktown and Gloucester Point were strongly fortified by water batteries, bastion forts, field redoubts, rifle pits, a series of bastion forts and redoubts connected by a line of breast works from Yorktown to the source of Warwick River, thence extending the western bank of that sluggish and boggy stream to Jones' mill (where Warwick Road crossed) thence to the mouth of the river at land's end and flanked by enemy works on Mulberry Island, constituted the main line of defense.

Brigadier General J. B. Magruder commanding about ten thousand infantry holding this line whilst the advanced line consisted of about one thousand infantry and five hundred cavalry and were about twelve miles in front of the main line.

The enemy had now about fifteen or twenty thousand men stationed at Fortress Monroe, Hampton, and Newport's News. Our cavalry picketed within eight miles of Hampton and Newport's News and about eight miles in front of our Bethel line. We had to go on picket about once a week, a detail of about 75 going out every day to relieve the posts, and also kept up a regular camp guard. So that he who got off with two days guard duty a week besides details to go after rations, forage, on scouts, he was deemed fortunate.

As the weather was very wet we were necessarily very uncomfortable during the winter. We had no winter quarters but we had good tents and owing to easy transportation and plenty of sawmills we had plank furnished to us to make bedsteads and floors. We learned then the art of making various sorts of wooden chimneys and these kept the tents quite dry. The most popular mode was to build these up three-sided to the arch, then run a four-corner stem and, driving stobs in the ground inside and about eight inches from the sides of the chimney, ram dry dirt into the space between, very tightly. The stem we afterwards daubed. The fire would soon burn the stobs away and leave a wall of firmly cemented dirt to protect the wooden frame.

We got plenty of oysters this winter and a plenty of choice sweet potatoes.

The health of the men was tolerably good after frost fell in October though the country is very flat and much of the surface is submerged during a long rainy season.

About the 1st of March, Captain Douthat was promoted major and put in command of the battalion of cavalry at Gloucester Point. Lieutenant Benjamin H. Harrison, a genial companion, fine officer, and accomplished gentleman, became captain of Company D.[1]

The first week in March we left our camp and went into "winter quarters" at Young's mill, built by an infantry regiment, 11th Georgia, (Colonel [Alfred] Colquit). While here our most efficient captain, William A. Perkins, resigned and an election was held to fill the vacancy. I was again induced to be a candidate for 1st lieutenant. But I would not electioneer atall. An offer was made of about sixteen votes if I would carry the vote of my supporters for a particular candidate for junior 2nd lieutenant. I very promptly, and I have since always felt properly, refused.

My competition was George H. Matthews, Jr., he was a very great wire-worker, the best of his age I ever knew.[2] He was very active and used arguments and persuasions which I scorned to use against him. I was sent off on picket and learned afterwards upon undoubted authority, that the offer above referred to was made to and accepted by him. The election came off March 10th. Lieutenant James Isbell was unanimously chosen captain, Matthews was chosen 1st lieutenant. The vote stood Matthews—43, Hubard—18.

Taking 16 away from 43 leaves 27, adding 16 to 18 gives 34. So that had I thought fit to make a combination, I should have been elected by about seven majority. A few weeks afterwards an election was held for junior 2nd lieutenant, the resignation of 2nd lieutenant B[enjamin] W. Allen having been accepted and Palmore being now 2nd lieutenant. As the bargain has previously been closed through Mr. S[amuel] E. Garrett, Peyton R. Browne was now, without difficulty, chosen junior 2nd lieutenant.[3]

We had for sometime been excited by rumours of an ironclad monster being built by our government from the hull of the steam frigate "Merrimac" [CSS *Virginia*], which vessel had been practically burned at Norfolk. It was said this vessel would not only clear James River of the wooden craft floating in those water, but be able also to batter down the walls of Fort Monroe. This, in connection with the mysterious pile of scaling ladders laying near one camp, which our quartermasters had orders to be ready to transport at any time on their wagons, tended greatly to excite high hopes.

We never dreamed of anything but success in spite of disparity of numbers and equipment. For we thought that "one Southerner could whip three Yankees any time and anywhere." Oh! How proud was the heart, how stiff the neck of the Southerner of that time. And how soon, alas! was he to be humbled by disaster filled with anxiety for the result and taught how vain is the pride, the courage, the strength of *man*!, (unless indeed that God, who ruleth our destinies, should be pleased to smile upon our cause and speed our missiles of destruction into the hosts of the foe).

When, on the night of March 8th, we saw a bright light toward Norfolk, we all readily guessed what was the matter. Our guesses became convictions when we were ordered to be ready to move out of camp next morning at sunrise with twenty rounds of ammunition to the man. General Magruder, with about six thousand men, went within four miles of Newport's News and ascertained that, though the "Merrimac" had sunk the "Cumberland" (44-gun frigate) and blown up the "Congress" (44-gun frigate), and temporarily driven out the garrison of the point, she had been compelled to put back to Norfolk for repairs.[4]

As we had never had any experience in charging across ditches, scaling breastworks, etc., and as we believed cavalry were not especially adapted to such purposes, I can't say we felt any great disappointment or regret when we heard the familiar command, "By fours, left about wheel, march, column forward."

Besides, we had the satisfaction of seeing the mastheads of the sunken

"Cumberland" rising out of the water and, knowing that the "Merrimac" had done no little mischief. It is due to the gallant officer commanding the former vessel to say that he stood to his guns manfully and fired his last gun as his vessel went down. He and most of the crew perished.[5]

During our stay at Young's mill in March our company was smartly recruited by conscripts who came in anticipation of the Conscription Act of April 16 passed by the Confederate Congress.[6] Among them was my neighbor, James A. Grigg. His brother Edward had gone into service when I went and made a fine soldier.[7]

Major [James M.] Goggin, connected with the Adjutant General's office in Virginia, came down in March to ascertain which of us were willing to enlist for the war.[8] The sentiment among the troops was very averse to re-enlistment. They had volunteered, found the life not exactly "what it was cracked up to be," didn't like the restraint and discipline of the army, found their families needed their attention as did also their business concerns, and that a great number of men had stayed home willing enough for the safety and comfort that home afforded and the chance of making money, to resign all "the glory," etc., of the war to the volunteers. The volunteers now desired to exchange places with these sleak gentlemen and fatten a little themselves.

Having no family and no business, I and six or eight others of my company volunteered for the war before the 16th of April. Generally, throughout the army there was not more than about one-tenth part who voluntarily re-enlisted for the war. All Virginia troops were originally mustered in for one year. From some southern states many regiments were originally mustered in for the war. It appears rather discreditable to the Southern character that after one year's war, with so much to stimulate to exertion, they should have lost so much of their spirit. *But facts are facts.* And the people of Virginia witnessed, with sorrow and disappointment, the rapid decline of that martial spirit, that patriotic ardour which seemed to pervade every Southern breast in April, 1861.

But Virginians were not, in all respects, more deserving of credit than the others. Much of their enthusiasm had died out, too. Yet it is undeniable that, all through the war, she stood her ground better than any other state. And when the war became a burden, laws which in other states could not be enforced, because frowned down by public sentiment, were rigidly enforced here and without a murmur, till the blessed, and ever dear, ever noble Old Commonwealth found herself stripped of nearly all her property, the railroads destroyed, the country laid waste, and nearly all of her daughters sighing for her absent sons. For so rigidly was the conscription enforced that General Grant, himself, remarked that to fill ranks, we had "robbed the cradle and the grave."

3
"Our Little Peninsula World"

Our little Peninsula world had now become a real "Theater of War." [George B.] McClellan had advanced from Fort Monroe with 120,000 men and on the 11th April, Brigadier General Magruder withdrew all his little force behind his Yorktown and Lee's Mill line of works and stood ready to defend them. On the 12th a strong column of "blue jackets" came in sight on the Warwick Road and, deploying right and left in front of Lee's Mill, began to skirmish heavily. Another strong column appeared in front of the line near Yorktown, deployed, and "felt our position." My regiment, with a battalion of infantry, was ordered to defend a portion of the line about half a mile long. The shallow, sluggish stream known as the Warwick River, being very small near its sources, five dirt dams had been thrown up between Yorktown and Lee's mill to back up the water and make it spread out into the marshes on either bank. These dams afforded a good passage for troops two abreast.

Hence, our first business was to throw up earthworks in front of and commanding them. I really felt like laughing when, with one squadron of dismounted cavalry and one company of infantry to hold down dam No. 3, I began collecting old broken logs and pieces of brush wood to shield my precious person from the view and the fire of the enemy. The rest of the regiment and the battalion were in line of battle in rear, being a "corps de reserve." Armed as we were with muzzle-loading, smoothbore carbines and the infantry with smoothbore muskets, I trembled to think of the stampede and awful gap which would be made in the line if some ten or a dozen really good riflemen had posted themselves a hundred yards off across the dam among the thick trees and opened fire on us.

Would we have run? Why, yes, like clever fellows for there we were on a damp, rainy day in a flat with miserable popguns which probably wouldn't go off. And if they did, couldn't hit an elephant a hundred yards off.[1] Besides, we knew that we had only 11,000 men and McClellan 100,000 or more.[2] We felt that Magruder was playing his old game of "Bluff" and that, if the enemy seriously attacked us, we must depend on our heels as our only salvation.

But smart old Joe Johnston with his quick, restless eye and ready ear was now energetically and laboriously working his weary way through the heavy Peninsula mud, eager to succor and to support us. He had withdrawn from McClellan's front at Centreville in March, sent a portion of his forces to Richmond and halted the rest at Orange Court House. When McClellan made his great advance on Manassas and captured the wooden cannon and abandoned works, he was greatly chagrined and almost lost his place. It was not long after this time that H[enry] W. Halleck, who left the Missouri Department on 9th April to the command of the Department of Tennessee, superceded McClellan as general commanding-in-chief and the latter adopted the Peninsula route for the 2nd "On to Richmond" as this campaign was called.[3]

And now, when the sun had set and nothing was heard save the occasional crack of a picket's rifle along the line, our regiment withdrew to camp to feed our poor beasts and ourselves and to get such rest as we could upon the wet ground with the continually dripping rain to keep moist our faces and the rheumatic limbs throughout the night. As we stood weary and thoughtful and anxious and gazed upon the feeble, unsteady flame which rose from the wet sticks we had piled together and dolefully thought of "tomorrow," a trooper galloped into camp and shouted, "Glorious news, boys. Old Joe's at Yorktown with five thousand infantry and plenty more coming." And this was indeed glorious news, a great load was taken off each heart and a bright smile lit up each face. A buzz of happy voices bespoke the universal joy and we gladly talked of the morrow. Yes, gladly for our Southern hearts were then proud and brave and confident. We believed that with Old Joe and his 25,000 men behind our works we could do up McClellan about right.

Instead of our usual bugle, artillery sounded reveille next morning.

It was nothing serious, only our batteries firing on some general and his staff reconnoitering or on some artillery company which had boldly advanced on our front and were trying to flank a battery.

That day a large number of our regiment were detailed as couriers for the different infantry generals and colonels and the rest formed a mounted courier line and were stationed three together on our skirmish line at intervals of about one hundred yards. After this had been kept up for four or five days it was abandoned and all the cavalry withdrawn, except couriers, and held as a reserve in camp.[4]

General Johnston's army kept pouring in and at last came Brigadier General J[ames] E[well] B[rown] Stuart with his distinguished cavalry brigade, the 1st, 4th, 9th cavalry and, I believe, other regiments.[5] General T[homas] J. Jackson remained in northern Virginia with his division and [Turner] Ashby's cavalry. [Irvin] McDowell was at Fredericksburg with 25,000 troops and McClellan's original plan was for that officer to march with his column and take Gloucester Point, then advancing up the river to turn our position at Yorktown. This was a good plan and would have succeeded but Lincoln, fearing General Jackson, would not consent to leave Washington City unprotected so he ordered McDowell to remain in front of Washington.

Our infantry strengthened their works daily and the [Federal] sharpshooters got so near that it was dangerous to show one's head. The artillery practice, too, improved considerably and there was much of it. McClellan brought heavy siege guns and mortars up York River and threw up powerful works in front of ours.

I was detailed about the 15th of April to report to Brigadier General George Anderson commanding a Georgia brigade composed of 7th Georgia, Colonel [William T.] Wilson, 8th Georgia, Colonel [Lucius M.] Lamar, and the 11th and 12th, forming a reserve to the force at Dam Number 1, which consisted of the 15th North Carolina Infantry, Colonel [Robert M.] McKinney. Anderson I found to be a tall, broad-shouldered, dark-skinned man of about 45 years, evidently a plain man but free from vanity and haughtiness.[6]

He received me kindly and bade me partake of his frugal fare, crackers, fried bacon, and peas. A day or two after, as he and I were riding along by a commissary wagon where there were some good-looking pieces of lean meat and crackers, he said he felt hungry and cutting off a slice of raw meat, ate it with relish. I expressed surprise. He said it was fine and he had frequently eaten it during the Mexican War. I have frequently since been only too happy to get a fat piece of raw meat to eat with my dry cracker.

On the 17th at 8 or 9 a.m., the enemy opened on Dam Number 1 with eighteen pieces of artillery.[7] We had one 18-pounder and four rifled 6- and 12-pounder guns with which to reply. By noon they had disabled two or three of our guns and rendered the position of two more untenable so that only one could be used. Seeing this, the attacking force of ten thousand men now opened a tremendous fire while a battalion of picked men advanced as a forlorn hope to the edge of the swamp.

The 15th North Carolina, feeling safe and not apprehending that the enemy could get across were busily at work on a second line of rifle pits when their skirmishers came running in and reported the enemy nearly across. The brave McKinney, whom I knew, lost no time but forming a hasty line, his men, having seized their guns and cartridge boxes, hurried forward and opened a sharp fire. It was too late. The battalion were across the swamp, having waded to their waists, and other regiments were hurrying over.[8]

Anderson, hearing the fire of small arms, lost no time but rapidly advanced in column. Gaining the hilltop, he learned that the enemy had our front line and the 15th North Carolina was retreating. "7th and 8th Georgia," said he, "remember Manassas, your old leader (Francis Bartow who fell on the 21st of July was colonel of the 8th) and your state. Do your duty. Fix bayonets! Give them the load you have and then the cold steel. Colonel Wilson, deploy and forward at a charge. Colonel Lamar, do the same. Orderly, repeat the order to the 11th and 12th and gallop off and bring up the 1st Kentucky at once."

I heard the loud command "Forward!" as I galloped off to the last named regiment and returning in ten minutes to the General. He said, "We have made quick work, sir. Wilson, with hat in hand, galloped up to their line and the 7th and 8th scattered them at once. They are now back over the marsh and we are pouring it into them."

A heavy fire of small arms was kept up till night. No further effort was made to cross. It was the first real fight I had been in and as the bullets hissed by me and the huge cannonballs came tearing through the woods, I felt rather uncomfortable.

The gallant colonel [McKinney] of the 15th North Carolina was killed early in the fight. We lost besides about one hundred killed and wounded.

The enemy loss was rather heavier some two or three hundred, perhaps. This was McClellan's grand effort to penetrate our lines and, almost successful as it was, he was convinced that the position could not be taken by a direct attack and gave up all idea of breaking through our lines.

General Joseph Johnston had conferred with the authorities at Richmond and it was now rumored about camp that General Huger was evacuating Norfolk, the troops retreating to Weldon and Petersburg, and that we would retreat in a few days. This was sad news.[9]

It was ascertained that McClellan was preparing to move a heavy column around Gloucester Point to the river above, compel its evacuation, open the river to his ships, and if possible, cut us off from Williamsburg. There was no longer any doubt. Stores and supplies of all sorts were sent up the river, reserve artillery and troops sent to Williamsburg, etc.

Saturday, May 2nd, the retreat commenced in good earnest.[10] The cavalry were dismounted and put on the skirmish line about 10 p.m. and the last of the infantry withdrawn. Reliable hands were employed burying "tor-paddos" as an Irishman called them, all about inside our camp and at about 1:30 a.m. the signal guns were fired, (three shots in rapid succession), for us to retire within the works and mount our horses.[11]

The night was dark and gloomy. I felt awfully gloomy. There were our strong works, the labor of months, lined with 120-pounder, 98-pounder, 64-pounder, and 32-pounder guns, large magazines of ammunition, quantities of stores of all sorts to be left to the enemy.

As the first streaks of gray light lit up the eastern sky on the [4th], our regiment was busily engaged in the work of destruction on the wharf at Yorktown. Stationary tents, bales of cloth, barrels of horseshoes, carpenters tools, picks, spades, shovels, all sorts and descriptions of things lay there in abundance and into the river we were hurling them as fast as we could.

Presently there was a large succession of explosions and then, "To horse!" called out our commander. What is it? What is it? Well, someone mistaking a house full of shells and other ammunition for one full of flour, attempted to force the door to which a torpedo was attached. An explosion was the result and the officers well knew that signal would inform the Yankees of the whole truth. The shells continued to be hurled through the air, bursting as they went. A dense cloud of smoke arose and then the house was wrapped in flames.

A loud "Huzzah! Huzzah!" was now heard and lo! Our breastworks were blue with Yankees. By fours left, about wheel, and off we go at a walk along the Williamsburg Road. Making a mile, we halt, wheel about again, and dismount. Up gallops a courier to Colonel J. Lucius Davis commanding the two regiments we now have together.[12]

"What d'ye see?"

"A squadron or more of horse, sir, slowly advancing with a few flankers out."

"Prepare to mount. Mount! Draw sabres."

A mighty rattling of sabres is now followed by—the silence of death! The haggard sleepy faces now look more haggard but not *atall sleepy*. Oh no! This is no time for sleep.

"There they are. Yonder they come, and with drawn sabres, too."

A courier from the rear now rides up. It is 9 a.m. the sun is rising bright and warm.

"His horse is foaming, Colonel Davis."

"The General says return slowly, don't fight if you can help it, and instead of going to Williamsburg, take the left at Lebanon Church and Grove Wharf.[13] If you find the enemy at Lebanon Church when you get there, flank round about them."

"What, are they advancing on that road?"

"Yes, sir. A heavy column in four miles of the church when I left and you are slow, now."

"Return sabres, by fours, left about wheel, forward march."

And now we are crossing the road from Lebanon Church to Williamsburg and we hear Yankees *above us* on this very road! We are puzzled and uneasy but *obey orders*.

1 p.m. [and] we are with Stuart on the road from the church to Grove Wharf. He orders us to feed our horses. We do so. But what are they unlimbering and planting those cannon on the hill there for?

"Bum—m—bum"

"Ah, yes. There they are. See those two of our regiments going off with drawn sabres. No time for feeding now. I'm going to bridle my horse."

"To horse. Form ranks. By fours, march."

"What orders?"

"General says follow Colonel Goode up the Williamsburg Road along the river there. The enemy have gotten above us and 'dog' if I don't b'lieve they are all 'round us. A captain was taken prisoner right yonder in those woods, just now."

"Bum—m-bum"

"Hear that? Look, they're limbering up those guns to leave. *Take care.* I'll *declare* that shell didn't miss you five inches."

"Bum—m—bum, bum—m—bum."

"*Steady, men, steady.* They are merely straggling shot. Don't disgrace yourselves. Halt!"

Plop—a—lop, lop—a—lop, lop, plop

"What's that?"

"Small arms."

"Goode into it a-ready?"

"Yes, and he's *coming back, too,* in a hurry!"[14]

"bum—m—bum"

"Ha. They're firing artillery at him!"

"Captain, there they are. Can you put a shell in the point of those woods, where the road emerges?"

"Colonel, attend to your men there. Quiet them. There is no occa—"

"Bum—m—bum"

"That's it, another in the same place. There's no occasion for all this excitement."

"Lieutenant Jones is shot through the body, Major Phillips, and one Mecklenburg trooper killed, one wounded."

"Captain Carter, detail two men to take Lieutenant Jones to the river and aboard a boat. Lieutenant White, see to your wounded man."[15]

"Captain, fire four more shots in those woods and make for Grove Wharf as fast as possible," said Stuart.[16]

"Colonel Goode! Forward to the wharf and *try the beach from there to King's Wharf.* Lieutenant, tell Colonels Lee and Davis and Chambliss to do the same."[17]

"Steady, men," cry the captains, "steady."

"Halt those men dashing towards the river, there. Halt, halt. Where the h——l are you going, there? Halt, halt you d——d cowards. What are you officers fit for? Attend to your men. Keep in your places, boys. We'll soon be out of this."

Talking is no use. *A stampede is* a stampede. Elijah Grigg and several others have just been captured between us and Williamsburg. Colonel

Goode is driven back by 5,000 Yankee cavalry and no road but that from King's Wharf, if we ever get there. Here we are, on the beach: "Splatter to splatter" in the water two to three feet deep. Bluff fifty feet high right above us. Suspicious looking men already seen up there. They'll shoot at us presently. Here go saddlebags, india rubbers [rubberized blankets or ponchos], blankets, everything to lighten horses. Don't know how far we've got to run. The wharf itself is two miles off!

But there stands the C.S. War Steamer, *Roanoke*. Ah!, she has just fired one of her biggest guns at the rascals! The coast is clear. We are no longer *cut off*. Oh, the horrid words!

We are in the works at Williamsburg, at last. A chain of square forts running north and south and the boys seem glad to see us. And we *are* glad to see them. They have been fighting, too! Yes, old Joe Hooker has actually hurried up and put [Samuel P.] Heintzleman [*sic*] into it right smartly and Colonel [Williams C.] Wickham of the 4th [Virginia Cavalry] has been making a charge, forgot to draw sabres, got cut on the back.[18] But his men made the 6th [U.S.] Regulars run, sabres or no sabres. The enemy were worsted smartly and withdrew.

The night closed dark and dreary and dripping. We were tired, so tired, and hungry. No camp, no fire, no water, no anything. At last we were drawn up in a wheat field where our horses were ankle deep in mud, ordered to dismount and "go into camp." There was a general rush to the fence to tie our horses and then a few minutes after, the fence was nearly all carried away to make fires. The horses got loose, the wood refused to burn. We got some crackers and a little meat and were glad enough to eat it raw.

Captain Isbell, poor fellow, looked very faint and sick as he sat back against his tree, (for he had found one tree and actually had a little fire). 1st Lieutenant Matthews and I tied our horses to a tumbrel cart and slept in it, such sleeping as we had.

By midnight the rain poured down in torrents and continued till 3 a.m. when we saddled up and went out in front of Williamsburg into a field, drew up in line, dismounted and took the reins. But there was a crumb of comfort in all this. Johnston had retreated during the night. Nothing remained but the cavalry and two regiments of infantry with a battery of 6-pounders and these were to withdraw presently.

The morning was propitious for the clouds hung very low and as the rain slackened, the rising vapor formed a dense fog and one couldn't see four hundred yards. How deceptive are human calculations. The rising sun of that morning ushered in the great Battle of Williamsburg.[19] The previous winter and the spring were remarkably wet and the roads were in a condition really terrible to a retreating army. Wagons, ambulances, and artillery sank nearly up to their hubs and every fifty yards some one or the other would become fast stuck in the mud or else some faithful mule sank in the mire exhausted from over-exertion and died where he fell. The poor, weary, wet, and shivering foot soldier struggling along through the brushwood, in avoidance of the awful road and balking teams, cursed his calling and the war and, sighing for his comfortable home and tender wife, dropped his gun, kindled a little fire, and laid down to rest. Thus, laboring, balking, and straggling, the immense train and the Army of Northern Virginia trudged along the road to New Kent Court House.

As I stood on the field by a feeble fire made of fence rails, holding my bridle, I noticed two pieces of artillery, which had started off, coming back again. I noticed the picket firing for the last five minutes had been growing more rapid and, here and there through the thick mist, could see two men carrying off a litter with a wounded man stretched upon it. These things made me apprehend that covering the retreat was going to be anything else than pleasant this murky, dripping, [fifth] day of May.

All at once there was a loud blast of the bugle and every man vaulted into his saddle and took his place in line. Then I saw the regiment on our right wheeling to the right and, marching to the front, they formed line of battle facing the enemy. A lieutenant of artillery now passed along by us with his section, two guns, halted in front of the cavalry line, and under the direction of General Stuart, unlimbered, loaded, and aimed his guns. Then with a sharp, crashing sound two rifle shots were hurled through the air and, as they went whizzing along their rapid course, all felt that *a battle* was at hand. A few moments after, two more guns opened and the four now kept up a very rapid fire at what, I could not see from where I sat—but something, evidently, for presently a shell tore up the ground very near the General. Another and another followed in quick succession and, passing a few feet over our heads, buried themselves in the ground. It soon became evident that our force was plainly seen by the enemy.

We were moved a little to the right and formed behind a little rising ground. To our left, on the centre of our line, stood Fort Magruder, a bastion fort with wings or curtains extending some distance to right and left, on the flanks of which work stood three or four forts in a line as before described.

Looking toward town, I now saw a fine column of infantry marching in quick time toward the several forts to our right. Presently, two guns opened on the enemy from the fort nearest us and soon after we had eight or ten guns firing rapidly. I now learned that Major General James Longstreet's command, nine thousand strong, had turned back and [George E.] Pickett and [Roger A.] Pryor's brigades were engaging the enemy pretty hotly. These troops leaving the forts advanced across the opened field nearly a thousand yards and entered the thick woods to the right, when you face the east, of the Yorktown Road. Here they had their hands full for a long time.

The fight now raged heavily for hours, but being in the woods, nothing could be seen of it and there was no immediate use for the cavalry. So we marched back to our camp and let our horses graze on green wheat for about two hours. Returning to the field about 2 p.m. we met a number of wounded, all of whom said, "We're driving them and have taken several pieces of artillery. Our boys are *piling* them up over yonder but they have piled up a heap of our poor fellows, too."

Here I saw a handsome youth about 19-years-old walking cheerfully along holding a comrade's arm with a fearful hole in his breast and one corresponding in the back. Shot through by a musket ball, he was yet cheerful and spoke like a hero. I breathed a prayer for "length of days and happiness" to the noble patriot and rode on.

The firing had receded from the right and presently news came that "their left is routed and their centre is giving way." Then the gallant Stuart, galloping to the head of his line of 2,500 cavalry commanded, "Draw sabres! Gallop—March!!" We dashed away in a beautiful column of fours 200 yards long, raised loud cheers and waving of hats from the forts on the right and left and we felt proud to have a chance to do our part and hoped to distinguish ourselves by breaking the centre and making the defeat a rout. Presently we got in range of the enemy muskets and their first fire emptied a dozen saddles in front. But gaily floated our chieftain's plume at the head of the columns and still we were dashing on when a courier from General Longstreet, (Robert Page of Cumberland), arrived and ordered a halt.[20] The enemy's centre had swung around on the right and was now making a bold stand.

I was now detailed with twenty men to go after ammunition. It had been impossible for any ordnance waggons to get back and all the ammunition brought that day a distance of four miles over an almost impossible road was brought by such details except only what the troops brought with them.

General Johnston and staff arrived about this time. He had halted his whole army. I found, however, that they had not turned back as I did not come up with them.

About 6 p.m. a Federal force under General [Winfield S.] Hancock crossed a little stream and occupied the fort on the extreme left in which we had no force. Partly because of the natural strength of that position and partly for want of troops, we had only two regiments near there. One of these, a North Carolina regiment, charged the work but were repulsed and then General Hancock, says a Yankee writer, waving his hat said, as General Hancock *only could* say, "Gentleman, charge." Whereupon his brigade charged and cut up the North Carolina regiment right badly before it got back to its support.[21]

Night came on. We had been perfectly successful everywhere, with the exception just stated, and held all the battlefield to the right of the Yorktown Road. I do not remember the loss on either side but it was considerable and the enemy much heavier, as will be readily understood, when I state that the enemy's force was ascertained to be 30,000 strong actually in line. We took, I think, eleven pieces of artillery but brought off only six guns. The rest were disabled or had the horses killed or carried off. We took several hundred prisoners and crippled the enemy so that the rest of our retreat was almost free from annoyance.[22] The Federal cavalry, only pursuing, harassed us but little as Stuart was a full match for them. Our cavalry returned that night to *their wheat field* and grazed and ate raw meat and slept.

Next morning was clear and as the sun was rising we marched through town *back to the battlefield* but *not* to *fight*. Our line of mounted pickets were slowly firing and retiring. A heavy, dense, blue column of Yankee infantry were emerging from the woods along the York Road and a few cautious cavalry pickets were slowly firing at ours and willingly awaited the approach of their supports.

At length the glittering bayonets had reached Fort Magruder, only three hundred yards off. I glanced around. There stood our brigade, (the 3rd Regiment was now part of Stuart's Brigade), alone. Not an infantry soldier, wagon, or cannon was there. They had all quietly slipped away during the silent hours of the night! Nothing now stood between the ancient Capital of Virginia and McClellan's grand army but Stuart's Brigade. Then we wheeled about and sadly and heavily filed through the dreary streets. They, indeed, were impassible and here and there the wreck of a cannon or ambulance bespoke the trouble our poor teams had had and the oaths their drivers had uttered. We did like many who had gone before. We rode on the sidewalks and threw yet more mud on the already thoroughly bedaubed railings and houses. There stood weeping the unhappy mothers, there with heavy bosoms were the lovely maidens, all forlorn. We too sighed and wept sorrowfully and marched away.

4

"The Enemy Were Worsted"

What effect Hancock's slight success might have had if Johnston had fought another day at Williamsburg, I cannot tell you. But as Johnston was trying to retreat to Richmond without a fight, and as that great commander well knew the danger of delay with bad roads before him and flanked by the rivers, the army retreated before daylight of the 22nd.[1]

As we marched up the road we only came up with a wounded man here and there trying to escape on foot. There was nothing like the spirit of our troops at that day notwithstanding conscription. I saw men with terrible flesh wounds in the legs that had not been dressed, marching steadily on. We, following the example of the main body, divided, a portion of the cavalry taking the Stage Road via Diascund Bridge, the other the road to New Kent Court House.

On the 6th the head of our column was attacked by a flanking column that had landed from York River near Brick Church.[2] After a heavy skirmish of two or three hours, the enemy was driven to their boats with a loss of two or three hundred men.

Colonel Fitz Lee of the 1st Virginia Cavalry, commanding a portion of 1st and 4th and all of 3rd regiments, was unexpectedly charged on two roads at Slatersville by squadrons of the 8th Pennsylvania Cavalry and was rather worsted at first. But as we outnumbered the enemy greatly, we drove them off as soon as we got over the shock. They lost ten or eleven men and we about the same.[3]

From this time till about the 10th of May, (when we took up our line near Seven Pines), our cavalry had daily skirmishes and were sometimes supported by infantry. We kept up a picket line in front of our infantry lines from quarter to half a mile.

Such an immense amount of rain had fallen during the retreat and such was the fare, (crackers and pickled pork), that as the weather became warm, the troops became greatly afflicted with scurvy, dysentery, and a low camp fever. It was undoubtedly the roughest army life I ever experienced. For ten days my clothes and blankets were almost constantly wet and we slept without shelter.

Notwithstanding all these difficulties, by bringing over [Benjamin] Huger's Division and reinforcements from the south, General Johnston got together at least 75,000 men. McClellan stated that he landed on the Peninsula with 120,000 effective men. He afterwards received reinforcements and probably had at this time 110,000 to 115,000 men.[4]

McClellan had selected a line confronting ours and running across the Chickahominy [River] at what was called McClellan's Bridge. We had destroyed the bridges below Mechanicsville. Taking advantage of the heavy rains, Johnston determined to attack the forces on the west side of the river consisting of a corps of about 35,000 men, hoping to destroy these before the troops from the other side could cross the swollen stream. Among his superior officers at this time were Major Generals G[ustavus] W. Smith, second in command, Huger, Longstreet, D. H. Hill, A[mbrose] P. Hill, and Magruder. I think [G. W.] Smith's and A. P. Hill's divisions were on the left with Magruder's in reserve; Huger's and D. H. Hill's on the right with Longstreet's in reserve.

Huger was ordered to commence the attack on the Stage Road at 6 a.m. Owing to the terrible storm the night before and some other cause, he did not make it till 12 noon.[5]

I was in reserve that day and did not see the fight and haven't a very distinct recollection of the details.

But about 2 or 3 p.m. Brigadier General Robert E. Rodes carried Major General [Silas] Casey's fortifications and camp by assault just as the enemy were about to enjoy a very sumptuous dinner. It fell into the hands of worthier and hungrier men. Rodes was driven back to the fortifications, but being reinforced, held them and after, after a while, the entire camp was retaken and our line advanced a mile and a half or two miles.

On the left we were not so successful having to give up the ground we took and would probably have been smartly worsted but for the gallantry and skill of Magruder's support.[6] General J. E. Johnston, while deeply interested in the progress of the battle and resisting an impetuous charge of the enemy, was shot in the body and fell from his horse. He was carried from the field much hurt by the fall and seriously wounded. G. W. Smith took command and the troops slept on their arms. It became evident that by the delay in our attack the enemy had been enabled to reinforce the corps attacked with at least another.

Next morning my company was detailed to bring off muskets and cartridge boxes from the captured ground. We made a number of trips and together with other troops, secured some 1500. By 12 noon the enemy opened so hot a fire on the camp that we were withdrawn and soon after our troops began to retire to their old lines. The fighting was principally in dense woods made almost impassable in some places by bamboo and grapevines, in others by swamps. We suffered heavily both days for our men, advancing, would come right upon the enemy before they knew it and were mowed down. I never knew the exact loss on either side. We captured some five or six guns and some few prisoners and lost some prisoners. As a part of this battle was at the Fair Oaks railroad station and part ran across Seven Pines farm, the Yankees called it by the former and we by the latter name.[7]

Fearing the effects of Johnston's wound on the army, the government was very secret about it. He was carried to Richmond to a private house on Clay Street and ropes stretched across the streets to prevent vehicles and horses passing near it. General Johnston was a great favorite and the army would have been inconsolable but for the arrival of General Lee to take the command. He soon convinced his army that he didn't mean to give up Richmond without fighting for it and readily gained their fullest confidence.

Stuart was now made a major general, Fitz Lee and Wade Hampton his brigadiers. The 1st and 2nd North Carolina, 1st and 2nd South Carolina, Cobb's Legion and Jeff Davis Legion and the 10th and 13th Virginia Cavalry made [Wade] Hampton's First Brigade. The 1st, 2nd, 3rd, 4th, 5th, and 9th Virginia Cavalry made Fitz Lee's 2nd brigade.[8] The 1st North Carolina and 3rd Virginia Cavalry under command of Colonel [Laurence S.] Baker of the 1st North Carolina were placed on the extreme right of our lines. I believe now I am a little too fast. The above promotions were not made till after the battles around Richmond.

To proceed, the 4th Virginia was on our extreme left towards Ashland. Our lines were now along [the] south bank of the Chickahominy from Yellow Tavern to New Bridge, thence to Seven Pines and White Oak Swamp and James River. McClellan held his own between Seven Pines and Bottom's Bridge and extended his right beyond Meadow Bridge towards Ashland.

Just before the battles began, Stuart went out by Hanover Court House to White House via Crump's Crossroads, across the Long Bridge into our lines again.[9] This was regarded as a great feat at the time. But was it really a great exploit? Riding around McClellan's army, burnt some wagons and stores, sunk a steamer, took some prisoners, and broke down his command on the eve of a great pitched battle that was to decide the fate of Richmond! A daring adventure which built up Stuart, broke down his horses, and did the country no great service is about all it deserves to be regarded.[10]

General Lee had now nearly 80,000 effective men. McClellan had 110,000 or somewhat more. The latter was entrenched near Mechanicsville at Gaines Mill and Cold Harbor with very strong natural advantages of position. On the 26th day of June, 1862, the "two Hills" crossed the Meadow bridges about 12 noon and moved up gallantly upon the enemy's right. Not being very strong here, he [General Fitz John Porter's V Corps] slowly withdrew contesting the ground as he went till he got into his works beyond Mechanicsville.

General James Longstreet now, (about 2 p.m.), threw his divisions across rapidly at this point and advanced up the hill. These three splendid divisions now engaged the enemy hotly and towards night had him in full retreat across the little stream flowing by Gaines Mill. [Thomas J.] Jackson had communicated with Lee and promised to be into it bright and early next morning. He had over 12,000 men. Lee had with him nearly fifty thousand while about thirty thousand, under Magruder and Huger, were left to cover Richmond.

On the 27th Longstreet, with the Hills on his left, advanced to the attack of the enemy on the Gaines Mill line. The fighting soon became tremendously heavy and raged for hours. At length, the low mutterings of distant artillery were heard and Lee learned that Jackson was at his post. He ordered an assault on all points. The Hills rushed forward triumphantly. Longstreet had a difficult task, to cross a millpond over a narrow causeway swept by artillery. Nothing daunted, he pressed forward with that bulldog ferocity that characterized his fighting and, though many a noble soldier fell by the way, he crossed and charged position after position till at last he quietly looked on from the hills and felt he was master of the situation.

The day closed upon a disordered and retreating foe and our victorious forces lay down on the battlefield and slept by their arms. Jackson has done great service by his flank movement, the enemy had been compelled to give up a position which otherwise would have been impregnable to any assaulting column.

The morning of the 28th again ushered in a terrible conflict. Cold Harbor was a strong place and there was a heavy fight. Jackson now swung around between the enemy and his base of supplies. Magruder was ordered, if possible, to cross the Chickahominy and attack the enemy opposite him. He did so, made several efforts to carry his works, but was repulsed with loss. This changed the feature of the fight, somewhat. We carried the works at Cold Harbor and Jackson was in the enemy's rear. Had Magruder been successful, perhaps the Army of the Potomac would have surrendered.

McClellan threw his whole force across the river that night and sent his trains down the banks of the Chickahominy toward James River. Jackson crossed McClellan's Bridge on the evening of the 29th and drove the enemy's forces from Savage Station, (Magruder cooperating with him), capturing their hospitals, etc. The rest of our forces crossing at New Bridge moved southwardly across the Stage Road to the Charles City and River roads. We, thus, formed a line from the upper part of White Oak Swamp to James River on the 30th and Jackson attacked the enemy rear and drove it across the swamp.

Colonel [Laurence S.] Baker, having received orders to reconnoitre the Quaker Road [on the 29th] proceeded down it with our regiment and his own [1st North Carolina Cavalry], the latter in front. At Willis Church he came upon a squadron of U.S. cavalry and we charged them at once. They fled precipitately, we pursuing when all at once, turning from the road, they exposed to view two pieces of artillery supported by artillery about 200 yards off. These opened on us with grape at once. We kept on a few yards but the fire was so withering that we were compelled to fall back with a loss of fifty or sixty killed and wounded. The loss fell on the North Carolina regiment as we had only one man hurt, Cary Allen of Cumberland, arm disabled.[11]

On the 1st July there was great delay on account of Magruder's and Huger's divisions missing their way and therefore failing to get between the enemy and river as General Lee wished. Jackson sent word that he had crossed the swamp, was in position on the enemy's flank and had been waiting *four hours* for the attack to commence.

We were marched round toward the river and shelled by gunboats so that we had to retire. The enemy were worsted in this day's fight but we suffered considerable and effected nothing.[12] He retired to Malvern Hills [sic] and there Magruder made his memorable attack. The chaplain of my regiment and one company, (Charles City), were with him [Magruder] as a bodyguard and all testified that he was not drinking that day as is often alleged.[13]

We encamped on the left flank of the army that night and next morning set out in a drenching rain to New Kent. Here we paroled a number of sick and wounded men, returned next day to Bottom's Bridge and crossed by letting the horses swim while we walked over on the sills of the old bridge. Such was the nature of the ground that the cavalry had but a small share in those great battles. With the exception of Baker's command, they were most of the time acting as supports for batteries of artillery.

When I returned to camp I went to bed and found myself right far gone into a spell of fever. I lay in a miserable tent on a bed of boards covered with two blankets till I got so weak I could scarcely walk and then after about a week's confinement was allowed to go to Richmond, (only two miles off), where I got into private quarters (at Mr. A. T. Harris') where I received every attention which a kind and hospitable family could give.

Ten days after, I got home greatly to my delight and stayed till the middle of September, being confined to bed six weeks. Captain Isbell of my company was taken sick shortly before me and died on August 5th. Matthews became captain, Palmore, 1st lieutenant, and S. E. Garrett, 2nd lieutenant.

By or before 1st of August, Jackson was "on the pad". [John] Pope was at Culpeper Court House with about 15,000 men, [Franz] Siegel [sic] at Rappahannock Court House with an equal force while another force of 15, 000 or 20,000 was at Fredericksburg. "Old Jack" hoped to crush three armies in detail. Pope passed through Culpeper Court House confident and boastful. Jackson masked a large portion of his forces in the woods on Cedar Mountain, while Major General A. P. Hill was marching up with the remainder [on 9 August].

The enemy came on confidently and rushed headlong upon us. The fight was severe and of varying success for hours. Brigadier General Charles Winder was killed early in the action.[14] At length, A. P. Hill having gotten up, our forces charged the enemy and drove him across the run. Owing to some unaccountable delay of General Hill's command, the battle was not fought as soon or terminated as early as Jackson had calculated. In consequence of this, Siegel got up in time to prevent our turning the defeat of the enemy into a perfect rout. They retreated, however, to Culpeper Court House before he joined them. General Jackson, on the 10th of August, finding his plans frustrated and himself confronted by a force at least double his own, retired to Orange Court House.[15]

About this time or soon after Major Generals Thomas J. Jackson and James Longstreet were promoted to lieutenant generals.[16] Towards the latter part of August, the Army of the Potomac, having sailed down James River, debarked at Fredericksburg and at Alexandria and moved up towards Manassas plains. General Robert E. Lee, thoroughly understanding the whole movement, was on the Rappahannock with the whole Army of Northern Virginia by the 20th of August. Lieutenant General Jackson, with a whole "corps d'armee" was sent by Culpeper Court House and [blank space] to gain the enemy's rear. He was preceded by Major General J. E. B. Stuart with a portion of his cavalry division. General Lee, with the remainder of the cavalry and the "2nd corps d'armee," Lieutenant General Longstreet commanding, marched directly by Warrenton Springs towards Manassas on the night of the 22nd of August.

Stuart charged a camp of the enemy at Catlett's Station, drove them out in great confusion, captured and destroyed a large train of wagons and made his way to Lieutenant General Jackson with some very valuable information as to the disposition of the enemy forces.[17]

On the 28th of August, to the utter amazement of the enemy, Jackson's artillery opened on *their rear* near Centreville. After a sharp fight, they retired before him towards Bull Run. The next morning he renewed the fight with great vigor. His position was now very critical. With a force of about 25,000 men and a very limited supply of ammunition, he had placed himself between Washington city and the Army of the Potomac numbering over one hundred thousand (100,000).

But this army was now commanded by Major General Pope who had succeeded McClellan and was greatly inferior to him. He was a great braggart, headed his dispatched "Headquarters *in the Saddle,*" and in general orders announced to his army that they were now going to Richmond and that that army should "never present its *back* to the enemy." Our people always spoke of this movement as the "Third On to Richmond."[18]

Well, Jackson soon found himself fighting vastly superior forces but still fought with heroic bravery inspiring his troops with implicit confidence and great enthusiasm. He had a giant's task to perform; nothing but the iron will and undaunted courage of Jackson could have succeeded. But Lee knew him. He *knew* when he sent Jackson around Pope's rear success was certain and new laurels would be added to the already famous "A. N. Va."

Towards night Jackson's right flank had been pushed so far south of Bull Run that it almost communicated with Longstreet's left. And now his command were overjoyed. A great load was lifted from their minds. They felt *hopeful* at first that all would be well, now they *knew* it and slept soundly.

Up to this time Longstreet had scarcely been engaged atall. The leaders held council during the silent hours of the night and prepared for the great struggle of the morrow. They knew that the vain-braggart Pope would give them a desperate fight to save his capital [*sic*] and, last though not least, his own *reputation.*

At last the morning star peered through the night vapors and shot upward through the skies. Then the drums beat and the bugles sounded the reveille of the mighty armies and the air, a moment before peaceful and still, was now filled with the mingled sounds of braying animals gnawed by hunger, swearing quartermasters angry at the loss of their morning nap, of loud commands oft repeated by impatient officers and of the hum and bustle and merry laugh of the gay soldier boys as they prepared their frugal meal.

Lieutenant General Jackson's left rested on Bull Run whence his line extended southwest and his right stood at the upper, (or western side), of the inclined plain over which our left fought at the First Manassas battle. Not far from this point, the interval occupied by cavalry, was the left of Lieutenant General Longstreet's line which extended thence southeastward to the Orange [and Alexandria] Railroad. So our line was very nearly in the shape of a "V" with Pope's army enclosed on two sides of a triangle having one open to him.

As was expected his troops fought with great desperation and the issue was long doubtful. At length, Longstreet's forces began to drive the enemy. Rushing madly against "Old Stonewall" and being again driven back with great slaughter, they at length became disheartened and fled. Lee now pressed his advantage with vigor and inflicted severe loss on the retreating column. We captured about twenty guns, many stands of colors and small arms and inflicted a loss of over ten thousand on the enemy, losing ourselves around six thousand.[19] The enemy gained the road along the Potomac from Fredericksburg to Alexandria, got under the protection of his gunboats, and was reinforced by a column under McClellan from Alexandria.

At this time I believe the Army of Northern Virginia was commanded as follows: General Robert E. Lee commanding army; Lieutenant General Thomas J. Jackson commanding 1st corps composed of 1st Division, Major General A. P. Hill commanding, 2nd Division (Jackson's) Major General R[ichard] S. Ewell commanding; 3rd Division, Major General Edward Johnson commanding; Lieutenant General James Longstreet, commanding 2nd Corps; 1st Division (Longstreet's) Major General Richard H. Anderson commanding; 2nd Division, Major General Samuel Garland commanding; 3rd Division, Major General L[afayette] McLaws commanding. Major General D. H. Hill was commanding near New Berne, N.C. Major General Ewell lost a leg at Manassas on the 29th or 30th [of August] and consequently was not with his command for sometime afterwards.[20]

I have inadvertently omitted to mention in the proper place the change which occurred in my regiment at the re-organization of the 25th of April, 1862. Of the general effect of this provision, of the Conscript Act, I have never had but one opinion: that it was a disgraceful piece of demagogism, that did more than all other things combined to bring about our final defeat.[21] Not only did the men as a general rule select, in preference, the most *amiable* men, who would indulge them most or the most unprincipled who resorted to all kinds of intrigue to secure success, but ever after during the war officers feared another "reorganization" and never dared to enforce discipline.

Thus, our magnificent army fought *without discipline,* from patriotism and courage during 1862 and part of 1863. Then when the constant fighting increased hardships and exhaustless resources of the United States depressed their spirits and their high hope began to give place to despair, the want of discipline began to be felt. Every effort of our commander to supply it was unavailing because of the character of his regimental and company officers and the influences operating upon them. Thus General Lee, who if sustained by proper men of those grades would have kept up the high tone of his troops to the last and commanded always the finest army in the world, was doomed to see his army gradually losing its "espirit de corps" and growing weak in its *morale* much faster than in its *numbers.* Thus did it come to pass that an army which once went into a pitched battle with the wildest enthusiasm against twice its numbers learned towards the close of the war to distrust itself (and some portions of it, at least), feared to encounter the enemy on equal terms.

Having lost its unity, it lost its self-reliance. Having been subjected to no restraint it was sometimes guilty of the most shameful depredations upon the very people whom it professed to protect. I have in my own experience known men to break open houses and rob clothes chests, to steal provisions and fowls and beehives, and yet the regimental and company commanders, while having it almost in their power to identify the parties without inquiry, would make fair promises to the injured civilian and do nothing more, never even so much as reprimanding the offender.

All these things were of frequent occurrence. I witnessed them till I was shocked and disgusted beyond measure and in October, '64, wrote a communication to the "[Richmond] Examiner" (newspaper) urging the adoption of some means to rid the army of such worthless officers and expressing the opinion that, if it was not done forthwith, we would be subjugated in the next campaign. The editor, through tenderness towards that class of officers, I suppose, did not, (I think), publish the article.

Other causes which we could not control doubtless had much to do with our final defeat. But I shall always regard this as the ever present and principle cause of the reduction of our armies, to that paucity of numbers and standard of morals which caused their surrender.

I could not accurately recite the history of my regiment if I longer postponed giving a list of its officers during this campaign. And I can say with pride and satisfaction that its *material* was of such a high order that want of discipline did not any time affect its *morale* very sensibly. The tone of each company was so good that plunderers and rogues were frowned down and not tolerated. Yet, in the winter of 1864, even among us, were found some who forgot their duty and were guilty of gross outrages.

Its officers were: Field and Staff

Colonel Thomas F. Goode—elected 25th April, 1862

Lieut. Colonel John T. Thornton (Captain, Co. K)—elected 25th April, 1862

Major Jefferson C. Phillips—re-elected 25th April, 1862

Adjutant Henry B. McClellan—appointed May, 1862

Quartermaster John A. Palmer—appointed May 10, 1862

Commissary Leroy M. Wilson—appointed May 10, 1862

Surgeon John Randolph Leigh—appointed May 10, 1862

Asst. Surgeon Alexander T. Bell—appointed May 10, 1862

Chaplain John McClelland—appointed July, 1862

Quartermaster Sgt. Tyree G. Finch—appointed April, 1862

Commissary Sgt. James T. Harriss—appointed April, 1862

Orderly Sgt. John James Crowder—appointed April, 1862

Company A

Captain William H. Jones—elected April 25, 1862

1st Lieutenant George D. White—elected April 25, 1862

2nd Lieutenant [Robert F.] Sturdivant—elected April 25, 1862

Jr. 2nd Lieutenant William Townes Boyd—elected April 25, 1862

Company B

Captain Jesse S. Jones—promoted July 2, 1862

1st Lieutenant John Wray—promoted July 2, 1862

2nd Lieutenant N[athaniel] Gammel—promoted July 2, 1862

Jr. 2nd Lieutenant William T. Smith

Company C

Captain Thomas H. Owen—elected 25th April, 1862

1st Lieutenant John A. Chappell—elected 25th April, 1862

2nd Lieutenant James W. Hall—elected 25th April, 1862

Jr. 2nd Lieutenant Samuel Ragland—elected 25th April, 1862

Company D

Captain Franklin Guy—promoted July 1st, 1862
1st Lieutenant John Lamb—promoted July 1st, 1862
2nd Lieutenant B[ernard] Hill Carter—promoted July 1st, 1862
Jr. 2nd Lieutenant William H. Harwood—elected August 2nd, 1862

Company E

Captain William R. Carter—re-elected 25th April, 1862
1st Lieutenant John K. Jones—promoted August, 1862
2nd Lieutenant Alex B. Jones—promoted August, 1862
Jr. 2nd Lieutenant P[atrick] H. Fitzgerald—elected August 2nd, 1862

Company F

Captain Telemachus Taylor—elected 25th April, 1862
1st Lieutenant [William Edmund] Clopton—elected 25th April, 1862
2nd Lieutenant James Christian—elected 25th April, 1862
Jr. 2nd Lieutenant Jones R. Christian—elected 25th April, 1862

Company G

Captain George H. Matthews, Jr.—promoted 5th August, 1862
1st Lieutenant Charles R. Palmore—promoted 5th August, 1862
2nd Lieutenant Robert T. Hubard, Jr.—elected 25th April, 1862
Jr. 2nd Lieutenant Samuel E. Garrett—elected August, 1862

Company H

Captain Henry Carrington—elected 25th April, 1862
1st Lieutenant Isaac J. Tynes—promoted August, 1862
2nd Lieutenant James V. Garner—promoted August, 1862
Jr. 2nd Lieutenant Joel Hubbard, Jr.—elected August, 1862

Company I

Captain William M. Feild—elected April 25, 1862
1st Lieutenant Edmund O. Fitzgerald—elected April 25, 1862
2nd Lieutenant [William H.] Rogerson—elected April 25, 1862
Jr. 2nd Lieutenant Berryman J. Hill—elected April 25, 1862

Company K

Captain Peyton R. Berkeley—elected April 25, 1862
1st Lieutenant Richard H. [Watkins]—elected April 25, 1862
2nd Lieutenant James Bell—elected April 25, 1862
Jr. 2nd Lieutenant John H. Knight—elected April 25, 1862[22]

The promotions above occurred by the rule of seniority as vacancies occurred in the various companies.

General Lee might justly feel proud of an army which had accomplished so much during this campaign. Naturally might he confide in the fidelity, patriotism, and endurance of men who had proven themselves so faithful and enduring a succession and variety of hardships as his army had done since the first of May. Yet his expectations were not fully realized. His confidence was in some measure too great. That sadly injurious and strengthening agency of democratization referred to in the preceding pages was already at work, already being felt. Its effects were already exhibiting themselves. Our timid Congress had deprived our generals of that usual authority over their commands so essential to the discipline of an army, so entirely indispensable to success in a military enterprise. I mean the power to enforce *obedience* to their lawful commands. It became customary for subordinate officers to disregard orders entirely or merely to go through the form of complying with them.

5
"A Little Stream of Limestone Water"

Now that Richmond had been relieved by the defeat of McClellan first and again by the recent defeat of the same army recruited and heavily reinforced, the government resolved to try the bold expedient of invasion. I do not know whether Lee advised it or not. Jackson was certainly in favor of it. In Virginia Lee's army had accomplished so much he might very naturally believe it capable of accomplishing almost anything. It is to be presumed, therefore, that he prepared to obey the order of the President for an advance cheerfully and hopefully.[1]

Soon there was a great flutter at Washington. Rumors came thick and fast. Squadrons of rebel cavalry had been seen on the south bank of the Potomac at various points. Suspicious characters, believed to be rebel spies had been seen in Hagerstown, Frederick, and other parts of Maryland. Then came a definite statement that Leesburg was swarming with "rebs." And at last, the news spread like wildfire through the north: "Lee's army had crossed the Potomac this morning and is moving toward Frederick. The rebel General Stuart crossed the Potomac this morning opposite Poolesville, charged a body of our Federal cavalry at that point, and captured forty or fifty. McClellan's army is now marching through Washington to meet the enemy. Heavy reinforcements expected from Philadelphia and New York, etc."

So it happened when General Lee reached the Potomac and directed that such soldiers that were entirely barefooted should not be required to go forward but remain in Virginia with the reserve trains, a very large number of shoes were thrown away, etc, and the effective strength of the army was greatly reduced. As I went on through Madison and Rappahannock counties returning to my command, I met numbers of deserters, more than I had ever seen before, claiming to have hospital tickets, etc.[2]

General Stuart's column moved from Poolesville to Frederick. The infantry struck the Baltimore & Ohio Railroad near the Monocacy bridge. This they blew up and destroyed the railroad for some miles.

Lieutenant General Jackson was ordered to invest Harper's Ferry and, if possible, capture the garrison. Coming up very unexpectedly he carried the Maryland Heights by assault after a fight of brief duration. Meanwhile a portion of his forces occupied Loudoun Heights. From these positions he succeeded by the evening of the 2nd day in forcing the enemy from all their positions and they agreed to surrender next morning. Their cavalry, however, cut their way out and captured one of our trains, 75 or 80 wagons near Hagerstown.[3]

General Lee, finding that McClellan, restored to command and heavily reinforced was advancing rapidly, retreated from Frederick towards Hagerstown through South Mountain to effect a junction with Jackson and sent him couriers to hurry him up to his support.

On the morning of the 15th September according to agreement, the whole force of 11,000 marched out from the Ferry and stacked their arms in front of our lines. And immediately after the necessary arrangements could be made, General Jackson, leaving but a small garrison, set out with his corps towards Sharpsburg.

General Lee, determined to check the advancing foe on the South Mountains, formed his line of battle and quietly awaited the onset. On, on they came in brilliant array across the plains below and up the mountain grades. Presently the pickets were driven in, the enemy's skirmish line deployed, supported by formidable lines of battle. His artillery was wheeled into position on the mountain spurs in our front and the battle was joined. It raged till night when Lee, having accomplished his purpose, to gain time, retreated along the road to the little village of Sharpsburg. Major [Brigadier] General Samuel Garland, of Lynchburg, was killed in this fight.[4]

About thirty pieces of artillery and a wagon train had taken the Hagerstown Pike and gone into camp just beyond Boonsboro. Brigadier General Fitz Lee's Brigade, covering the rear on this road, was ordered to check the enemy on this road till these trains could get off.

Next morning at sunrise Fitz Lee, pressed by cavalry and infantry, and the artillery had not yet gone. He sent orders to it to push off as fast as possible while, like a true soldier, he resolved to defend it at any cost and against the field.

The odds were greatly against him. At length when he retreated through Boonsboro, the enemy were on both his flanks and rear and his command was fired upon from the houses. Not liking to be hurried too much, he wheeled a squadron or two and charged back through the village with some success and considerable loss. The cornfields on his right and left concealed the enemy on his flanks while the dust in the road was perfectly suffocating and blinding. He hurled squadron after squadron upon the overwhelming columns of the enemy until, broken and confused by the flank fire and countercharges, he could no longer hold his own and retreated in disorder. He was always blamed by his men for making this unequal fight but it seemed to be quite a feather in his cap, for of it he might say, "They have whipped me but *I saved the artillery!*"[5]

2nd lieutenant James Christian of Company F, 3rd Virginia Cavalry, was killed. The lieutenant colonel of our regiment, John T. Thornton, commanding, distinguished himself greatly in this unequal fight. Descended of a good blood, he inherited the spirit of his ancestors. When the war broke out he had never been in political life. But having risen by force of his genius to be one of the most prominent lawyers in the Southside, it was only because he had been unwilling to have office that he had not had it.[6] He was a little over 40 years of age, practiced in Buckingham, Cumberland, and Prince Edward counties, resided in Farmville and was attorney for the Commonwealth in the latter county. His practice was worth about $3,000 per annum. He accepted a seat in the Virginia convention as a conservative state-rights man. When the Peace Conference, of which John Tyler was president, adjourned he declared for secession in a beautiful and eloquent speech which elicited great applause. Whilst shrinking from no duty, he was a man of too much sobriety and of too literary a turn to take any pleasure in or to enjoy a military life. Hence, some said he was cold and haughty, others that he was a slow and cautious "old fogy," etc.

Colonel Goode had gone home sick in June and left Thornton in command. Before, he had never had a fair chance. He soon showed his administrative and executive talent. All began to feel that they had a sensible, wise, efficient commander and at *Boonsboro* they learned what before they had doubted, that they had a truly chivalrous, dashing leader!

But alas! On the 16th as his regiment was marching out to take its place in line, (a battle was expected), he was struck by a cannonball which shattered his left arm dreadfully. Private Edward N. Price, Company K, carried him from the field to a little house, where, after great loss of blood, and before any reaction had set in, the arm was amputated at the shoulder joint by our youthful assistant surgeon A[lexander] T. Bell.[7] This noble chief breathed his last about daybreak of the morning which will ever be remembered in history as the day of the battle of Sharpsburg! His remains were brought to Farmville and his general paid a high tribute to his worth in general orders to his command.[8]

Rushing down from the mountain gorge a little stream of limestone water, about 30 feet wide and from two to three feet deep flows swiftly by the village of Funkstown and gliding along its course between steep banks very near the village of Sharpsburg, it empties itself into the Potomac River. This is Antietam Creek (pronounced An-tee'-tam). After this creek the Yankees named the battle; we named it after the village.

As the shadows of the evening before began to gather around, an officer with an escort galloped up to the headquarters of the general commanding and reported the surrender of Harper's Ferry and that Lieutenant General Jackson's forces were marching up rapidly and would soon be in place. Lo, when the angry signal gun announced the mortal strife of the 17th, Jackson *was* in place. Like a true son of Mars he rode along the fatal lines that day as if invoking death. Believing in the over-ruling power of God and confiding his life to him, he devoted his whole soul to inspiring the troops. And there, too, was the *noble Lee* and the *invincible Longstreet*. Under such great commanders, what soldier would hesitate to fight!

As these great men rode among their troops high above the rattle and din of musketry and the deep roar of the hoarse artillery could be plainly heard the loud, hearty cheers of our patriot army. On, on rolled the tide of war, column after column of impetuous soldiers were hurled upon our *single line*. The enemy brought up line after line, division after division and heavily and furiously they rolled down upon our line; and *we* had but *one*! There was no relief for them and *no support*.

Now borne down by the resistless force of the mighty wave of human beings our line would shake and waver and bend here and now there. The great heart of Lee bled for his gallant men who were falling thick as autumn leaves but it palpitated for his country and he calmly gave his stern command to hold the ground at every cost.

And now the quick eye of Jackson saw the line about to break and with glistening blade and eloquent appeals he urged them to stand and *die there* rather than yield an inch. And they gave a loud cheer and charged their cartridges home.

Now Longstreet saw his guns exposed and half-worked from loss of men and the enemy about to charge. He dismounted with his staff and couriers, pointed a gun and made them fire and load and fire until the charge was made and the charge was *repulsed.*[9]

Under the inspiration of Jackson our left had swung a little across the creek and forced back the enemy's right some yards. By greatly superior force the enemy had crossed below and forced back our right and equal distance, as it is at last night!

Ten thousand men on a side would not cover the number of human beings who now lie dead upon the field or awaiting patiently the insertion of the surgeon's probe in the gaping wounds. McClellan had lost fully 20,000 men and as his officers report how they have lost, one a fourth, one a half, another two-thirds of his command. He sighs and "gloomily he thinks of the morrow."[10]

Lee and Jackson and Longstreet have held their council and have resolved "we will stand our ground." All is calm and still on the field save the low moan or the feeble cry for help of some poor boy who has not been found by his friends, whose parched lips crave a little, only a little, water. Lights pass to and fro. In the hospitals the surgeon's knife is busy and the stimulants pass freely among the pale, exhausted wounded and *too* freely among the doctors!

The day's work has been hard, very hard upon the nerves and upon the muscles and the men of each army, forgetful of the proximity of their foemen, forgetful of sorrow and care, sleep soundly sweetly. Oh how blessed a thing is sleep at such a time.

Day breaks, the sun rises. Here stands the Army of Northern Virginia, *defiant.* There stands the Army of the Potomac, *irresolute.* The latter attacked yesterday, gained nothing, and suffered greatly. Shall it attack again? We shall see. The sun ascends the heavens, is now in the zenith, at length declines, descends toward the horizon, sinks behind the distant woodlands. *Yet,* all is *still.*

The silent hours of the night were gliding by when two brigades of cavalry marched solemnly from their place in our line of battle towards our skirmish line. They dismount. Hist! What sound is that? Was it there a rumbling of artillery wheels? Wasn't there the measured tread of infantry. No, no. Fancy, fancy.

Day breaks at last. McClellan's army awakes at the sound of reveille and behold! What? Far as the eye can reach beyond the stream no troops can be seen save here and there a squad of cavalry slowly retiring, now disappearing in the distance. The ford at Sheppardstown was very rough, the banks steep and entrance narrow. But on the morning of the 19th the Army of Northern Virginia reposed quietly on the southern bank of the Potomac.

Note: I was always told that our strength at Sharpsburg was only 35,000 when it might have been 50,000 but for the causes previously mentioned in this chapter. It was a rule never to allow the Army of the Potomac to be less than 100,000 and it was at least that strong on this occasion.

That night I arrived at Winchester from Flint Hill and stayed with the brigade sick camp. Here, thanks to the poor discipline of the army I found a large portion of the brigade. Next day I went on towards my command and got to the wagon train that night and on the 21st joined the command not far from Sheppardstown. They had been suffering very much for want of forage. And the men were beginning to learn already the art of "foraging" for themselves.

Next morning having nothing to feed on I myself actually did pluck half-a-dozen ears of corn from an adjoining field to feed my horse. Subsequently while on picket between Charlestown and Harper's Ferry, I did the same thing. These things I never attempted to justify but thought there was much in extenuation of it for it was not merely our private interest we had to consult. The lines had to be held and guarded, the horses couldn't live without food and where none was furnished there was almost a necessity of taking some, when we were actually confronting the enemy and might be engaged at any time.

General Lee kept his army between Winchester and the Potomac till the latter part of October to avail himself of the supplies which abounded there. Our cavalry were stationed a part of the time at Leetown and picketing to Sheppardstown and a part at Charlestown picketing towards Harper's Ferry. We always found the people very hospitable. We had a sharp cavalry skirmish near Leetown about the last of September, in which I had a horse wounded, and another at Charlestown.[11]

While we were at Leetown, General Stuart went on an expedition which he thought would result in the capture of a number of horses to remount his cavalry, as he learned that the enemy had a large horse camp near Chambersburg, Pennsylvania. He took about half the cavalry of the two brigades, crossed the Potomac near Williamsport, went to Chambersburg, then to Frederick, Maryland, and recrossed near Leesburg. He found no camp of horses but he got a number of them from farmers along the route. He, however, broke down more than he secured, I think. Yet it was regarded as very smart and made a sensation.[12]

Stuart had an extremely gallant and promising artillery officer commanding one of the horse batteries, (batteries attached to the cavalry), by the name of [John] Pelham. This officer and T[homas] L. Rosser, colonel of the 5th Virginia Cavalry, spent more of their time at the General's headquarters as the latter were at the Bower where there were two or three charming ladies, Misses Dandridge.[13]

On the 29th of October our brigade passed in review on a large field at Leetown and then marched to Berryville camping just beyond on the road to Snicker's Ferry. Next morning we crossed the ferry and gap and encamped that night in Loudoun. We now learned that the whole army was retreating to Culpeper. Brigadier General W[illiam] E. Jones, (successor of General Turner Ashby, killed at Port Republic), was left in the Valley and also some infantry.[14]

On the 31st October, General Stuart went on a reconnaissance to Aldie. Before getting there the 2nd Cavalry charged and routed several squadrons on picket. With our regiment coming up, the pursuit was continuous through the village till we came upon a largely superior force.[15] Retiring then with a considerable lot of prisoners to where the brigade was, we had hardly time to form before we were charged by a fresh regiment. Wheeling about, we charged and drove them off. I rode down and captured a prisoner myself on this occasion and had my horse wounded.

We went into camp at Union and next day skirmished till night at Philamont. The next day we repeated the same opposition at Union, the next at Upperville. We were retreating slowly before the advance of McClellan's army, so as to allow ours time to get off with its immense trains to the south side of the Rappahannock. It was on this occasion

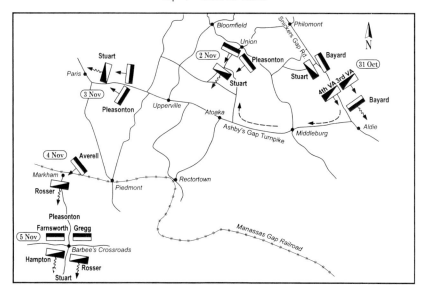

2. Loudoun Valley, 31 October–5 November 1862

that General Stuart acquitted himself with real credit and won a much greater title to renown than by any of his foolish raids. With about 5,000 cavalry he kept General [Alfred] Pleasanton, commanding about 10,000, in check and only permitted him to advance when he was free to retire without prejudice to our army.[16]

Brigadier General Fitz Lee had been kicked by a mule and disabled pro tempore. Colonel Wickham of the 4th Virginia was in command but at Upperville a piece of shell wounded him on the neck and Colonel Rosser took command. Our brigade marched that night to Markham Station on the Manassas Gap Railroad while Hampton stopped near Piedmont. Early the next day the enemy began to press us and Rosser did not handle the brigade very well. We didn't have the directing hand of Stuart with us. We at length got off, however, without much loss at Barbee's Crossroads. Here Hampton joined us on the left and about night the enemy charged us and were handsomely repulsed.

Next morning our regiment was sent with Colonel Rosser to Warrenton to reconnoiter, taking with us our gun. [George D.] Bayard's U.S. cavalry brigade nearly cut us off on the way back but with the aid of a good guide we got across the river near Warrenton Springs and rejoined our command near Waterloo Bridge.

We gradually fell back to Culpeper Court House, the army retiring behind the Rapidan. We were glad enough now to have some rest after our frequent skirmishes and constant marching. But, about the middle of November, Stuart went on a reconnaissance to Amisville, got into a slight skirmish but whipped the enemy. Here my horse was again wounded in the leg and disabled.

I was soon sent in command of a party to take the disabled horses of the regiment to Albemarle along with others of the brigade, all under command of Major [William A.] Morgan of the 1st Virginia Cavalry. We went into camp near Gap's School and remained ten or fifteen days. When relieved I got eight days leave to go home.

Our major, Jeff Phillips, was made lieutenant colonel of the 10th Virginia Cavalry in July. Senior Captain Jones had resigned.[17] So the next in rank were promoted. Thomas H. Owen became lieutenant colonel and William R. Carter, major.

6
"Stuart Set Out on a Raid"

Immediately after the battle of Sharpsburg it became evident that some general policy must be adopted to ensure the efficiency of our cavalry. Under Brigadier Generals [John] Buford, Bayard, and others and under the management of Major General Pleasanton, the Federal cavalry was improving greatly in efficiency. Stuart's raids had taught the enemy the necessity of keeping up a strong cavalry force to protect his communications and defend the country from raids in the future.

Whilst the boundless resources of the United States enabled the government to keep all of its cavalry well mounted on horses of its own, this, it was early determined, our government could not do for want of money and also from its inability to keep up larger recruiting camps because of scarcity of supplies. Hence our cavalrymen always *mounted themselves.*

Now previous to this campaign our horses had not been over marched or half fed and consequently the general condition of the horses was good. So when three or four men in a regiment had broken down horses it was no great matter to give them short furloughs to home after fresh ones.

But now the case was different. The men were far from home and there were from one to two hundred men in a regiment totally dismounted or with horses which could never do service again till recruited. Something was to be done or the cavalry would be broken up. Hence, it [had been] decided to send home from Winchester all soldiers with unserviceable horses who expressed themselves as able and willing to bring back fresh ones in 15 to 20 days.

In November Major General Stuart established recruiting camp in Albemarle. But there was no depot of supplies and after about three weeks experiment it was abandoned as wholly impracticable. From this time forward the practice, notwithstanding occasional interruption, was to detail the soldier to go to his home for the purpose of getting a horse and return in a certain number of days in this form:

Special Orders No.
                                    Headquarters, Cavalry Div.,
                                    Army of Northern Virginia
                                    December _____ 1862
The following named soldiers being dismounted are hereby detailed to go to their homes in Cumberland County, Va. To remount themselves. They will return to their commands in (20) twenty days or else be treated as deserters.

        Private W._____G._____Company G, 3rd Virginia Cavalry

Appd. By orders of   By command of
Gen. R. E. Lee   Major Gen. J. E. B. Stuart
R. H. Chilton, A.A.G.   R. Channing Price, A.A.G.
December, 1862

This method of keeping up the cavalry was subject to *very great* abuse. Men would purposely neglect their horses to break them down and get these details so that the indifferent soldiers and worthless men, (for they were synonymous), were nearly always home or on the road and the good men had all the fighting to do and all the hard drudgery of military life. Yet this would be the case anyway where the *discipline* could not be enforced as was the case with the Confederate soldiers. And it might be said on the other side that had not this indulgence of occasionally going home been accorded to the soldiers, the worthy men finding all the burden on their backs and no favor whatever shown them might have much sooner grown faint and hopeless.

As it was, towards the close of the war the cavalrymen held out better than the infantry. That is to say, there was not so great a proportion of desertions, absences without leave, etc. And I believe it was in a great measure due to this fact that the infantry soldier could never get home to see his family except that General Lee allowed four furloughs to every hundred men during the winter months. Under this detail system a regiment of 800 men would average 300 men actually present for duty in the saddle if they were even moderately fed.

I returned from home across the country halfway, (having gone as far as Richmond by railroad), and during an exceedingly disagreeable spell. I reached the encampment on the 8th of December, a bitter cold day. They were on the road from Spottsylvania [*sic*] Court House to Fredericksburg. The ground was covered with snow. My brother officers Matthews, Palmore, and Garrett had just put up a small tent without clearing away the snow and were now piling up some large logs in front of it to make a hot fire. There I was, fresh from home, from all the comforts of warm rooms, feather beds, hot fires, sumptuous meals, etc., standing *out in the woods* in snow ankle deep, had to spread my gum cloth and blankets on the snow to sleep, had nothing to feed my horse with that bitter cold night but *wheat straw*. Nobody to clean him off but *myself* and after making my dinner had to be thankful if I could get one moulded cracker and a piece of rancid meat for my supper! Yet this was but a sample of what afterwards became so common as to be almost *everyday life*!

From here we picketed on the Rappahannock from the mouth of the Rapidan to Fredericksburg. General McClellan had been relieved from command and the Army of the Potomac was now commanded by Major General Ambrose E. Burnside, a very conceited officer who proposed to lead his army to Richmond, "by a way they knew not of." So he marched from Fauquier County directly to Fredericksburg.

Our Richmond *newspaper generals* expressed the confident belief that General Lee would be able to make a stand somewhere about *the North Anna River*; at all events, that he would not fall back to Richmond without a fight! To the amazement of these persons and of General Burnside when the latter reached Falmouth, the heights near Fredericksburg were bristling with Lee's artillery! Yea, "Mas' Bob," as the soldiers loved to call him, had determined to meet him right there.

After fortifying sufficiently, each party began to prepare for an immediate battle. They had about 200 guns on a side. The enemy [had] many heavy guns: 32s, 64s, etc. We had but few if any heavier than 32-pounders and no great number of them. Lieutenant General Longstreet had been sent to Norfolk with McLaws' and Hood's (successor of Garland) divisions, 20,000 men.[1] I think we had perhaps as many as 40,000 men. Burnside had, I believe, about 120,000 men.

On the night of the 12th December he succeeded in throwing two pontoon bridges across the river, one below and one just above Fredericksburg; though at the upper bridge he was very hotly opposed by Brigadier General [William] Barksdale's gallant Mississippi Brigade. The latter withdrew in the morning and took its place in our line of battle.[2]

Our cavalry were drawn up and dismounted on the Plank Road six miles from town to guard that flank and had no part in the fight. Brigadier General Thomas Cobb of Georgia was behind the stone wall below Marye's house. This position was charged by [Thomas F.] Meagher's Irish Brigade who left three hundred dead on its front. I myself saw this sickening sight after the fight.

It was beautiful work everywhere for us except near Hamilton's Crossing. Here a powerful column landed under cover of the bank. As the approach to the river here is in three distinct terraces, they were enabled to approach very near our men before the latter could do any execution. They broke our advanced line and began to shoot the artillerymen at their guns. But our hero, Jackson, placing himself at the head of a fresh brigade and charging, hat in hand, restored the line and saved the day.

The defeated enemy retreated to the protecting bank of the river and the town of Fredericksburg. So severe had been their loss, so complete the repulse of their desperately furious onsets, that they were all the next day in a state of demoralization near akin to a panic. It was always said and believed that Jackson believed them to be in this condition and consequently favored an advance on the 14th in the hope of driving them into the river or compelling them to surrender. It certainly was in keeping with his character. And there is some reason to believe that had we attacked the next day the surrender of Burnside would have followed.

But Lee was not only cautious he was also a very human man. He knew that all the hopes of Virginia and of the Confederacy perhaps rested upon his army and he was unwilling to *endanger* that army in any offensive movement. Jackson, self reliant and strong willed would stake *everything* on the issue of a single battle because he was *determined* to succeed. Lee probably reflected also that a fight *in* the town would ensure its destruction and the death of hundreds of helpless women and children, that if he advanced across the wide bottoms to attack a force much greater in numbers and which had retired in pretty good order from the battle the day before, Burnside's two hundred guns might create such confusion and demoralization in his own army as to cause its defeat by a vigorous attack of the enemy's infantry.

Burnside, I think, acknowledged a loss of nearly 20,000 killed, wounded, and missing.[3] His troops threw a large number of their killed into a *big ice house* in the suburbs of town and half filled it!

Among those who particularly distinguished themselves in this battle was Captain Pelham of "Stuart's Horse Artillery." He made the artillery he commanded, (a whole battalion), act the part of real flying artillery on this occasion; silenced the enemy's field-pieces on this side [of] the river and played havoc with his infantry.[4] I think it was here that he won his commission of major of artillery and he was succeeded in the command of our battery by Captain [James] Breathed, of whom more hereafter, he himself commanding both batteries of our division.

For some time all remained quiet along this line. Burnside, making occasional feints in the neighborhood of Port Royal and causing some little change in the position of our troops, nevertheless took very good care to remain where he was. Our brigade went into camp at Guinea Station, Richmond, Fredericksburg & Potomac Railroad, and drilled frequently in regimental drill. We got here about five pounds of corn and six or eight pounds of hay per diem to the horse. Our own rations were plain but wholesome but sufficient. Hampton's brigade was meanwhile picketing on the upper Rappahannock having his camp near Culpeper Court House.

On the 30th December Stuart set out "on a raid" with our brigade and two pieces of artillery.[5] January 1st we crossed the Rappahannock and encamped not far from Bealton [*sic*]. Next day marched towards Aquia Creek and on the 3rd we attacked Dumfries having on the way there pursued and captured eight richly loaded sutlers' wagons. One disconsolate looking German-Jew, as he passed along behind a gay trooper by a party who were testing the merits of a lot of bottles labeled "Old Bourbon Whiskey," being asked what he lost in the fracas replied, "Me lose twenty tousan' dollar."

The 3rd Regiment was stationed on the Fredericksburg Road facing in that direction to oppose any force which might come from the camp at Aquia Creek while the other regiments dismounted and made quite a vigorous attack. But the enemy had two regiments of cavalry and two

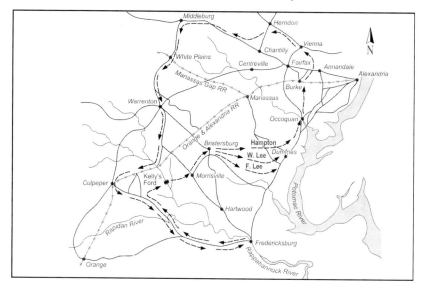

3. Dumfries Raid, 26–31 December 1862

or three of infantry, so though we drove them from their position and across the creek beyond Dumfries, Stuart found there was no hope of capturing them and might himself be attacked in rear by the arrival of other troops so he withdrew westward about night and at 1 a.m. we went into camp about 10 miles off.

Our four days rations had given out the day before so the men broke in the captured wagons and had nothing else to eat than the notions they got therefrom. I remember full well I had one cracker left that night and enjoyed it very much sweetened with some choice syrup from the wagons furnished me by a friend. We found hay hard by camp and our horses were kept eating till day broke.

Next morning I breakfasted on a small bit of cheese, (scarcely a mouthful), and two or three sardines. When we moved out all thought that we were going to return but presently a courier reported the capture of one of our pickets, (lieutenant, and a dozen men), and Stuart turned towards Occoquan. Passing by a cornfield, the quartermasters called upon the colonel for details to get top fodder for the command. One man in four turned out and got his turn and under charge of a lieutenant, they came on behind their respective regiments.

Presently someone said, "Yankees are about," and then came the order to throw down that forage and take places in the ranks. Fitz Lee moved straight ahead with three regiments while ours was ordered to report to Colonel Rosser of the 5th. That officer, mounted on a bob-tailed black charger of high metal, appeared to great advantage. Making a detour to the right with the two regiments, we drew sabres and put out at a gallop hoping to gain the enemy's rear but Lee got into him rather too soon and put him to flight at once. (I think his force was the 11th and 14th Pennsylvania, two regiments I know). We joined in the race. We did considerable execution killing about twenty and taking some forty prisoners before reaching Quantico Creek.

Here they made a stand but we crossed under their fire and pursued them to and through their camp which we destroyed, tents, baggage, and all. It abounded in crackers and meat, sugar, coffee, and "notions." Being now very hungry I enjoyed some crackers and peach jelly *hugely*. Some of the Yankees, (we afterwards learned), fled to Occoquan while others kept on to Alexandria.[6]

A regiment presently came down the road from Fairfax Court House and worried us a little but were soon run off with a loss of six or eight prisoners. After feeding on the shelled oats we found in camp we took a by-road and passed by a station of the Orange & Alexandria Railroad, destroyed some stores and intercepted a telegram from Major General Heintzleman, commanding at Washington, to Brigadier General Slocum, commanding at Fairfax Court House stating "the rebel General Stuart is on a raid with 5000 cavalry. When last heard from was marching towards Fairfax Court House. Be sure to notify officers commanding at Centreville and Annandale. With proper precautions his escape is impossible." Stuart forwarded a dispatch better calculated to serve his purposes and moved on.[7]

About 9 p.m. he struck the turnpike from Alexandria to Fairfax Court House about twelve miles from the former place, charged a picket we found there, and moved on at a trot toward the Court House where there were 5000 infantry and eight pieces of artillery. We all involuntarily fell to thinking of the fitness of cavalry for assaulting breastworks, of the capacity of our own particular beast for clearing ditches, of the effect of night frosts upon a fresh wound, etc. Presently there was a loud cheer in front and we found ourselves going faster. Then there was a tremendous volley, a blaze of fire in front, and a sudden halt. Chattering teeth and anxious agitated inquiries one of another showed clearly that all thought "somebody was hurt." Then came the inevitable "by fours left about wheel." To cut matters short, Stuart charged the pickets, etc., to create the impression of an intended assault while really at that very moment Hampton's command, (a portion of which was with us and in our rear), was moving off along a by-road to the right towards Chantilly. We had charged upon an infantry picket and had one horse killed.

Stuart withdrew only some three hundred yards and had hundreds of campfires kindled to create the impression that we were going to stay all night, *at least*. Leaving the 3rd and 5th under Rosser to cover the retreat, he pushed off. A flag of truce came after a while to know "If these are not our men we have been firing into." Rosser replied rather affirmatively and said, "Tell the General I'll report in the morning." Fifteen minutes after, we were gone and presently a section of artillery, which we had plainly heard coming down from the court house, opened furiously on our camp. We laughed and rode on.

The night was very cold and what with empty stomachs and loss of sleep we all suffered a good deal. Next day we reached Annandale by an hour by sun, drove off a regiment of Yankees, captured a major and captain, fed horses, and breakfasted on a few sardines. We passed on thence without serious difficulty by Aldie, White Plains, and Culpeper Court House back to Guinea Station arriving there about the 10th January, 1863. I have unavoidably encroached a little upon 1863 in this chapter devoted to the "Second Year of the War." In this expedition we captured about one hundred prisoners altogether and some dozen wagons or more.[8]

Correspondence, 1862

Hd Qs., 3rd Va. Cav.
Wagon Camp, Wednesday
Dec. 17, 1862
Dear William,

We have had stirring times. "Richmond has been *conquered* at Fredericksburg and *occupied* by the army from Suffolk and the Rebel army of the East is crushed." (Herald) Many criticisms will be passed on our glorious Lee. His name will be lightly spoken of by many. But I assure you he has acquitted himself nobly.

He told his generals Wednesday night to be ready. The enemy would attempt a crossing next morning. One hour before day two great signal guns were fired and presently the enemy were discovered stretching the bridges and at the same time their heavy batteries opened a tremendous fire. The regiment of sharpshooters [Barksdale's Mississippi Brigade] placed on the river bank by Lee pretty well destroyed the "Irish Brigade" in their attempt to cross the bridge and kept the Yankees back all day.[1] That night he [Lee] withdrew his troops to his own line of battle and let the Yankees cross.

Friday there was skirmishing in town nearly all day. That evening General Lee put all of his commanders on their guard telling them the enemy would attack him in the morning. Orders were sent us on picket up the river to hold ourselves in readiness to cooperate and if possible annoy the enemy's right during the fight. Hancock's corps [division] advanced in beautiful order Saturday from the river bank across the flats to the bluffs where our lines were. A deathlike silence was followed by a tremendous roar of artillery and crash of fearful musketry. The earth shook and Hooker's veterans quailed before the fearful storm of grape and musket shot which was fast melting their ranks away. A line five miles long of splendidly disciplined troops made charge after charge against the impregnable position of General Lee. It was all in vain. Shattered and broken, the old brigades which had so often fought for the Stars and Stripes were again forced to retreat in disgrace and disorder.

I saw the enemy's extreme right, an open space (intersected by small lot fences) about the size of the three houselots at Chellow, on yesterday. It had been commanded by the hills on top of which was artillery, at the bottom our infantry behind a strong stone wall. About 1000 dead Yankees were still lying on the ground. Our men lost only about ten or fifteen killed opposite this point. In forty yards of our line was a plank fence enclosing a lot of about 1/2 acre which contained at least two hundred dead Yankees. Just behind this fence and for ten yards from it they lay about as *thick* as men could be put without piling them. About one dozen dead bodies were in twenty yards of our men.

I had a view of the Yankee army on the other side of the river but could not see very distinctly. They retired so suddenly yesterday morning that they left about 500 men this side in town. They were captured.

General Lee was right in not attacking them in the flats on Sunday for their numerous and heavy batteries commanded the flats completely and he probably would have lost 20,000 men without killing and taking more than 25,000 or 30,000 Yankees. He has a splendid army and needs every man of them. It would be foolish to murder them merely to kill a few more Yankees without making his victory any more complete. He estimated the Yankee loss at 15,000 or 20,000. It is thought ours will not exceed 3,000. Hooker is said to be killed. The Yankees are gone, where I do not know.

I have been quite sick from Wednesday till yesterday but kept with the regiment as I thought they might get into the fight. I had the worst thirst I think I ever had (headache and disorder of the stomach). I am a great deal better now.

I hope we will go into winter quarters soon. A young Daniel of the 2nd Virginia Cavalry got pretty tight some days ago. Fowler of my company says he's the judge's son. The latter was Adjutant of the 11th Infantry but may be turned out.

Your Affectionate Brother, Robert T. Hubard, Jr.

Year 3
1863

7
"One of the Best Cavalry Fights of the War"

Our brigade now marched via Bowling Green to Mangohick Church in King William County and went into camp. We didn't build huts but had about ten tents to a company to which we built wooden chimneys, got straw to put on the ground for our beds, and made ourselves tolerably comfortable.

Our horses only fared tolerably well getting sometimes five or six pounds of corn and same amount of wheat straw, sometimes nothing but top fodder. Horses were now worth from $400 to $800 Confederate money according to quality.

Our mess cook, Effard Jenkins, was taken by the Yankees while having a turkey cooked at a house near Middleburg in November. We had now, (Matthews, Palmore and I), two yellow boys from Ca Ira, Robert and Thruston Smith, and a black boy, Giles, belonging to Palmore, as our servants.[1] The first was an excellent cook, the other two attended to the horses[,] blacked our boots, etc., for blacking was not too dear to be used in camp. We had a rude table made of pine plank laid on some poles, a tolerable dinner service of tin plates and cups and plain knives and forks. Sweet potatoes sold for $2.50 a bushel, turkeys about $5 each.

On the 9th day of February we marched for Culpeper Court House via [Mt. Carmel] Church and Summerville Ford on the Rapidan. We encamped on a piece of woods north of the Court House 1 1/2 miles belonging to Reverend Mr. George. Nothing occurred to interrupt the monotony of a dull camp life till March.

Hampton's Brigade had gone off to the Southside counties to forage. Our's had to picket the river from the confluence of the Rappahannock

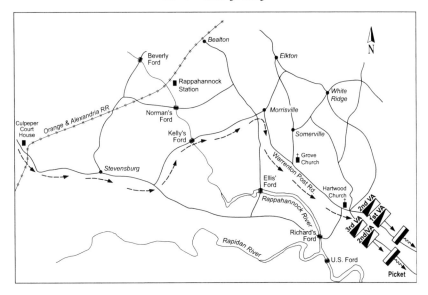

4. Hartwood Church Raid, 24–25 February 1863

and Rapidan up towards Crigglersville. Brigadier General Fitz Lee did, however, go on one little expedition which I had like to have forgotten. With about three hundred men of the 1st, 2nd, and 3rd Regiments he went across at Kelly's Ford and turning down towards Falmouth, came up with a regiment of [William W.] Averell's Brigade near Stafford Church about seven miles from Stafford Court House the next day. This was the latter part of February.

We charged the enemy and routed them, capturing about 75 prisoners. After securing our prisoners and plunder, a fresh regiment came up and we retired until we had entered a body of woods, then several squadrons were drawn up and awaited the enemy's advance. They presently charged our rear guard into the woods when we sallied out, met, repulsed, and drove them half a mile capturing eight or ten more prisoners.

Lee, thinking his little command might be overwhelmed by a larger force if he remained longer, now withdrew and marched till late at night, encamping near Groveton. The snow was about eight inches deep on this occasion and made it rather heavy work charging. Captain Richard Watkins, (Company K successor to [Peyton R.] Berkeley [who had] resigned), lost his horse in the charge. He fell with him and then [the horse] ran off to the enemy.

Lt. Palmore, being a good doctor, was left with the wounded and had a pleasant sojourn of three weeks at the headquarters of the 3rd Pennsylvania Cavalry where he met with his old friend, Effard Jenkins, who was now cooking for some of their officers.

Averell followed us up to Kelly's Ford but we got across safely and returned to camp by 4 p.m. of the next day. I think the fight was on the 27th February.[2] Our loss was one or two killed and five or six wounded. The enemy lost several killed and wounded. Brigadier General Averell determined to retaliate.

So on the 17th day of March, 1863, he crossed at Kelly's Ford with 4,000 cavalry and four pieces of artillery. Fitz Lee heard of his arrival the day before at Groveton and increased the pickct at Kelly's Ford to eighty men including the Buckingham troop, Captain William A. Moss. This squadron of the 4th Regiment had a sharp fight and three times repulsed the enemy in their efforts to get across. But at length they made a vigorous effort and succeeded.

Our men under Captain [William B.] Wooldridge now retired about a mile and a half and met General Fitz Lee coming down with all of the brigade he could get together, in all about 800 men of the 1st, 2nd, 3rd, 4th, and 5th Virginia Cavalry. William H. F. Lee had been made a brigadier general and commanded the 9th, 10th, and 15th Virginia Cavalry and was down in Essex, etc., counties wintering.

We found the enemy advancing rapidly, turned to the left in a field and formed. As soon as it was done, Colonel Owen made a charge driving a regiment before him but, being unable to get at them because of a stone fence, kept along their flank till he had gotten directly in front of the enemy's whole line which was drawn up behind the wall to our right. Circling around to the left, we galloped into line of battle fronting the enemy and halted.

Rosser, now coming charging down our front with the 5th and wheeling, formed on our left. Seeing the situation in which we were and thinking that we might get at the enemy through a lane on our left, these two colonels rcsolved to try it. Wheeling to the left by fours, the 5th trotted into the lane and we followed. The 2nd now made a charge on the right but were flanked and fell back. The enemy now advanced a regiment, dismounted, to the fence and poured a hot fire into our flanks. The lane did not give us any way to the enemy and we were compelled to retire, (as we couldn't advance), from under the hot fire, over the next hill.

Lieutenant [Benjamin W.] Lacy, Company F, was wounded in the leg, several others wounded. Major [John W.] Puller of 5th and Sergeant [George] Betts of the 3rd [were] killed under that fire.[3]

The enemy now advanced their dismounted men on us and mounted men on the left. The 1st and 4th charged the latter beautifully and drove them back, while the 3rd charged the former and drove them. Stuart was on the field with Surgeon [John B.] Fontaine, Major Pelham and others of his staff but left direction of matters to Fitz Lee.

Our whole line now drew back a quarter of a mile, reformed and awaited the enemy. They advanced vigorously and Major Pelham, while entering with great zest into a beautiful charge of the regiment on the right was mortally wounded in the head. Fontaine had his horse killed while with us. I was in command of my company and had thirty men on the field.

The 5th now charged a body of dismounted men behind a fence (of rails) but were repulsed. The 3rd then tried but were likewise repulsed, (just when they seemed about to succeed), by a *galling crossfire*. We had several men wounded here, Hugh Goodman, Company G, among them.[4] My horse was shot but not hurt much.[5]

The enemy now opened with two pieces of artillery and ours hadn't been brought up. So Fitz Lee resolved to fall back a mile across a wide flat and take up a line at the foot of a hill on which his two guns were placed in charge of Captain Breathed. Our position here was very good, the level ground in our front was 600 yards across, bordered on the other side by woods. The road to Kelly's Ford ran through the centre, from us directly across, with a cap-and-stake fence on either side. At right angles to this road, a plank fence crossed the centre of this plateau. Our regiment was drawn up "in line of battle," i.e. in two ranks, from left to right in the following order: 1st, 5th, 3rd, (our right nearly at the road), 2nd, and 4th. The plank fence was broken in places except in front of the 2nd and 4th who had to halt and break it down to make their charge.

Our mounted skirmish line presently fell back from the woods in our front and took position behind the plank fence. The enemy's skirmishers could be presently discerned by the little puffs of white smoke curling upward in the air along the line of the woods. After a while they became bolder and advanced steadily out into the open field. They were mounted about five yards apart in single file and extended along our entire front [of] half a mile. The skirmish now became very brisk, indeed. Our line was only about one-third the thickness of theirs but still they held their ground beautifully.

General Fitz Lee now rode along our line and told the colonels [that] immediately after two shots from his cannon, he should command a charge on the extreme right and wished the regiments to gallop off in columns of squadrons, their front into line "en echelon." That is, in such a way that the regiments would be situated towards each other very much like a flight of steps thus

The dark blue lines of Yankee regiments now appeared to skirt the woods and they began to unlimber their artillery, one piece in the road, two to the right of it a few yards, and one out some distance. Then about 3 p.m. our signal guns now fired, then we heard the loud voice of Fitz Lee commanding, "Forward gallop march," saw the gleam of his battle blade, and dashed onward to the charge. It was a beautiful, splendid charge, the prettiest I ever witnessed. We drove the gunners from their guns and but for the tremendous odds, could have gotten them. But we were compelled to draw off to our position.

Yet, such was the moral effect of this charge that Averell was frightened. He thought we had been supported and after awaiting where he was for about a half an hour, began to retreat! The enemy poured grape and shrapnel shot into us during this charge and in it alone the 3rd Regiment lost about twenty men and an equal number of horses. The regiment had 240 officers and men present and lost four killed and about twenty-four wounded. Our whole loss in brigade was over one hundred men and nearly 150 horses killed and wounded. I never ascertained what Averell's was.[6]

By this little fight we defeated an expedition designed to reach and destroy Gordonsville. I always regarded it as one of the best cavalry fights during the war. A fight which reflected credit on the men and no less credit on the gallant young officer who, without support, relying on the moral effect of a charge such as he knew his command would make under his lead, hurled his 800 against 4,000 with the result of so far discouraging and demoralizing the latter as to induce them to retreat from the field and abandon a carefully prepared for and elaborately planned expedition! This fight won for our brigade a high reputation, a reputation which it strove to successfully maintain ever afterward.[7]

J. E. B. Stuart, who spelled his name very much as it is done here, [facsimile of Stuart's signature], began his career in the Confederate Army as Colonel of the 1st Virginia Cavalry. The 2nd Virginia Cavalry was commanded by Colonel [Richard C. W.] Radford, an "Old Army" officer till April, 1861. The 3rd by Colonel Robert Johnston, likewise an officer in the Old Army for the same time. The 4th by Colonel Beverly Robinson [Robertson], the 5th by Colonel Rosser, both formerly officers of the regular army.

The 1st Virginia Cavalry was made up of the Amelia Troop and companies from the Valley. The 2nd [was made up] of 2 companies from Albemarle, one from Amherst, 2 from Campbell, 1 from Bedford, Botetourt, and Roanoke. The 3rd I have before mentioned. The 4th [was made up] of companies from Powhatan, Chesterfield, Buckingham, Hanover, Madison, Culpeper, Fauquier, and Prince William.[8] The Madison and Fauquier (Black Horse) companies were so large they were counted as squadrons. The 5th Virginia was [made up] of one company from Petersburg, Richmond, James City, Gloucester, Matthews, etc. These regiments it will be seen were mostly composed of an independent class of country farmers with an unusually large proportion of the elite of the counties from which they came. Their material and the officers who taught them the rudiments of war were a sufficient guarantee of their future success and distinction and it is not to be wondered at that this brigade won a reputation second to that of no other cavalry, if indeed, of *any* other brigade atall in the Confederate service.

In 1862 Stuart, having been made brigadier, William Jones succeeded him as colonel but at the election in April, Fitz Lee was elected colonel of the 1st Virginia Cavalry with R. Welby Carter, lieutenant colonel, and William Morgan, major. (*Correction: The lieutenant colonel was [James H.] Drake who, afterward, became colonel, Carter, lieutenant colonel, etc. Drake was killed in the Valley of Virginia in 1863, I think.) Radford of the 2nd was turned out and Thomas T. Munford was chosen colonel with [James W.] Watts, lieutenant colonel, and Cary Breckinridge, major.

Robert [Johnston] was turned out and Goode elected colonel of the 3rd as stated. He having resigned, [on] 18th November, 1862, Lieutenant Colonel Owen was promoted colonel with William R. Carter, lieutenant colonel, and Henry Carrington, major.

Robertson became brigadier and went to North Carolina in July, 1862, and Wickham became colonel of the 4th Virginia Cavalry with Robert Randolph, lieutenant colonel, and William Payne, major.

Of the 5th, Thomas L. Rosser was colonel with H. Clay Pate, lieutenant colonel (killed at Yellow Tavern), and [J. W.] Puller, major (killed March 17, 1863).

The following are some of the changes which had occurred in my regiment by resignations, etc. "A": G. D. White, captain, Boyd, 1st lieutenant, [David D.] Gayle and [John P.] Puryear, 2nd lieutenants; "B": same captain and 1st lieutenant but [William T.] Smith and [C. C.] Miller 2nd lieutenants; "C": Chappell, captain, J[ames] W. Hall, 1st lieutenant, [Samuel H.] Ragland and [James W.] Hall, 2nd lieutenants; "D": John Lamb, captain; "E": J. K. Jones, captain, A[lexander] B. Jones, 1st lieutenant, [Patrick H.] Fitzgerald and [Franklin W.] Guy, 2nd lieutenants; "F": J. R. Christian, captain, B[enjamin] W. Lacy, 1st lieutenant, [Henry W.] Stamper and [Edgar M.] Crump, 2nd lieutenants; "H": William Collins, captain; I[saac] J. Tynes, 1st lieutenant, etc.; "I": [Joseph H.] Bourdon, Jr. 2nd lieutenant; "K": Watkins, captain, [John H.] Knight, 1st lieutenant, [Archer A.] Haskins and [Henry T.] Meredith, 2nd lieutenants.[9] On Fitz Lee's promotion [R. W.] Carter became colonel of the 1st Regiment.

We had a quiet season of rest after the battle of Kellysville until the 27th of April. Despairing of success at the hands of Burnside, Mr. Lincoln removed him and placed Major General Joe Hooker in command of the Army of the Potomac. That officer, leaving about 30,000 men under Burnside immediately opposite Fredericksburg, moved the main body up the river a little as if to cross at the fords just above town and began to make strong feints. Then suddenly throwing a column of 30,000 men across the Rappahannock up at Kelly's Ford, he attempted to flank the position of General Lee. His movement was very successful at first. The pickets at Kelly's Ford and thence down were all captured. But an inside picket on the Culpeper Court House Road took the alarm and reported to Stuart.

He, taking his division, marched down towards Kelly's Ford, saw a heavy column moving down toward Germanna Ford and shelled their trains all day so that they could not follow. Taking some prisoners, he got from them some hints and telegraphed General Lee from Culpeper Court House. But the latter had no cavalry with him except the 10th Virginia Cavalry under Colonel J. L. Davis. Colonel Owen was ordered to proceed by a forced march with two squadrons of his regiment across Raccoon Ford, then as near to Germantown as possible, send out scouts, get what information he could, and await further orders.

The night was dark and rainy. Reaching Locust Grove about 12 o'clock, we threw out pickets and sent off two scouting parties, one towards Germanna, one towards the ford below Ely's. Marching on further we halted at about 1 a.m. and slept in the rain till 3 a.m. on the 30th April.

A dispatch was then received from Fitz Lee directing us to move forward, if possible, get between the enemy and Fredericksburg, delay him all we could, and give General Lee all the information we could get. Hearing nothing from our scouts we went ahead, struck the Germanna branch of the Plank Road five miles from that point, and sent a scout of five men in that direction. They came back presently reporting they had discovered a large encampment of infantry, estimated over 20,000, and a force of several thousand cavalry drawn up and forming to move off. The other scouts finally came up and reported as above and also that a column of infantry and a large wagon and artillery train were across at the other ford and in motion towards Chancellorsville.

After a while the enemy appeared in our front and began to skirmish. Then a courier we had sent to Chancellorsville came back and reported that the infantry regiment on picket there were skirmishing with Yankee cavalry and falling back along the Plank Road. We did not stay any longer but went on down this road towards Chancellorsville. Getting to the fork of the Plank Road and learning that the enemy were on the road between us and Chancellorsville not more than 1 1/2 miles off, we turned to the right to Todd's Tavern.

On the way by direction of Colonel Owen, I, acting as adjutant, wrote off a dispatch for General Lee on a miserable bit of paper upon my knee and while it was dropping rain. So do trifles sometimes prove to be matters of great moment. This little bit of paper carried to General Lee [was] his first positive knowledge that a flanking column was moving upon him! For Stuart's dispatch was uncertain and gave no definite information as to whether this was a *heavy flank movement* or some little feint.

Jackson's whole corps was immediately put in motion. It was some miles below Fredericksburg. When courier [William] Bruce delivered the dispatch to Adjutant General [Walter] Taylor he said, "The General is asleep but must see *this at once*" and woke him up immediately. The only force we had above Fredericksburg was Richard H. Anderson's Division at Zion Church about eight miles from town up the Plank Road.

We attempted to go directly across from Todd's Tavern to the Plank Road but found a heavy force in our front and had to deflect to the right and come up considerably in Anderson's rear. Stuart, coming on down that night ran into this same body of cavalry between Todd's Tavern and Spottsylvania Court House, was well nigh captured while riding on ahead and then our brigade had a right sharp fight in the dark killing about twenty-five Yankees and losing ten or fifteen men.[10]

The way being opened, they joined the troops on the left of our new line, which faced to the west. The 4th was sent over to where we were and Colonel Wickham took charge of this command, the 4th and part of the 3rd Virginia Cavalry.

The arrival during the night of Jackson's forces gave us a very respectable body of troops to meet the flank movement next day. [Ambrose R.] Wright's Brigade, Anderson's Division, went forward that evening and saw nothing but cavalry who retired before them and he began to think it was all a humbug, sort of a false alarm which the confounded, sorry, good-for-nothing "calvary" had gotten up. For when an infantryman general or private wished to show his spite, and they were *all* very spiteful towards us, they would call us derisively "calvary." Perhaps the only good reason for this spiteful feeling was that opined by my servant, Davy. As, while he and I were riding by some infantry one day, they called out "Here's your calvary." He said, "Dey jes' do so cause dey down in de mud while you on good horse."

8
"Our Brigade Advanced to Aldie"

The morning of the 1st of May dawned upon us through the clouds and fog. But gradually the vapors arose and floated away and the lessening clouds were at length parted asunder by the dissolving rays of the sun and a warm, pleasant May day breathed its sweet influence upon us. Lieutenant General Jackson passed by us as we lay about in our roadside camp awaiting orders and presently I was called upon by my colonel to detail two detachments, each under a lieutenant, to report immediately to Lieutenant General Jackson. One of these was 1st Lieutenant Charles Palmore of Company G.

Having made the detail I walked up the road to where the Lieutenant General was standing and entered into conversation with my collegemate and his Assistant Adjutant General, Major Alexander Pendleton.[1] He told me that Brigadier General Wright and Major General Anderson were both of the opinion that this movement of the enemy was only a reconnaissance in force and that he thought the Lieutenant General was of the same opinion. The latter was standing at this time dressed in a military glaze-covered cap pulled down over his eyes, grey frock coat with short skirt, grey pants and without his arms, with paper and pencil in hand, sketching some of his plans and pointing to Lieutenant Palmore, who stood at his side, the point on the extreme right which he wished him [Palmore] to occupy for observation.

Presently Palmore turned to go, mounted, and carefully turning his horse, the head of the latter rubbed against the General's shoulder, turning him half around. Never taking his eyes off his papers, the General continued his reflections without being in the slightest degree disturbed.

Another detail was ordered to report to Brigadier General Wright, now about to advance. Of this, Lieutenant B. Hill Carter of Shirley took command and was sent forward to find the enemy while Colonel Owen, with the remainder of his force, advanced parallel and to the right of the infantry.

We soon captured a major of Burnside' staff making his way from the headquarters of Hooker to General Burnside.[2] This important capture gave us some valuable information about the disposition of the enemy's forces. Pressing forward, Lieutenant Carter soon got into a hot skirmish and was himself mortally wounded while acting with reckless daring.

Our lines were advanced four miles and came up with a heavy force entrenching themselves on the heights of Chancellorsville. This is not a very precipitous elevation but one rising gradually to a considerable elevation about the country to the west, south, east, and north of it. Nothing beyond a heavy skirmish occurred today.

Saturday, the 2nd, Lieutenant General Jackson, with permission of General Lee, undertook the bold plan of getting around the enemy's right flank and attacking it in rear by the difficult way of "the Wilderness."

He marched off with from 27,000 to 28,000 men and his entire artillery and wagon train. The enemy got a glimpse of the latter and flattered themselves with the pleasing fancy that the "rebs" were in "full retreat for Richmond." A vigorous attack was made on this train by a division of infantry and would doubtless have been successful but for the great gallantry and obstinate fighting of Lieutenant Colonel William R. Carter commanding three squadrons of 3rd Virginia Cavalry and a battalion of infantry who held the enemy at bay till the trains could move off and a brigade came to his relief. This affair was near the "[Catherine] Furnace" southeast of Chancellorsville.

Jackson was, meanwhile, noiselessly, rapidly, pushing forward now across Orange Plank Road, now across Germanna Plank Road, and now plunging out of sight into the dense, almost impassible chinquapin and red wood copse of "the Wilderness."

About 5 p.m. the commanding officer of the right corps, (the 11th, I think), of Hooker's army was sitting with his staff in front of his tents.[3] His men were busily digging and throwing up a formidable line of works facing southeast. They were talking, (said one of them, a prisoner), of the discovered movement southward of the wagon train and canvassing the probable motive of Lee in making this hasty retreat without a fight and making merry over the triumphant pursuit which they would inaugurate tomorrow when. . . . .Lo! The earth trembled beneath their feet and there is a great crashing among the trees at the discharge of twenty-five pieces of artillery upon their rear and not over a half a mile distant! Surprise and excitement gave way to confusion and confusion to a wild, *perfectly uncontrollable panic.*

The "rebels" now filling the air with terrific yells made a tremendous onset with fixed bayonets. It was all over in a breath. The 11th Corps fled from the field and Jackson pressed forward toward the centre. Hooker made haste to swing his centre around sufficiently to face him and awaited his attack.

Night coming on, Jackson, with Major [Colonel Stapleton] Crutchfield and others of his staff, rode through his lines to reconnoiter, telling his men he wouldn't return that way and that they must fire on any body coming from the front. Five minutes afterwards a body of men came galloping to the very point he had left. The commands, "Ready—aim—fire" were answered by a heavy volley and Lieutenant General Jackson reeled and fell from his horse fearfully wounded! Several of his escort were killed, the Major and others wounded badly.[4]

It seems that a moment or so after leaving his own lines, the General came suddenly and, to him no doubt, very unexpectedly upon a strong line of Yankees advancing and close at hand. It was supposed that, wishing to appraise his command of the near approach of the enemy, or possibly flurried by so nearly running into the enemy, he forgot what instructions he had given his troops. Thus, while nobody was to blame perhaps, our greatest military hero fell at the hands of his own troops, by whom he was loved with a devotion never surpassed. And our Confederacy received a blow greater than any other that could have been inflicted, not excepting the total defeat of the Army of Northern Virginia.

Couriers were sent off for Major General J. E. B. Stuart by direction of General Jackson, who appointed him to take his place. In one hour Stuart was calmly giving orders, restoring things to rights, and making the necessary arrangements to follow up the success of "the great flank movement of the war!" Major General Lafayette McLaws Division had arrived and gone forward on the original front where Lee commanded in person.

Jackson was tenderly cared for and carried off gently to a house near Hamilton's Crossing. He was badly wounded in one arm and the hand of the other. His staff surgeon, Hunter McGuire, amputated his arm and hoped to save the other hand. Though deeply distressed, the country hoped that our noble Christian soldier might recover and live to strike again those giant blows which never once failed to tell upon the enemy and bring success to our colors. General Lee wrote him a letter worthy and characteristic of him congratulating him upon his great victory and chiefly to his own exertions, expressing profound sorrow at his misfortune and declaring that, had it been the Divine pleasure, he would have preferred that the blow should have fallen on himself than on him.

The General's medical attendant pronounced his wounds doing well and expressed hopes of his recovery. But unfortunately he was attacked with pneumonia, sank rapidly, and expired on the 10th May.

All the states of the Confederacy felt that they had sustained a common loss. The government and the Army went in mourning for him and even the Yankee papers passed eulogies upon the illustrious dead. He spoke and acted always the true Christian and felt that he died a Christian martyr. As he requested, they carried his body to his home at Lexington, Virginia, where he had long lived as an honored professor in the Virginia Military Institute. His mortal remains now quietly sleep beneath the green sod of the Valley and his spirit has fled to the realm above "where the wicked cease from troubling and the weary are at rest."

He distinguished himself highly in the Mexican War and was brevetted major. His private character was upright to a degree that inspired his meanest enemies with respect while it awed them into silence. He lived fully up to the sentiment "verite sans peur et sans reproche."[5]

His patriotism was with perfect devotion and without one selfish thought or aspiration. Cheerfully, freely, fully he gave himself to the cause for which he lived and died. And though dead, he still liveth; liveth not only in the world beyond but also on this earth in the hearts and affections of his countrymen. And his noble influence is passing about and disseminating itself like a celestial spirit among the thoughts and feelings of those he has left, to affect generations yet unborn and beget in them those noble impulses, the greatest, the brightest and holiest actions of which human nature is capable.

Reverend Robert L. Dabney, professor in the Union Theological Seminary, Prince Edward [Court House], Virginia, who was for a time Assistant Adjutant General on his staff has written his biography and it will doubtless, ere long, issue from the press.[6]

Sunday morning, the 3rd, Major General Stuart commanding the 1st Corps advanced to the attack upon the enemy's centre. At the head of his splendid body of troops, ably supported by the forces on our right under Major General R. H. Anderson, General Robert E. Lee was present on the field in person commanding the army. The fight raged furiously for hours. At length the glad tidings reached us on the extreme right "the enemy are in full retreat towards the river."

Our bugles sounded and all the necessary arrangements were made to hurl a brigade of cavalry upon the flanks of the retreating enemy. We mounted and moved off at a trot. After a while we were halted and everything seemed to be paralyzed. Our troops along the whole line halted! Yes, halted in the moment of victory just when a great prize seemed in our grasp.

But not without good reason did they halt. Courier after courier came galloping in from Brigadier General [Jubal A.] Early, (who had been left at Fredericksburg with his division), with 1st: "A large force is moving down to the river opposite—a heavy artillery duel in progress." 2nd: "Despite most strenuous efforts the enemy has succeeded in throwing across a heavy force. I have retired to Marye's hill and hope to hold it." 3rd: "After a most sanguinary struggle the enemy flanked my position. I evacuated it and am falling back up the plank road." Early with about six thousand men was retreating before Burnside at the head of (25,000) twenty-five thousand. Our lines in front of Hooker had to be greatly weakened and our only fresh division, McLaws', went to reinforce Early.[7]

Now was Hooker's great opportunity for presently another division under Brigadier General [Cadmus M.] Wilcox was sent off to Early. Never before had a general greater opportunity to retrieve his fortunes. But from incapacity or some cause unexplained he failed to improve it and remained idle. After an obstinate fight for some hours Burnside was defeated and driven in disorder across the river. McLaws' Division returned that night and all the orders were issued for an early attack next morning.[8]

Hooker retreated to the north side of the stream during the night and saved us from another severe fight and at least a doubtful victory. The loss in this battle was not much if anything short of ten thousand on a side killed and wounded. We took a number of prisoners, I don't remember how many.[9]

Our cavalry was sent scouring through the dense woods between Chancellorsville and the river to pick up stragglers. While this engaged, I came upon two infantrymen who attempted to make off through the copse. Having halted them in vain, I fired several shots at them with my pistol and called for some comrades who were near to assist in surrounding them. They now halloed to me to come and take them and surrendered. On being asked why they did not surrender when I fired at them they replied it was true they had heard me *shoot* but thought I fired in *another direction*. This was a poor compliment to my accuracy as a shot. Our wagon train having been stampeded about the commencement of the fight and thrown away all of our baggage, I was under the necessity of taking an extra shirt and pair of drawers which I found in the knapsack of one of them.

After this our cavalry were concentrated at Culpeper Court House and General Lee began his arrangements for the next campaign. Major Generals R. S. Ewell and Ambrose P. Hill were now promoted lieutenant generals and the army was divided into three corps: First [Corps] Longstreet's, Second [Corps] Ewell's, Third [Corps] Hill's. The Second Corps had as division commanders: 1st Major General Edward Johnson, 2nd Major General Jubal Early, 3rd Major General Robert E. Rodes. The Third Corps had 1st Major General Henry Heth, 2nd Major General [Joseph B.] Kershaw, 3rd Major General Cadmus Wilcox while Brigadier General Pickett became a major general under Longstreet.[10]

Lieutenant General Longstreet had been entrusted with an expedition against Suffolk and was engaged in it several months but quite unsuccessfully. He now joined the Army of Northern Virginia again.

Our adjutant, Henry B. McClellan, was appointed major and assistant adjutant general of the [cavalry] division on 2nd May and at the urgent request of Colonel Owen, I gave up my position in the line and became adjutant of my regiment with the rank of 1st lieutenant, losing thereby all chance of promotion by seniority and having to depend upon the very slender chance of promotion for merit which, owing to the legislation of Congress was very unusual. My pay was now $110 per month Confederate money.

During the month of May, Brigadier Generals Fitz Lee and Hampton were reinforced by Brigadier Generals Beverly [Robertson's] North Carolina Brigade and William H. F. Lee's Virginia Brigade, whilst William E. Jones' Brigade was in the southwest of Virginia, [John D.] Imboden's and A[lbert] G. Jenkins' in the Valley.[11]

About the 7th of June, Stuart had a grand review of the 4 cavalry brigades first mentioned in the large field in front of the Kennedy house near Brandy Station.[12] His force numbered between nine and ten thousand. The enemy got wind of it and on the 9th General Pleasanton with about 12,000 cavalry crossed the Rappahannock on a "reconnaissance in force." Stuart met him near Brandy and we had a sharp fight resulting finally in the repulse of the enemy and his retreat across the stream with a loss of about 200 prisoners and some 500 or 600 killed and wounded. Our loss in killed and wounded was nearly as great. Colonel Sol Williams, 2nd North Carolina, was killed, Colonel [Matthew C.] Butler, 1st South Carolina, lost a leg.[13]

On the 10th we set out for Sperryville and found that a heavy column of our infantry was marching along our left. Meanwhile, Lieutenant General Ewell with his corps and Jenkins' cavalry brigade had advanced against Winchester. His plans were complete and, but for some unfortunate mishap, he would have captured the whole force of 6,000 or 8,000 men. Early advanced right down the Valley Turnpike. Rodes and Johnson moved on the rear by way of Berryville. The enemy by a precipitate retreat got off with a loss of about 2,000 prisoners, all his artillery, wagon trains, and supplies and reached Harper's Ferry in a totally demoralized condition. Ewell pressed this advantage, sent Jenkins with his and Imboden's brigades across the Potomac at Williamsport while he marched to and occupied Harper's Ferry and then crossing the river, pushed on to Hagerstown, Maryland.[14]

On the 17th June our brigade advanced to Aldie reconnoitering. It was supposed that Hooker's army was marching towards the Potomac and would probably try to get up as high as Leesburg. Colonel Munford commanding the 1st, 2nd, and 3rd Regiments went down the Snicker's Gap Road while Colonel Wickham commanding the 4th and 5th and two guns went to the left of Middleburg and then entered the turnpike and thence to Aldie.[15]

Sending on foragers, etc., to pick out a camp and procure forage near Aldie, Colonel Munford halted to feed at Mr. Carter's house about two miles from the village. While there about 3 p.m. the 1st Regiment, which had been sent forward to the heights half mile this side of Aldie, was attacked vigorously by a body of the enemy's cavalry. We mounted and formed hurriedly and moved off at a rapid trot with drawn sabres. The booming of artillery on the right now showed plainly that Wickham was also getting into trouble. We just reached the hills in time to hold the place and save the 1st from disaster. Our regiment drew up in line on the left, the 2nd on the right of the road while the squadrons of carbiniers were thrown forward as skirmishers and secured a splendid position behind a stone fence.

The 1st Massachusetts Cavalry, supported by the 4th New York battalion, and having a Maine regiment on its left, now came on to the charge. They were twice repulsed with heavy loss but reforming they moved up steadily and now it was doubtful whether our skirmishers could continue to withstand them as they advanced firing heavily with carbines.

Colonel Owen was ordered to charge down the road, Lieutenant Colonel Watts commanding the 2nd, to charge on his right. I rode by the side of my colonel and we were in front of the regiment. It charged splendidly and when we got in ten paces of the Yankees they wheeled about and slowly retreated. I had never before so beautiful an opportunity to use my sabre but unfortunately I was riding a wild Morgan colt who became frantic with excitement and wholly unmanageable. I was, therefore, compelled to put up my sabre and use my revolver. The Colonel being, fortunately, mounted on a horse that was well broke did considerable execution. I saw him cut down two men, myself.

The Maine regiment on our right gave way before the 2nd Virginia and into them I fired with, I hope, some effect. Coming upon a party of five who couldn't get over a fence, I and two others captured them and sent them to the rear.

The regiment was now charging by fours down a lane, the Colonel commanding "Halt" with all his might. But not being heard, more than half kept on with the Lieutenant Colonel [Carter] and I galloped on to try to get at the head of and stop them. The road was blocked up considerably with dead men and horses.

Rosser, with the 5th, came thundering on behind us, overtook me and we both, descrying a regiment about 100 yards to our right firing on us, he ordered his regiment to turn to the right and charge them. Just then our men, having in their excitement run plumb into a brigade, came rushing back and Rosser wheeled about and fell back out of the lane.

A piece of artillery now opened on us from the rear firing right down

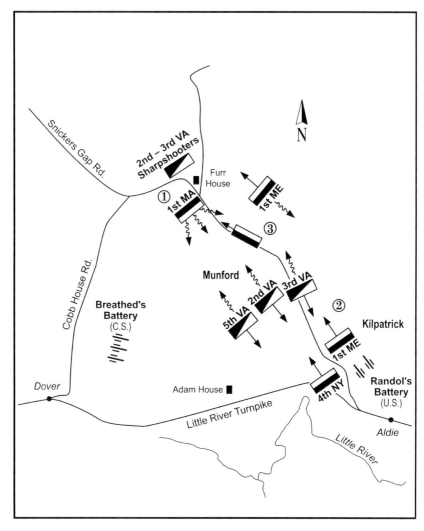

5. Aldie, 17 June 1863

the lane, fortunately a little high, while the regiment on our flank kept
up its fire. It was now perfectly evident that Pleasanton's whole command was coming up.

While doing my utmost to preserve order and prevent a stampede, my
horse went down, caught my right foot and threw my head between the
hind legs of a horse which was dying already on his back scuffling and

kicking powerfully. Making a desperate effort to get up and partially arising, some fellow jumped his horse over me and kicked me flat again. I thought I was in a fair way to be trampled to death. But just as the last of our men were passing and the head of the Yankee column in twenty yards of me, I extricated myself and sprang over the fence. My horse never rose and must have been killed or had a leg broken. The Yankees passed me in an instant but seemed not to notice me so bent were they on their pursuit.

Our skirmishers, being [at] the stone wall, stopped them, however, and gave the regiment time to reform, when Colonel Munford, seeing he was fighting fearful odds, withdrew rapidly towards Snicker's Gap carrying off 200 prisoners.[16]

Our brigade lost about seventy prisoners and thirty or forty killed or wounded, while the 1st Massachusetts alone acknowledged a loss of 200 men out of 400 with which they left camp. We had about 180 men present in our regiment of which forty were skirmishers. We lost twenty-five or thirty men in the fight. It was decidedly the most effective charge I ever knew the regiment to make. Had they stopped when the Colonel ordered, they would not have retired in the least disorder and scarcely lost a man. As it was, most of the loss was occasioned by horses falling in the hasty retreat through the obstructed lane before reaching our skirmish line which had been kept stationary as a support.

Returning to myself, I had an open field of 400 yards to cross before I could possibly get out of sight of the Yankees, knew they were going to hold the ground, was in ten steps of the road up which they were passing, with an empty scabbard, ([I] lost my sabre in the fall), and an empty pistol. My only chance was to drop them and run for my life while the enemy were engrossed with the charge and before they could halt and look around. This I did.

Getting to a little branch behind a slope which concealed me from those Yankees nearest me, I stopped to rest being exhausted. Finding from the firing that our men were retiring, and rising to go I beheld a dismounted Yankee in a few yards of me putting a cap on a carbine. Looking around for a chance to escape his observation, seeing none but discovering a disarmed comrade trying to snake off like myself and beckoning to him, I resolved to try a game of *bluff*. Springing behind a little tree the size of my leg I called out in as commanding a tone as possible, "Lay down your arms, sir, and come here."

"Who are you?" was the audacious reply while that formidable carbine was half-raised most significantly. This was extremely awkward. Must I now cry out for quarter? I determined on one more effort and repeated my command while my comrade, (Private [Thomas B.] Johnson of Dinwiddie), who was coming nearer cried out, "And if you don't, we will shoot you."[17] Whereupon he came up to me and delivered his carbine.

We three now put out for the woods. On getting half way across the field I saw another dismounted but armed Yankee to my left making for the woods. Turning, I also saw a squadron of Yankee cavalry formed facing me in the field about where I got over the fence. Getting in about 30 yards of this fellow, I called to him to surrender. He threw down his arms where he was and came to me. My comrade had a shoulder out of place and could carry nothing and I had a carbine and was so tired I could scarcely carry that so we abandoned the arms and pressed on with our prisoners.

After going some distance through the woods we met with some ladies who lived in the house where our charge commenced having in charge a wounded horse with colors of one of the Yankee regiments, the 1st Massachusetts I think, which they had picked up and were making to the rear, that is, out of harm's way.[18] They delivered these to me but the horse being nearly dead I abandoned him and not thinking to tear the colors off the staff, hid them in a thicket. We had to make a circuit of about sixteen miles to get back into our lines, reaching Union next day at 12 noon and turning over the prisoners.

I went on to Mr. Dulaney's house near Middleburg where I was most hospitably entertained, supplied with a leghorn hat in place of mine lost in the fall the day before.[19] I rejoined my command that night and got leave the next morning to go to Clarke County after another horse. My brother William, who was on a visit and travelling with me, went along also.[20]

The evening of the 17th, Stuart, judging from our firing that we were hotly engaged started to reinforce us with Robertson's Brigade but encountered a brigade which had gotten around Wickham's right at Middleburg and there had a sharp fight. But a splendid charge of the North Carolina regiment put the enemy to rout with the loss of over 100 prisoners.[21]

On the 18th our brigade holding the road to Snicker's gap, Hampton's, Robertson's, and William Lee's brigades formed line of battle at a cross-road between Upperville and Middleburg and awaited attack. Nothing occurred, however, but some sharp skirmishing. Next day, the 19th, the enemy advanced in heavy force of cavalry and after a very severe fight of some hours duration, he brought up infantry and forced Stuart back into the mouth of Ashby's Gap where McLaws' division lay in ambush. The next day, the 20th, the enemy couldn't be found anywhere west of Aldie.[22] Stuart's loss on the 19th was 4 or 5 hundred, the enemy's perhaps smaller. A. P. Hill's Corps pushed across the river at Shepphardstown and advanced to Hagerstown. Longstreet followed. General Lee left Stuart with the brigades of Hampton and the two Lees to follow up the enemy rear and join him in Pennsylvania by such route as he thought proper. Robertson's Brigade was to hold the gaps till the enemy crossed the Potomac, then to move on to Chambersburg via Williamsport.

Having bought a fine bay horse in Clarke County for $800 Confederate money ($100 in gold) and parted with my brother at Bunker Hill, I went with Robertson's Brigade, it being impossible to join Stuart who was off again on a raid via Annandale, Vienna, across the Potomac at Seneca Falls via Papertown, Westminster, and Hanover to Carlisle, Pennsylvania, then back to Gettysburg marching, fighting, and capturing canal boats, wagons, and prisoners without stint. Crossing Hooker's track he brought out 1000 horses and mules, burned 200 wagons, etc., etc.[23]

Jenkins' and Imboden's brigades which went in advance became so scattered and demoralized by plundering that they were of little service. Ewell had pushed as far as the Susquehanna River and threatened Harrisburg. Stuart by a strange mishap crossed the track of the other two corps and went off to Carlisle before he discovered his mistake and was too late, therefore, to be of any service. Longstreet's and Hill's corps turned to the right at Chambersburg along the Gettysburg Pike and, without any warning of their proximity, Lee's advance encountered that of the Army of the Potomac, (now commanded by Major General George G. Meade), about 2 p.m. near the little village of Gettysburg.

A sanguinary battle now raged till night with every advantage on our side. But having no cavalry with him, Lee didn't know, certainly, that he had engaged the whole army and worsted it so considerably as he had. So he lost his golden opportunity of charging Cemetery Hill when they retreated to it that evening. He might then, it is thought, have dislodged them without difficulty. Ewell had followed and joined him before this fight.

A council of war was held. Longstreet, A. P. Hill, and most of the major generals were clamorous for an assault the next morning and confident of success. Ewell was undecided, as he always was, after the loss of his leg at "2nd Manassas."[24] Robert E. Lee disapproved of the scheme but for the only time during the war yielded his opinion to his comrades and ordered the attack.

Brigadier General [William N.] Pendleton commanding the artillery was ordered to open with 200 guns and, after silencing the enemy's batteries, the charge was to be led by the division of Major General Pickett followed by others.[25]

Crossing through South Mountain Pass on the 3rd with Robertson's brigade about 10 a.m., I found our wagon trains nearby and soon joined a party going on to the regiment. Stuart got up with the cavalry the night before and was now fighting the Federal cavalry on the left. I had about eight miles to ride and finally got with my regiment after some difficulty about two hours before the fight closed and at a time when none but our skirmishers were engaged. Indeed, during this great battle the cavalry of each army seemed content to act on the defensive and guard its flank.

The artillery firing was tremendous for about two hours, (200 guns firing on a side), when the enemy was silenced and his forces were driven out of their works. Under shelter of a hill, Pickett now set out at a charge at least a half a mile from their works, upgrade with some ditches and a large stone fence to cross. By [the] time the men began to get in musket range of the enemy, they were dreadfully scattered and nearly out of breath.

Our artillery having stopped when the charge commenced, the enemy showed themselves. Seeing their advantage they re-opened their artillery fire directing it at Pickett this time, occupied their works again, and opened a murderous fire of musketry. A part of our forces had gotten into a portion of these works but no troops were in proper supporting distance and, being flanked in addition to the galling fire, Pickett ordered a retreat.

Our supply of artillery [ammunition] was so near exhausted, (some guns having not more than two or three rounds), Pendleton couldn't fire a shot to cover the retreat of the division.

It lost, I think, every brigadier and every field officer killed, wounded, or captured and out of about 6,000 men, only some 2,000 could be mustered several days afterwards.

This was, of course, not the whole fight. Other divisions were considerable engaged along the lines but this was the charge which was to wring victory from the enemy or destroy the hopes of a successful invasion. Upon the charge was staked every hope of carrying Cemetery Hill. *That failing,* the attempt was to be abandoned, the campaign given up. For from here to Baltimore the country was in favor of the enemy almost the whole route. And besides, we were compelled to await the arrival of the fresh train of ammunition which was now near Williamsport and which Lee hoped to have gotten before being compelled to fight a great battle.

The enemy made no attack, having narrowly escaped total defeat he was content to remain in his position, at least during the night. Having awaited attack till about 11 a.m. or 12 noon next day, Lee commenced slowly retiring. The rain poured down in torrents nearly all day.

We remained where we encamped the night before, grazing our horses, eating green apples, and taking the rain. At night we started and marched behind the artillery, halting very often while the rains poured down and the roads were becoming very bad, indeed. The only sleep I got that night was *one hour* wrapped in a very wet blanket under a little apple tree so destitute of leaves that it didn't shelter me atall, scarcely.

Lee lost in the two fights at least 20,000 men. The enemy probably as many as we, took several thousand prisoners (I think nearly 6,000).[26]

We passed through the gap about 2 p.m. and went into camp nearby. Next day, July [5th], going southward along the foot of the mountain, we came to Funkstown, Pennsylvania, [Maryland], and at length got into a turnpike leading to Greencastle which we passed through on the [6th]. On the evening of the [6th] we got near Williamsport where Imboden was having a sharp fight against the Federal cavalry (who were trying to get the trains of our army collected there), with his brigade and Company "Q."

I must now explain what is meant by this term, Company "Q." It originated in this way: a body of mounted men were marching along one night when somebody seeing them inquired what company that was. It being customary to designate companies by the first letters of the alphabet, some wag, knowing this to be a party of men with broken down horses going to recruit, responded "This is Company 'Q.'" As soldiers have a very lively appreciation of anything ludicrous or witty they readily detected the humor in this application of a final letter to a party who were used up, or to use an army phrase "played out," and it spread like wildfire throughout the army coming to be applied finally to all used up parties, whether cavalry or infantry who were following after the wagon train instead of being in line.[27]

Imboden made a handsome fight and repulsed the enemy completely. Next evening, the [7th], we marched near Funkstown, Maryland, and went into camp. The infantry marched from Chambersburg to Hagerstown, four miles from Funkstown, and went into camp. July [8th], next day, our brigade, William Lee's and Hampton's went towards Boonsboro and there we had a sharp skirmish with Pleasanton's command, driving them back into the gap of South Mountain. The [9th], we having camped near the scene of yesterdays operations, formed our line and awaited attack. They soon came forward, we had a sharp skirmish, and in the evening had to fall back, it being evident that General Meade had come through the gap at Boonsboro.

The third day of our skirmishing, the [10th], came near being quite disastrous. Fitz Lee, commanding two brigades, kept us beyond the village skirmishing till the enemy had brought up a heavy force of cavalry and infantry and planted his batteries in half a mile of us. Then he [Lee] commenced a hasty retreat through Funkstown across the two bridges. The enemy shelled the village unmercifully and we sustained some loss. Private [D. B.] Ellyson, Company F, had his head shot off with a shell and 1st Sergeant [John M.] Jeffries, Company C, had a hand disabled and 1st Sergeant [Theophilus] Foster, Company E, had his head shot off with a shell, all about the same time with two or three horses killed in one regiment.[28]

Our infantry lines were along the western bank of Antietam Creek and they now commenced throwing up entrenchments. Colonel Wickham took one regiment and his own off down the Sharpsburg Road where Jenkins was skirmishing with the enemy's cavalry. Here we skirmished a while and a shell bursted in the 4th Regiment killing two men and two horses of the Black Horse Cavalry.

At night we went into camp on the left of the infantry. General Lee now issued a stirring order to his troops, telling them that everything now depended on their fortitude and endurance, that he would require another grand effort of them and felt that they would not disappoint the high expectations of the country. All eyes saw in this order unmistakable evidence that we were in a critical situation and that fighting was a matter of *necessity*, not of choice. This was, indeed, our situation. The almost incessant rains for the last week had raised the Potomac much above the usual height so that fording was impossible. All efforts to construct a raft at Williamsport were reported to have failed while one half the pontoon bridge left at Falling Waters had been destroyed, the remainder was fastened to the southern bank. Yet, General Lee was calm and undismayed. He knew that he had a fine army with him and he was hopeful still.

Unfortunately, the news now came creeping stealthily through camp that Lieutenant General John S. Pemberton had surrendered Vicksburg with 25,000 men to General Grant on the 4th July. Yet under all these adverse influences, the army was comparatively resolute and if not hopeful and cheerful was not despairing and demoralized.

Having given the enemy a fair opportunity on the 11th, 12th, and 13th to deliver battle, on the night of the 13th our army retreated, the 1st and 3rd Corps to Falling Waters, the 2nd Corps, (followed the next morning by the cavalry), to Williamsport.[29] This was, indeed, a gloomy occasion. The roads were a perfect series of puddles, the rain was falling night and day, everybody and everybody's "plunder" was ringing wet.[30] Scant rations were furnished the men and the horses lived upon hay and grass, many of them had their shoes off and were so lame they could scarcely get along.

When we reached Williamsport there was a string of *heads and arms* to be seen stretching across the river from bank to bank. While on the southern side, ascending the hills, were an irregular body [of] miserable looking creatures who evidently felt none the better for their ducking. And this, we were told, was *Ewell's corps.*

We entered the stream about 12 noon and crossed slowly by twos. The river had fallen some but took our horses within 12 inches of the top of the shoulders and wet our legs thoroughly eight inches above the knees, at least. The pontoon bridge below had been repaired and the 1st and 3rd Corps crossed easily. But there was an inexcusable piece of negligence on the part of somebody. [James J.] Pettigrew's and, (I think), [Thomas L.] Clingman's North Carolina Brigade of infantry were last to cross and, foolishly *taking it for granted* that the cavalry was still behind them and would cross there, the former stacked arms, lay down, and went to sleep.

A squadron of cavalry coming on about 2 p.m. were, *of course,* taken for "ours" by the few men who were awake until getting close enough to see the condition of things.[31] They charged right down upon this brigade. Half the guns were wet and wouldn't go off but still this squadron was presently repulsed. Being reinforced, however, they charged again. This time Pettigrew was mortally wounded in the bowels and his brigade stampeded and about 600 captured. The rest were saved by Clingman's Brigade.

General Meade having reported 1,000 to 1,200 prisoners captured on the 14th by his cavalry, General Lee came out in a card denying that "any organized troops whatever" were captured, that they were only stragglers who had gone off the night before to sleep in barns, etc., etc. Meade replied that he had too high an opinion of Lee to think he would purposely misrepresent but the facts were such as he had before stated and General Lee must not have been properly informed by his subordinates. Certain it is we lost 800 or 1,000 men that day.[32]

In other respects the retreat was successful and the army moved to Bunker Hill [Virginia].

During my brief sojourn in Pennsylvania the rain was almost incessant and sufficed of itself to produce an impression anything less than pleasant. These people were very vulgar and coarse, a very large majority of the country women were barefooted and of very broad, coarse figures, ugly, and not atall intelligent faces and had any amount of impudence. The town girls, though better clad generally, were evidently of the same species. The men were no better and seemed to tell lies as a matter of preference.

The country, particularly the Chambersburg valley, was really beautiful. The lands are of the finest limestone with crystal streams and formations divided into 60, 100, and 150 acre farms splendidly cultivated in oats, wheat, timothy, and clover. The dwelling houses [were] all very plain and their heavy style, or dingy red color afford unmistakable evidence of Dutch and German descent of the occupants. The barns, like those in the Valley of Virginia, are large and commodious costing from two to three thousand dollars. The cattle are mostly thoroughbred. The horses, like the women, belong to the heavy Dutch breeds. But few Episcopalians, Presbyterians, Methodists, or Baptists are to be found. The population were Lutheran, Dutch Reformed, Dunkards, Quakers, or

Menonites [*sic*]. As far as I could judge they seemed to feel no great concern about or regard for any God but *Mammon*.

A great deal can be said about the outrages perpetrated by our men during this invasion. I can testify on my own personal knowledge that it was nothing in comparison with what their own troops were every day committing upon our soil. Our men did take the horses and fowl and fruit of all sorts and our quartermasters did impress forage for the *subsistence* of the animals, and our commissary impressed such meat as was essential to supply the wants of the troops. Beyond this, private property was, (with some unavoidable exceptions), respected and spared. *We* never burnt their barns and mills, not their villages and towns, as *they* did ours and *had been doing* from the commencement of the war. In retaliating, we could have been justified after the awful desolation and destruction they had already inflicted on us and that, too, in the most wanton manner *not* merely to supply the wants of their army as was the case with us when we took their property.[33]

Many of our men offered to *pay for* every mouthful of bread they got at private houses in Pennsylvania. I was not so squemish as that but asked politely and thanked them for everything to eat they furnished me. I was, however, sufficiently positive when they appeared unaccommodating, to tell them that they *had to furnish something*, if not meat at least bread, butter and smeared! They called apple butter,(i.e. cut apples boiled down to the consistency of marmalade in cider), spread on bread, a "smear." A favorite expression for making known that they didn't have anything was, "*Indeed* and *double*, I h'a'nt got any *more!*"

It was subsequently ascertained that General Meade commenced to retreat from Gettysburg before Lee did. This accounts for the former crossing the South Mountains at Boonsboro instead of following Lee towards Chambersburg.[34]

On the 15th [July], Fitz Lee, commanding his own and Jenkins' brigades, was attacked near Shepphardstown by [David M.] Gregg's cavalry division and had a sharp fight. "Fitz" drove him back until he [Gregg] got behind a very thick and high stone fence where he made an obstinate stand. Lee, succeeding at last in enfilading it with four guns, opened and at the same time his brigade charged. The "blue bellies" couldn't stand that and retreated rapidly a quarter mile to another similar fence where they held their own till night and then withdrew. We drove them, in all, about a mile and considering they were twice as many, plumed ourselves somewhat on the fight. The loss was about 150 to 200 on a side.[35]

A few days after, the army retired to the Rapidan River, we covering the retreat and having some insignificant skirmishes. We suffered greatly for food but the immense crop of blackberries found along the road relieved our wants very much. One or two days we had nothing else. The horses had nothing but blue-grass and occasionally a little hay.

We went into our old camp near Culpeper Court House and remained until July 31st evening when our brigade marched off for Fredericksburg traveling all night to avoid the heat and went into camp two miles west of the town at Dr. Lawless' about 12 noon, August 1st.

About the 2nd or 3rd August, Stuart had a considerable fight near Culpeper Court House with Pleasanton's cavalry and was driven back upon the infantry. He had only Hampton's and Robertson's brigades against the whole Federal cavalry of two divisions. Supported by infantry he repulsed and pursued them across the Rappahannock losing in all some 300 men.[36] Out of his whole force of over 9,000 on the 1st of June, Stuart lost up to this time about 2,500 while General Pleasanton in his official reports acknowledged a loss of over 3,000 men and a large number of horses.

9
"To Gain Kilpatrick's Rear at Buckland"

While we were at Fredericksburg the Army of Northern Virginia lay quietly in camp along the south bank of the Rapidan, General Meade's forces being mostly beyond Culpeper Court House. Our life now was quite monotonous for a month. One division of Yankee cavalry were in camp about two miles from Falmouth and picketted the river opposite us. The pickets were civil enough not to shoot at each other.

About the middle of August we went into camp at Harrison's house, (brother of the historian of Virginia), our headquarters being in his yard. He was extremely civil to us and seemed pleased to have us near him.

In the latter part of the month Colonel Owen was sent with a detachment of 200 men from the 1st and 3rd Virginia and 1st Maryland Cavalry to cross the Rappahannock at Port Royal, come up on the other side, and cross the ford, (at low tide), just above Fredericksburg after dark. The object of this expedition was to intimidate the marauding parties from [H. Judson] Kilpatrick's Division who were daily going down the river depredating upon the people.[1] I went along as adjutant of the command.

We went into camp 1st night near Port Royal and next day succeeded after great difficulty in getting from the infantry division stationed there, possession of an old pungy and a barge [at] about 12 noon.[2] One of these wouldn't carry horses. The other one took about 8 at a time. It was soon found, however, that we couldn't cross in time unless the horses were carried faster. So the men who went in the pungy held their horses by the bridle, they swimming the while. It was soon found that many would be drowned in this way so they were turned loose and swam safely over.

Thus, after much difficulty, we all got safely across about 2 p.m. and started up the River Road.

Being sent on ahead to procure a guide, I dined with a very nice old gentleman, ([an] ex-lieutenant [in the] U.S. Navy), whose name I forget and then got Mr. Taylor, son of Dr. [Thomas] Taylor who lives at Fredericksburg, as guide. He informed us that there were, he believed, some Yankee foragers between us and Falmouth and thought our position rather hazardous as they might readily report this division and further that General Fitz Lee was mistaken as to when the tide would be low, (our only chance of fording) and that it would be certainly by 8:30 or 9 p.m. Although somewhat apprehensive, all went on smoothly and as we marched up a beautiful cedar avenue two or three miles below town, one or two scouts came out and, inquiring for Colonel Owen: "General Lee says all's right, come ahead and capture their pickets if you can."

The moon shone beautifully upon us and we came right upon the pickets who were so fully satisfied of our being U.S. troops that didn't challenge atall. Most of them, five or six, were captured and we crossed without accident.[3]

Fitzhugh Lee was, this time, made major general of cavalry and Wade Hampton the same. The latter commanded the 1st Division composed of the South Carolina Brigade (commanded by Brigadier General Butler of the 2nd South Carolina Cavalry), North Carolina Brigade commanded by Brigadier General Baker of the 1st North Carolina Cavalry [but] soon after succeeded by Brigadier General [James B.] Gordon, lieutenant colonel of the 1st North Carolina Cavalry, on [Baker] being wounded, and the Georgia Brigade commanded by Brigadier General [Pierce M. B.] Young, of Cobb's Legion cavalry. The former commanded the 2nd Division composed of Brigadier General W. H. F. Lee's Brigade, his old brigade (i.e. 1st, 2nd, 3rd, and 4th Regiments) subsequently commanded by Brigadier General Williams C. Wickham, of the 4th, and Lomax Brigade, 5th, 6th, and 15th [Virginia], commanded by Brigadier General Lunsford L. Lomax, late colonel of the 11th [Virginia]. Stuart was, henceforth, "Major General Commanding Cavalry Corps, Army of Northern Virginia."[4]

About [the] 1st September we moved up to Vidiersville [sic], Orange County, and went into camp. Meade's lines were now along the north bank of the Rapidann [sic] but our signal agents reported his main force about Culpeper Court House.

Our horses were now fed on a very scant supply of new corn, (while at Fredericksburg we got an abundant supply from [the] Northern Neck by boats).[5] Leaving camp after the 25th of September on 15 days leave of absence, I came home.[6]

Meanwhile, his arrangements being complete, General Lee resolved to force Meade back to Manassa[s] and by thus threatening Washington, prevent the sending of more men to reinforce [William S.] Rosecranz [sic] who, about this time, occupied Chattanooga, General [Braxton] Bragg withdrawing behind the Chickamauga River about 30 miles. Lieutenant General Longstreet was sent to reinforce the army of Bragg with Hood and McLaws' Divisions. Lee now had 25 or 30 thousand infantry, Meade 40 or 50 thousand.

About the 8th October, A. P. Hill's Corps moved off to Madison Court House. Meade discovered the movement by the 10th and that night fell back behind the Rappahannock carrying off all *his supplies and trains* in a masterly maneuver leaving the cavalry on the front and one corps of infantry near Brandy Station.

Lee ordered Stuart to move forward at daylight of the 11th followed by Ewell. Hampton's Division encountered Kilpatrick's and became hotly engaged. Wickham's Brigade, Colonel Owen commanding, crossed Raccoon Ford under fire and became hotly engaged at once. Lomax crossed at the ford below, (Morton's), and aided Owen. After the loss of two noble officers, Captains William S. Newton of Hanover and [Phillip D.] Williams of Prince William, both of 4th Virginia Cavalry, the Division was successful and drove the enemy rapidly to Brandy Station.[7]

Kilpatrick, being unable to resist the impetuous charge of Stuart and Hampton and hearing the fire in his rear, came thundering down behind Fitz Lee. The latter, not knowing he was being driven by Hampton, and having his hands already full, "made way for him." Our corps now drove them back upon their infantry and then went into camp. A. P. Hill was, meanwhile, marching for Warrenton via Waterloo Bridge and Ewell, pressing forward toward the [Warrenton] Springs.

Next morning early, the 12th, Stuart moved toward the bridge near the Springs, encountered the enemy again, and at evening drove him beautifully over the river and through the Springs' village, Ewell's Corps crossing after him. The enemy, meanwhile, through forward some cavalry towards Culpeper Court House driving back William Lee's Brigade [that had been] left there and then retiring again.

Next evening I reached the bridge above mentioned and stopped for the night with some wagons. Riding on early next morning, the 14th, I reached Warrenton by 9 a.m., found A. P. Hill's Corps and part of my command there, (joining the latter a few miles below about 1 p.m.). Ewell had gone to Catlett's Station to relieve General Stuart who had gone into the enemies lines near that point with Baker's, now Gordon's, Cavalry Brigade the evening before to reconnoiter. The enemy, meanwhile, moving in two parallel columns, caught him between so he couldn't get out and he remained that night with the brigade and a battery of 4 guns in a hollow within quarter of a mile of one road along which they [Federals] were passing without being discovered. He sent two couriers through to inform General Lee of his situation. They were dressed in uniforms taken from prisoners and thus escaped capture.

Early next morning he unlimbered his 4 guns and fired on the masses of the enemy while they were foraging. They now learned of his proximity for the first time and began to advance upon him both cavalry and infantry. Ordering his artillery to fire a few more shots at their advancing line of infantry, then limber up and place themselves in the center of his cavalry, his bugles sounded the charge which was led in splendid style by the 1st North Carolina Cavalry, commanded by Colonel Thomas Ruffin, former Member of Congress, full against the line into which the artillery was firing and which was now somewhat confused, thereby. Ewell's guns, having now opened, added to the confusion. The charge was perfectly successful and the entire command passed through[,] losing, however, some noble spirits, among them the gallant Ruffin.[8]

A. P. Hill, taking the road to Manassas, deflected to the right and advanced upon Bristoe Station, (next below Catlett's). Seeing here a thin line of skirmishers and supposing the force small, he ordered Major General Harry Heth to send forward [John R.] Cook's [sic] Brigade with a battery of 4 guns to disperse them and occupy the railroad. Beyond the little stream crossing the railroad here at right angles, a larger force of the enemy was seen and of these, Hill supposed, this was only the rear guard he was about to attack. The railroad at this station runs for 100 or 200 yards along an embankment about 4 1/2 feet and then through a cut of equal depth.

As Cook's Brigade came near and the artillery opened, the skirmish lines were easily driven across the railroad as if unsupported. Our men rushing up in the excitement of a charge to the embankment and cut received all at once a tremendous volley from a heavy force there posted. The shock was overpowering. They broke and fled with a loss of about 500, (1/3 their number). The enemy now charging and Heth being too far off with his other brigade to give support, succeeded in capturing the artillery.

Thus, by the most stupid bungling, a well conceived plan for enclosing one corps d'armee between Hill and Ewell and crushing it was entirely thwarted and instead of inflicting, we sustained a heavy loss, for Heth's whole division was very much affected by the disaster.[9]

It always appeared to me a great error of General Lee for not having General Hill removed for this and perhaps Heth, also, for he was a very indifferent officer. But all that General Lee ever did was to express some disapprobation verbally to Hill and the latter, riding up, thereupon, and asking if he had any further instructions to give, to add "I think you had better go out and bury your *unfortunate dead!*" Hill having sufficiently withdrawn, the corps Ewell was engaging passed quietly by and our cavalry followed up the enemy's cavalry to Manassas Plains.

On the 15th we went forward and after a little skirmish, drove his rear across Bull Run. This day and the 16th the cavalry command was entirely out of rations and had nothing but grass for our horses.

Encamping the first night on the Plains, next day early we commenced retiring [and] went, our division, toward Bristoe to the road leading from Warrenton and went into camp. Next morning early, passed Bristoe and after halting to feed, struck road from Warrenton to Catlett's, turned up towards Warrenton and then suddenly turned off towards Buckland, (a small village).

I now learnt that Hampton's Division had been followed up rapidly by Kilpatrick's Division towards Warrenton and that Fitz Lee had suggested a plan of attack which Stuart had accepted. The former was to gain Kilpatrick's rear at Buckland, secure the bridge across the stream at that place and then both parties to attack simultaneously.

Fitz Lee, getting in range, charged the pickets, etc., and we advanced beautifully till in 1000 yards of the bridge when a fire from 2 rifle pieces was opened on us from *across* the bridge. This was unexpected and caused some delay as we had to shell these guns off before we could get the bridge. Finally, a beautiful charge was made by the whole division, (part mounted, part on foot), and Hampton, driving [George A.] Custar's [*sic*] Brigade back.

Meanwhile, we got the brigade before it could cross but not till the others had gotten over, (many of them fording up the stream). Custar took across the fields and got across the stream a mile or so above, followed closely by Hampton's Division. We crossed at Buckland and pressed the enemy back vigorously till we came up with the infantry brigade, (which had been at the bridge, or a portion of it when the fight commenced), finding that a heavy force was just beyond and Meade evidently advancing again, we retired to Buckland and went into camp again a little beyond.

We captured two guns and four or five wagons in this fight and some forty prisoners. Our loss in killed and wounded was not over one hundred, I guess.[10]

Lee now retreated behind the Rappahannock leaving [Harry T.] Hays' Louisiana and [Robert F.] Hoke's North Carolina brigades occupying a semicircular fortification on the north side, connected by a pontoon bridge with the other side.

Our cavalry followed a few days later and went into camp on Welford's farm, a few miles above the railroad bridge. In the course of two or three days, Meade advanced, one column appearing in front of Hays at the railroad bridge and another commenced crossing at Kelly's Ford (five miles below). Lee designed hurling his force upon the latter column as soon as it got across, believing the other was only making a feint and would really cross at Kelly's.

In front of Hays there was a semicircular ridge of hills much higher than and about 600 yards in front of his works. Matthews' squadron, from my regiment, were on picket on these hills that morning and as the country beyond was an inclined plain offering an extensive view, he saw, (as did his men), also, the heavy column of the enemy march up and deploy within 1500 yards of him. [He] reported to Colonel Penn, the officer then in command of the fort, and suggested that by sending a section of artillery up on the hill, he could do great execution.[11] The latter replied that he had only some 1300 men, just enough to hold his works and didn't feel authorized to advance or bring on an engagement but reported facts through Major General Early to Lieutenant General Ewell, thence to General R. E. Lee. These officers all came down there and remained till a little before sunset.

At dusk our cavalry was all ordered across the river and infantry pickets stationed only some 75 yards in front of the works. The enemy having planted a battery of artillery where it could rake the bridge, suddenly opened on the bridge and charged under cover of darkness right over the little rifle pits our men had. [They] captured 800 of them and four guns. About 500 men escaped by jumping into the river and wading or swimming across. Only a few could get over the bridge.[12]

Thus, in this Manassas campaign we lost 1400 men and eight guns without inflicting a loss of more than two or three hundred. I always thought this latter affair the greatest military blunder Lee ever committed. The only way I could ever account for it was that, like a chess player when highly excited, he had become so intent upon his own plan, he didn't watch the movement of his adversary with sufficient care.

He [Lee] retreated during the night nearly to Culpeper Court House and lay in line of battle all next day. We followed at daylight but halted and skirmished two or three hours at Brandy Station and went into camp that night on Sperryville Turnpike.

Next day, Lee having retreated at night lay in line of battle at Cedar Creek [Cedar Run] and we went across to Jamestown village. That night Lee retreated behind the Rapidann and we crossed the same stream above him and took position on the left flank of the army, Hampton's Division being on the right, (from Germanna ford to Fredericksburg). We picketed across the Blue Ridge via Criglersville in Rappahannock.

Davy was with me on the last campaign and when I got up with the command, I sent him to the ordnance wagons to stay with them during the fighting, telling him that if anything bad should befall me to try and take care of my horse and baggage and take them home. One day when a heavy cannonade was in progress someone met Davy riding towards the scene of the action and asked, "Where are you going?"

Davy: "Gwine arter Massa's horse, sir."

"For what?"

"Case he tell me if he got kilt I must take care'n his horse and all dat firin' must ha' kilt him 'fore now."

On another occasion, walking up to where General Fitz Lee was sitting, he said, "Sarvant, Marsa." The General nodding, he [Davy] said, "Marsa, dey tell me you's Gineral Lee."

"Yes."

"Hi Marsa, you so young, you don't look no older'n Marse Robert [Hubard]. I thought ginerals, dais be ball [bald] an' have gray beards."

The General was highly amused and got into conversation with the old fellow. (He [Davy] is now about 57.)

Longstreet's command left for the South in August, (for the battle of

Chickamauga was fought on the 1st of September and he participated, indeed, it was always said that the victory was due to the superior fighting of his troops.)

Not long after we got behind the Rapidann, Kilpatrick's division drove in Lomax's Brigade near Madison Court House and pushed on towards Barboursville. Our brigade hurried up there that night and the enemy, getting wind of it somehow, retreated before day. We followed but couldn't overtake him before he got across the Hazel River.[13]

It was thought that Meade at that time contemplated an attempted to turn Lee's left flank. Soon after, about the 10th November, he crossed the Rapidan at Germanna and moved upon Lee's right flank. The latter, however, anticipated him completely and was quite well entrenched behind Mine Run, his line running nearly north and south. When Meade got up, the latter having felt his position pretty heavily on the 20th and 21st and gotten somewhat worsted, concluded to withdraw to his former position. This was a masterly movement of Lee and added a new laurel to his brow.

Things remained in statu [sic] quo for some time and about the 15th December, Lomax's Brigade being [on the] left on the line, was sent to Charlottesville to recruit but the day after getting there they were ordered to Harrisonburg to reinforce Imboden who had retreated to Brock's Gap before Averell at the head of about 7,000 men, cavalry and infantry. The latter took his cavalry, about 3000, and a battery and set out for Salem on the Tennessee Railroad. Our brigade had a "wild goose" chase after him and suffered greatly from cold and want of food, each regiment being reduced to less than 100 men mounted.[14]

Being off on three days leave of absence, I got to camp after they started and knowing the character of this expedition, made no attempt to join them till they reached New Market. Setting out with Ned Price and 20 others on December 26th we reached camp on Neff's farm on the 28th. On the 30th we started to Hardee [sic] [County, West Virginia] after cattle under Fitz Lee and crossed the North Mountain in a snowstorm on the 31st.

At sunset on the 1st of January we halted for nearly an hour on the top of Branch Mountain, the men in front having to clear away the snow and ice. Our route was a bridle path which the citizens said *they never* used in winter and they vowed we'd never get across in the world. We had to go up and down on foot. And in going down the men and horses fairly slid for ten, fifteen, and twenty yards at a time. Nearly every officer and man had his ears or toes frostbitten and several men like to have lost their feet.

We got into camp at 10 p.m. in a piece of woods entirely destitute of dead wood about two miles from Moorefield and had to get corn a mile off across the South Fork of Potomac which nearly swam the horses. The 2nd of January we spent in camp. The thermometer stood 4 degrees below zero at sunrise. I never have at any time suffered as intently from cold as then. But the boys all swore that Napoleon's passage of the Alps was fun compared to the crossing of North and Branch mountains.

We threatened Petersburg [W.V.] and, destroying all the stockades between there and New Creek Depot, set out to attack that place one day and went into camp near the top of a mountain at a little place called, very properly, Ridgeville.

It was snowing very hard but we built shelters in the fence corners, burnt rails, and got some hay for our horses. Captain Watkins, commanding the regiment, Ned Price, [William A.] Bruce, two couriers, and I got suppers at a house hard by after nearly having a fight with Lieutenant Colonel [Elijah V.] White of Rosser's (promoted in place of W. E. Jones) Brigade, who had occupied the house where we engaged supper and refused us admission, claiming it was his headquarters. A statement of facts being made to Fitz Lee, he and Major [Robert F.] Mason of his staff went to White and ordered him to give up possession of the house for the night to Captain Watkins. The latter, however, took nothing more than supper and allowed the vulgarian to stay in the house.

We set out before day, the snow still falling, but news being received that they had reinforced heavily and were ready for us at New Creek, it was deemed best to withdraw so we returned to Burlington halted and fed. Here I got a fine breakfast at the house of Mr. Vanmeter.

Taking the road to Romney, we marched through there that night. Next day passed through and encamped some miles beyond in Grass Lick Valley. Keeping down this valley, (though differently named lower down), crossing the Lost River, (a branch of the Shenandoah), almost every half hour. We finally passed through Brock's Gap and arrived at Harrisonburg. Going thence to Port Republic, we reached Charlottesville on January 10, 1864.

On this trip we captured a train of eighty wagons, about 75 prisoners, and some three or four hundred head of cattle. On the 21st January in consequence of the great scarcity of forage, difficulty of procuring, transportation (from wear and tear of railroads), and other causes, each company commander in our brigade was ordered to take his company to its own county to remain until April 15th or further orders.

Correspondence, 1863

Hd. Qrs., 3rd. Va. Cavalry
May 10th, '63
(near Orange C. H.)
My Dear Father,

Your letter by Phil Grigg reached me yesterday and was highly gratifying although you seem, as usual, inclined rather to discourage any attempt on my part to obtain promotion. In all kindness and reverence, I would like to ask if it had not occurred to you that your sons are too little inclined naturally to rely on themselves and to push themselves, and do we not need a spur to encourage our ambition rather than a bit to curb it? Had I pursued the course most others pursued, gone to work and gotten a company, I might now be a Colonel, instead of playing third fiddle to Matthews and Palmore. I have written this now in a perfectly good humour and am conscious that you wish me prosperity, etc., but it has been suggested by the general tone of your letter and I have often thought of it before. It arises, I know, from an affectionate desire to prevent our appearing presumptuous and ridiculous. But I fear that we are too much afraid of that always for our own good.

Colonel Owen has requested me to act as adjutant once he is officially notified of McClellan's promotion.[1] Everybody seems to think he will offer me the place; if he does I think I will accept it and hold on till I can do better. I have thought a great deal about it and am inclined to think it will give me advantages in the way of making the acquaintance of many men that I do not now possess. I doubt whether anything could be accomplished by applying to Seddon[2] through Uncle Edmund so you may let that matter drop. I will try to fight my way up before long.

It is rumoured that the brigades of mounted riflemen are on the way to Stuart from the southwest.[3]

And I hope we will finish Stoneman, yet. Stuart is said to have remarked the other day that after resting his horses a few days he would start after him. The white livered sons of bitches who have been scared so badly will, I hope, learn a lesson and furnish the government the forage necessary for our horses. They are to blame, not we, for what Stoneman did.[4] Hampton was recruiting south of James River.

The few men we could turn out were essential to Lee's success at Fredericksburg [Chancellorsville]. The active movements of his army were directed by the information we furnished him and we had to stay there partly to protect the weak points of his line (the 4th and 3rd Virginia Cavalry occupied a position in front of the whole army corps of the army) and partly to protect the trains. Jackson's wagons would have been captured but for the success of Lt. Colonel Carter of our regiment commanding a squadron of cavalry and some companies of infantry.

William [Rooney] Lee had two regiments down in Essex [County] foraging. In one of the others we had only 57 men for duty. They guarded our wagons. The 9th and 13th went with him after Stoneman but could not give him much of a fight.

The battle of Fredericksburg [Chancellorsville] was a grand affair. Jackson's flank movement was one of the greatest ever made. The enemy having sent out scouts in front of his right wing, they reported Jackson falling back toward Richmond having already disappeared. Some of our men who were prisoners were present. The general commanding there said, "Boys, we have the heights and Jackson has left our front. We rest tonight and tomorrow on to Richmond."

A few moments after six bomb shells burst in their midst. "Jackson is on our flank," they shouted. Officers and all took [to] the woods and the whole 11th Corps fled in confusion. Hooker attempted to rally them and his horse was killed and he reported wounded.

We had a hard time of it, short [of] food, loss of sleep, etc. Nobody was killed in our regiment but [with] Lt. [Col.] Carter several were wounded, several horses killed and wounded including several in our company.

A panic was raised in our train of wagons and my saddle bags thrown away and lost. But in scouring the woods when the enemy fell back I captured two Yankees after shooting at them twice and from one got black oil-cloth, haversack, canteen, one new pair drawers, and an excellent shirt. Have one pair cotton drawers, one cotton shirt, two summer flannel shirts, several pair socks, a handkerchief, a few collars, and a towel sent to me by express from Curdsville as soon as possible. As I have no way of carrying my clothes with me send them either in my old saddle valise or the little bank trunk upstairs according to what you think best. One will be about as apt to be thrown away as the other. I would have bought clothes here but there is nothing to be had, not even a pair of cotton socks.

We started from near Spottsylvania C. H. Thursday evening and reached here Friday evening travelling till 3 o'clock Thursday night.

Jackson had his left arm amputated and was shot in lower part of right hand, one bone broken.

I am well. Give my love to all. Your affectionate son, Robert T. Hubard, Jr.

～

Camp Near Hagerstown
Saturday, July 11th, '63
My Dear Father,

I take this opportunity of writing you a few lines. I rejoined my regiment on the left of our army at Gettysburg on Friday the 3rd while they were fighting. We had no charging that day.

We came back to Williamsport on Monday and Thursday attacked the Yankee cavalry near Boonsboro, driving them back toward the mountains a mile. At night we fell back and next day they attacked us and we fell back before them. They attacked us again at half past 6 a.m. today and pressed us very hard. We fell back under a galling fire of rifles and artillery to this [west] side of Antietam River at the village of Funktown on the other bank. The 7th Georgia Infantry came up to our relief and deployed as skirmishers. We had two men killed and two horses by shell while passing through the village.

Our infantry are in line of battle on this side of the Antietam. The enemy's infantry. who have been supporting their cavalry this morning are here and a great battle is at hand. May God in his mercy grant us a victory.

I must close. I am well. Love to all.

Your affectionate son, R. T. Hubard, Jr.

〜

Hdqrtrs, 3rd Va. Cav., Jefferson Co., Va.
Monday, July 20th, 1863
My Dear Father,

My letters of late have not been numerous and, owing to my worn out condition and want of time, have been, I fear uninteresting and badly written. Now, therefore, having had several days of rest in fair weather, feeling much refreshed and having leisure, I write with the hope of being more interesting.

I was very much gratified by the receipt of a letter from William dated 11th July at Chellow. But I was very sorry to hear that you were and had been quite unwell for some days. I fear that in consequence of my thoughts being so much engrossed by the exciting scenes around me I appear in my letters to think too exclusively of myself and not enough of you and my brothers and sisters. This is not the case in any respects. I assure you that I feel the most anxious solicitude about you all and never felt more strongly attached to you all than now. My first and most earnest wishes are always for your welfare. Nothing gives me more pain than to hear of your being sick. No children ever had greater cause to love and revere a parent than we. And I am sure that we all appreciate this fact and are anxious to do all in our power to evince our love and gratitude and make you happy. I hope you will soon recover from your indisposition and not allow the troubles of the times or any anxiety about me to [affect] your spirits or affect your health. If I survive this war, and I hope I will, my first wish is that I may find you at home to welcome my return, to aid me by your counsel and to participate in my anticipated joys. Your health is not good, I know, but I will indulge the hope that it may not grow seriously worse for some years to come.

I wish very much that I could be at home a part of the summer. I am very anxious to see all of you; to hear brother's speculations about house building, crop making, educating children, etc., sister Isa's accounts of the gradual progress of the illustrious Benjamin from crawling to walking,[5] Edmund's grandiloquent representations of the schemes devised and to be put into immediate execution with a view to the consummation of that object most devoutly to be wished; viz. a matrimonial alliance with some bouncing lassie. Lou's [Louisa's] intentions in regard to captivating and killing hosts of poor fellows with good intentions. Bolling's and Philip's views on the subject of education in general and their views of kings, in particular. All these things would be very gratifying, indeed. But at present you know much depends on the Army of Northern Virginia and every man must be at his post.

I hope, though Vicksburg and Port Hudson are fallen and probably Charleston, that Providence will yet bring us succour in some way. It may be that our very adversities will frighten France into giving us aid. Certainly Europe is not anxious to see the Union restored.

In going up the Cumberland Valley and crossing to Gettysburg I saw the finest wheat country I ever saw before. The country is divided into small farms which are in a very high state of cultivation. We marched our heavy columns through their wheat, oats, potatoes, etc, where the roads were bad; burnt their fences, stole their chickens and vegetables and gave them the longest faces you ever saw.

I talked with some of them; told them they were the greatest asses the world ever saw. That in giving Lincoln the power to free our slaves he had made slaves of them and that the change might be agreeable to them but I always thought a white man better than a negro and couldn't see what they had gained.

They seemed to think I was not far wrong—said that wished Lincoln at the devil—would turn him out soon, etc. But none of them seemed to care particularly for us—some men very bitter against us— all seemed attached to the Union. Though all professed to be Constitutional, none would confess that they voted for Lincoln.

In my letter to you from Maryland, I dated it Saturday, this was wrong—we skirmished heavily Wednesday, Thursday, and Friday and my letter was written Friday [July 10]. Our army did not all cross the Potomac by 7 1/2 a.m. Tuesday as I thought and stated in a letter to brother last Saturday. A. P. Hill's corps did not all get over at Falling Waters till 12 m. Heth's Division was in rear and off its guard, I suppose, when a squadron of Yankee cavalry charged upon Pettigrew's brigade who were nearly all sleep with arms stacked, killing Pettigrew and some others, but were annihilated themselves.

Our army is resting and I can't tell what will be done. The impression prevails that we will recross the Potomac but I hear that Longstreet's Corps is moving today towards Clarke County.

I was much pleased at hearing from Miss —— through William. I wish the little scamp would be more civil and correspond. But I know she loves me and must be content, I suppose, for the present.

I am feeling much better than a day or two ago and regaining flesh, I think. Hoping that this letter may find you well and the whole family in good spirits. I must close my letter.

My new horse is a good one but stuck a nail in his foot the other day and is quite lame. He will probably be so for several days, maybe a week. If my Osborne horse is, as brother thinks, well and a [illegible], you would find me a good servant and send him and the horse to me as soon as possible. I have not yet been able to buy a saddle but have a borrowed one. I am much in need of a servant, Matthews having retained his.

Your affectionate son, R. T. Hubard. Jr.

Hd Qs., 3rd Va. Cav.
Sept. 1st, 1863
My Dear Sister [Isaetta],

I take this opportunity of complying with my intention long entertained of writing to you. Regarding you and brother James as very completely one, I have concluded hitherto that you would not feel slighted, provided I wrote to him. But as you may be more gratified at the receipt of a letter yourself, I address this to you in person.

I received a letter from William a few days ago announcing his intention to contract to a matrimonial alliance about the 1st October. I was much surprised to learn who the young lady was. For though I had heard of his seeing Miss M., etc., I had received a letter from him which stated that he had called on Miss B. and had a very pleasant visit; and I thought from what I have heard of the young lady she would be more likely to suit William's tastes than Miss M. I would have immediately written him a letter of congratulations but I had to go off to Bowling Green with the brigade and besides, did not know whether he was still at Chellow. I am very happy to learn of his happiness and hope his fullest expectations may be realized. I hope that I shall be able to get a leave of absence sometime this month or next and will endeavor to attend the wedding or at least be present to welcome the happy couple home to Chellow.

My letter to Pa of a few days since will inform you all of the unhappy times in my love affairs. I do not wish or intend to trouble you with many words on the subject. But I deem it simple justice to Miss —— that I should state my real convictions in regard to her. I do not believe her a flirt or a false woman. I believe like many other young persons she was pleased with me when I saw her last and spoke what she did sincerely. My love may have been of too demonstrative a character. Or she may have been annoyed by the over zeal of some of her family or other friends of mine in my behalf. Thus, perhaps a sincere but transient feeling of regard may have been destroyed. I have no idea of what course I shall pursue but incline to the opinion that I shall not make any further efforts in that direction. If a young lady discards a man emphatically and finally now, while he is away fighting the battles of his country, he need scarcely hope to be able to bring any other more powerful influences to bear in future. This is no time for a man to indulge in personal griefs. I shall, therefore, strive to forget myself in the great struggle and devote my whole time and thoughts to the duties I owe the country. After the war I cannot believe I will be regarded so stupid or worthless as to be unable to find some one worthy of one who will be willing to love and accept my hand.

When the alarm was given at Richmond the other day that the Yankees were at Bottom's Bridge, several brigades of infantry were put in motion for the railroad depots and our brigade marched off Friday evening to Bowling Green, there to await further orders.[6] Nothing turning up, we marched back next day. So you will readily imagine it was a great relief to me to go on a little trip just at that time and have some prospect of a fight causing me to forget in the excitement of surrounding events matters of private interest.

Though it was quite dusty, Gen. [Roger] Pryor bore the trip like a philosopher. He was put on camp guard yesterday. I could scarcely suppress my inclination to laugh when the O[rderly] S[ergeant] marched him into the line and reported to the Sergeant Major, "Detail present from Company E. Brigadier General Pryor [is] the detail from Company E!" The antithesis was so great as to make it ludicrous. Because while it is in some sense a misfortune for Pryor to be thus degraded (in a technical sense), it is by his own choosing and cannot hurt him in the end.[7]

I suppose Edmund and Louisa were badly frightened at the Rock. Alum [Springs] by the approach of the Yankees and shall not be surprised to hear of their return home very soon.[8] I fear they have not met with very many interesting strangers but hope they have had a pleasant time of it jolting up and down the mountains and seeing some scenes new to them both.

I saw your brother frequently during the late campaign but have not seen him since we came down here.

How tall is Benjamin now and what is his weight? I suppose he can talk very distinctly by this. How I wish I could see the dear little fellow and will, doubtless under your training, make a man worthy of his parentage.

I must now close my letter. I and all the troopers from my neighborhood are well. Give my love to all at Chellow and remember me to your father and mother and Bobby when you write to them. Give Ben a kiss for his Uncle Robert.

Your Affectionate Brother, R. J. Hubard, Jr.

~

Hd. Qrs., 3rd Va. Cav., Vidiersville, Orange
Sept. 21st, 1863
To E[dmund] A. Hubard of Chellow
My Dear Brother,

I received a very kind, interesting letter from sister Isa a few days ago informing me that Lou and yourself had returned safely from the Springs after a pleasant trip. A few days before I had a letter from William informing me what a terrible dance he had been led by the Charming Alice. Whilst I did not like to intimate an[y] suspicion of the kind whilst he had confidence in her, I was apprehensive of the very thing which has happened. Having just been maltreated myself, I was predisposed to look out for squalls in his case. It is a singular thing in regard to women that those who would make devoted wives and sensible wives too often are to the last degree frivolous and fickle before marriage.

I am still in the dark as to what causes influenced Miss D—— in her last action towards me. Her letter does not give me any clue atall.

After expressing regret that I considered our relations as more intimate than she would wish, she said she wished always to be regarded
as frank, honest, and sincere, and spoke truly, therefore, in declaring
that she esteemed me as a friend but did not love me. From my knowledge of the girl I am satisfied that she meant not to deceive me at
first—but that subsequent events have convinced her that she did not
love me, or causes may have operated to destroy any such feeling as
did exist. I do not believe, therefore, that I have been flirted with. I
know that I did excite the strongest emotions in her breast. Her conduct destroyed it. And I experience a feeling of deep sorrow and sad-
ness when I reflect upon the happiness that both of us might have
derived from a marriage to which no one could urge an objection—
prevented now, perhaps, by some frivolous reason.

I confess, however, that I fear Lou's conjectures are nearer right
than any other. Miss S. is a sentimental girl and young Johnson of
Petersburg, being related to Mr. A. Warwick, puts up at the house
whenever he is in town. I think it quite likely that this young rascal,
having had better access to the young lady's society than I had, sup-
planted me entirely. It is very well to talk about philosophy in love affairs but human nature is human nature and will obey nature's laws.

I have not written to Miss D. but once since being dismissed and
never expect to write again. I shall call and see her if I get a leave of
absence any time soon but have very little hope of it resulting in anything.

If you think of courting Miss Munell or Miss Galt take care not to
love either too hard and not court either unless she is so cordial as
almost to ensure success. Being discarded is no pleasant thing and has
an inevitable tendency to sadden the brightest season of life. Women
are strange beings and yield every consideration of good sense and
propriety to a sickly sentimentality about exalted [illegible] etc. If any
artful rascal can convince them that he has something angelic about
him he wins surely. Profit by the experience of older brothers and do
not hastily plunge yourself into a situation which brings inevitable
disappointment and sorrow.

I hope you will be more successful than I have been. I fear that I
haven't the art of pleasing young ladies somehow. It is a mortifying
reflection that men of no worth are often, in politics, in the army and

in courting, successful where men of worth go unrewarded and over-looked. Such is the course, however, and it is idle to dream. What we cannot prevent we had best submit to with a good grace.

Who is it that Lou's been elevating lately? I'll venture a wagon he hails from Farmville.

We are stationed 17 miles east of Orange Court House. Our army confidently expected an attack yesterday and day before. They are in line of battle along the Rapidanne [*sic*] immediately north of us. General Hampton's Cavalry Division under command of General Stuart is on the left toward Madison. Major General Fitz Lee's Division comprising William Lee's, Lomax's, Wickham's brigades will operate on the extreme right, though we are at present in rear of the center. The army, except perhaps the North Carolina troops, is in fine condition and although McLaw's and Hood's divisions are gone to Tennessee, it is said we have as many effective men as we ever fought with.[9] Everybody here is in fine spirits and confident. Our regiment numbers about 300 officers and men for mounted duty and are in a fine condition, I think, to fight well.

Meade may not attack but I think he will. He will most probably cross on our right flank at Germanna and endeavor to occupy the strong works at Chancellorsville till he can establish his base of supplies at Aquia Creek again. Trusting in God, a good general, and a brave army, I shall confidently expect victory.

Direct your letters to "Third Virginia Cavalry, Wickham's Brigade, Fitz Lee's Division via Richmond."

I am quite well, the Griggs, R. Page, etc. ditto. Isham is quite well, attentive to my horses and contented.[10] He sends his compliments and expresses the hope that white folks and black folks may gather abundant crops of corn, peas, etc. Give my love to all the family, white and black, and receive assurances of the love and best wishes of your affectionate brother,

R. T. Hubard, Jr.

Orange Court House
September 24th, '63
Dear Father,

We marched up from Vidiersville day before yesterday and joined Hampton's Division just after the cavalry fight was over. Our division went that night to Barboursville, 6 miles from Gordonsville, and met Kilpatrick next morning; he heard of our move and fell back at 3 a.m. yesterday. We advanced at sunrise to attack him. But finding he had gone, had to content ourselves with following him beyond Madison Court House, across Robinson River and capturing about twenty of his guard. The 2nd Regiment was in advance and had sixteen men wounded. We were not engaged. We got back last night and the regiment moved down to Vidiersville today.[11]

I went over to Hampton's Brigade and collected the money on your o/c's. You were mistaken in the amount. There were two duplicate o/c's and one certificate relating to one of them; in all 180 bushels. They allowed $4 per bushel = $720.

Major McClellan says I'll get my leave of absence approved as soon as all is quiet.

I believe I gave my directions, 3rd Virginia Cavalry, Wickham's Brigade, Fitz Lee's Division.

I am very well and off for camp in haste. Your affectionate son, R. J. Hubard.

~

Hd. Qrs., 3rd Va. Cav.
Dec. 11, 1863
Dear Lou,

Our regiment moves to Albemarle tomorrow; the whole of Fitz Lee's division save Lomax's brigade has already started. We will be somewhere west of Charlottesville between the two railroads.[12] I want to get to Dr. Randolph's tomorrow night. I got a letter from H. Flood today. He said Miss S. was well and thinks from the way she carries on with Mr. McDonald of L. that she is a flirt. Very likely. I may however pay her a visit about Xmas. I don't [know] whether she will flirt with me again. Probably I may court Miss Emma Rives. Be surprised at nothing.

I was very much pained to learn from Ned Price that Mrs. Eppes died last Saturday.[13] I felt great reverence for her. She was one of the purest characters I have ever known. Were all like her, no laws save those of God would be required. I shall very fondly cherish her memory and strive to learn lessons of virtue from her pure upright example. May it be her privilege to be one of the most highly favored of those who worship around the throne on High. The legal [——]

will doubtless soon call for a division of the property and I hope almost against hope that Uncle Philip's improved financial condition will restore him to something like decency of life.[14]

I had a promise today from a brother of Major General Lee that he would try to induce the General to aid me in getting some promotion before long.[15] Some think there will be a reorganization of the army. I do not believe it.

Davy returned from Nelson [County] with a fresh horse some days ago. William had been affectionately riding about trying to buy me a horse, hence Davy's delay.

My letter by Bed Grigg did both injustice. William wrote hopefully concerning Miss F. M. and reiterated his inalterable purpose never to address A. B. again. I hope William is acting discretely and will be successful and happy.

And now, dear Lou, asking your forgiveness for having written in haste, such a scrawl, with an affectionate kiss and many a good wish for you all. I bid you adieu. *Please have my new uniform coat nicely bundled up and sent to Dr. Randolph's immediately* as I shall need it to do some courting, you understand. James and Elizabeth Grigg are both well. My regards to Mr. James Grigg and family.

Your affectionate brother, R. T. Hubard, Jr.

Year 4
1864

10

"Boys, You Have Made the Most Glorious Fight"

Matters were now very gloomy, the prospects of the Confederacy were very doubtful and many had despaired since the battle of Gettysburg and fall of Vicksburg and Port Hudson. Our currency was in a hopeless condition of depreciation. Our population had furnished nearly as many soldiers as it could naturally bear and the conscript laws therefore availed but little and the tax and impressment laws had nearly stripped the country of flour, grain, and meat and greatly discouraged production. Congress was weak-headed, weak-hearted, and weak-kneed resorting to every kind of temporizing expedient rather than boldly resorting to strong measures which alone could restore hope and confidence and provide the sinews of war. They gave their treasury notes a fatal stab instead of a healing dose by providing for their funding in a new issue of 33 1/3 cents discount on the dollar. None of our armies in the field were looked to with any hope atall except that of General Lee. And all that was hoped of it was to hold Richmond.

After Grant's great success over Bragg, he was appointed "Lieutenant General Commanding the Armies of the United States." He established his own headquarters with the Army of the Potomac with a view to crush Lee's army, take Richmond, and close the war.

Though President Davis had grown more sour and obstinate as matters grew worse and had no great fancy for General Joe Johnston, he yielded to the earnest wishes of the people and appointed him to succeed Bragg. The latter was called to Richmond to act as a sort of advisory and directory general. Being himself disappointed and soured, imagining everybody hated [him], he seemed to have taken to hating everybody else and was eternally getting up a mess between the President and some of the generals in the field.[1]

General Beauregard was now in command of Charleston, South Carolina. The enemy commenced to besiege it about the 1st of July, 1863, and kept it up until its evacuation in March, 1865.

Such efforts were made to remit and strengthen the Army of Northern Virginia as lay in the power of the nearly exhausted government. And we prepared now not to conquer independence directly but by prolonging the war another year, exhaust the Federal treasury, and thus through the "pocket nerve" of the Yankee, operate to bring about a cessation of hostilities and our acknowledgement. We didn't consider that in a fight, the man who has had strength and wind enough to get his adversary down generally has enough to hold him there till he cries, "Hold, enough."

Lomax's brigade, holding the left of General Lee's line, having been compelled to scatter about very much to get forage during the months of January and February, about the close of the latter month, General Kilpatrick, with 2 brigades, one which was commanded by Colonel Ulric Dahlgren, broke through the lines and came to Barboursville. There, dividing his force, a part threatened Charlottesville but were driven off by Major R. F. Mason of General Fitz Lee's staff and one company of Stuart's Horse Artillery.[2] The other pushed on to Gordonsville, burned the depot, etc., and tore up the track very considerably. They then united, struck the canal at Columbia, attempted in vain to blow up the aqueduct, and went on towards Richmond along the 3 Chopt Road tearing up the track and burning the depots between and including Frederick's Hall and Hanover Junction and burning the bridges across the South Anna and other streams. They thus cut off General Lee's supplies and now moved forward towards Richmond where we hadn't any troops, scarcely a regiment or two guarding prisoners, etc.

General Wise, who was on a visit to his brother-in-law, Mr. Stanard in Goochland, was almost captured but escaped galloping into Richmond with the *first news* of the approach when they were within 15 miles of the city![3]

All was now bustle and confusion. General Bragg managed to draw up enough recruits the next day to man the works. Had the enemy bolted ahead the day they came near catching Wise, instead of stopping to plunder the rich farms along the river, they might have taken and burned Richmond.

Hampton pushed forward in pursuit from Fredericksburg and we had two regiments of cavalry on the Peninsula which turned out scouting.

I received a telegram from Farmville on the 2nd March to notify the regiment to report by companies to General Fitz Lee at Richmond immediately, notified them, and reported in person with the Cumberland Troop the evening of the 4th.

The enemy divided [on] the 1st or 2nd, Kilpatrick with the main column going off safely to Old Church down the Peninsula. Dahlgren's party were cut off and, attempting to escape by the north side of the Pamunkey through the darkness of night, ran into an ambuscade, was himself killed, and his command dispersed. On his person were found instruction to his men to burn and sack Richmond and in some captured wagons were found turpentine balls and other combustible materials for this purpose. His corpse was taken to Richmond and buried in disgrace, secretly at night in an old burial ground.[4]

We now had an extremely disagreeable time until the 15th April being encamped in a very soggy piece of ground and exposed to almost incessant rain and sleet with indifferent shelter, but little wood and little forage for the horses. By the middle of April we put out for Fredericksburg where we had a very pleasant camp and good grazing with some corn for our horses.

On the 4th May, Grant crossed the Rapidann at Germanna, etc., with 112 thousand muskets, about 15,000 cavalry and two to three hundred pieces of artillery. On the 5th one division [of Confederate cavalry] marched up to Massaponax Church. On the 6th (our brigade, numbering about 2250 men, my regiment 30 officers and 494 men), we marched up beyond Spottsylvania Court House, dismounted and formed a line of battle about two miles east of Todd's Tavern where we skirmished with the enemy slightly all day. [We] had 2nd Lieutenant Puryear, Company A, wounded through the lung and one man of Company B killed.

Next day Brigadier General Rosser sent us word to advance and press the enemy as he had a brigade cut off. We impetuously assaulted the enemy and drove him back to Todd's and here, being backed by infantry, he made a firm stand and was unmovable. The 5th and 6th [Virginia] Regiments of Lomax's Brigade suffered severely.

Finding we could do nothing, we returned to our position and found

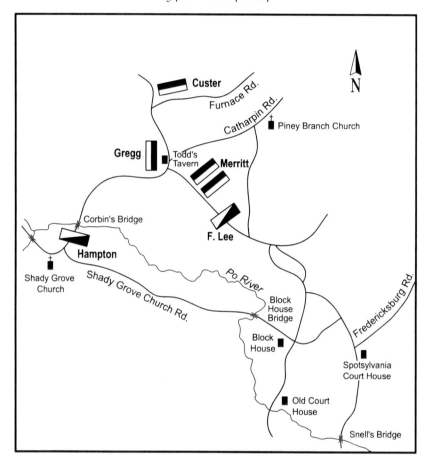

6. Todd's Tavern, 7 May 1864

that Rosser instead of a brigade had "cut off" two divisions of cavalry, several brigades of infantry, and one or two batteries of artillery and had to withdraw *without* his *game*.

Towards evening the enemy made a heavy movement on our front, at the same time threatening our right, which was guarded by Colonel Owen with three squadrons, Lieutenant Colonel Carter being hotly engaged in front with the other two. About 5 p.m. Colonel Owen was ordered to the front with one squadron on foot. I went with him. [We] double-quicked for half a mile.

We got up on the line, found our right driving the enemy some distance ahead while the left was being forced back almost upon the artillery. Halting only long enough to form a hasty line, not waiting for stragglers, the Colonel bolted right ahead into the thick woods with about fifty men. We halted in about 150 yards, deployed, and commenced firing. We saw but few men in our front. There was a heavy firing to our left succeeded by a profound silence. Presently somebody seemed to be firing upon our rear. I called out to them to desist and come up on the line or they would hit some of us. Then a sergeant on my left came running up to me saying, "The Yankees are behind us and I believe have captured the Colonel for I went to the left to look for him and ran into them."

Thinking him frightened, [I] told him to take his place and watch out. He had scarcely left me when turning around, I saw two Yankees, one in 15 yards of me. While hesitating to fire as he came from the rear and I feared I might kill a Confederate, he aimed at me. I had a carbine cocked in my hand and raised, aimed, and fired it killing him. I then called to the men to face about and right oblique. In this way we got out of the scrape and fell back upon the line which was now 75 yards further back.

It seems that the 15th Regiment on our left was driven back, leaving our flank exposed, when the Colonel and men nearest him were attacked in rear but repulsed, at least for a moment, those attacking him captured five or six and got out with the loss of one of the Colonel's fingers which was shot away.

That night we still held our position and awaited attack early the next morning. We now learned of the desperate fight of the Wilderness, which was fought near the ground over which Jackson made his great flank attack movement, on the 6th of May by A. P Hill's and Ewell's corps against Grant's whole army. The latter attacked and met with a bloody repulse. Longstreet's Corps, which had arrived from east Tennessee, had not yet gotten upon the ground, but was marching down from Orange Court House.[5]

This battle was fought almost exclusively on densely wooded grounds so that artillery couldn't be but little used. It is said that at a crucial juncture General Lee having ordered a desperate charge and, seeing the men hesitate a little, placed himself at the head of Heth's Division and called upon the men to follow him. They insisted that he should not expose his precious life and that they would charge whenever and wherever he wished and did make a splendid and successful charge.

Lee had, including Longstreet's command, about 45,000 effective infantry, about 8,000 cavalry, and some 200 guns. Though his army hadn't altogether the spirit it had commenced other campaigns with, it was yet self-reliant and went into the campaign with the hope that it was to be the last and with the determination that *General U.S. Grant should not whip "Mas' Bob."*

W. H. F. Lee was now major general commanding division composed of his own, now Chambliss', brigade and Rosser's [Brigade].

My regiment, Lieutenant Colonel Carter commanding, was left on picket the 7th and at 3 a.m. [May 8th] we heard the Yankee bugles sounding to horse. So we prepared for immediate attack and sent couriers to inform the generals. They took but little notice, however of the messages. We had heard a movement on our right as of a marching column with trains etc. but this, when told [to] Brigadier General Wickham and Major General Fitz Lee, was likewise little heeded; they turned over and "slumbered and slept."

Sending our horses to the rear, Lieutenant Colonel Carter formed the four squadrons with him in line behind the barricade and resolutely expressed his purpose to hold his ground. At 4 a.m. we plainly heard the commands not many yards down in the woods, "Battalion forward, guide center, march" and, in a few moments more, we were firing as fast as we could load, at a very heavy line of blue jackets. It was one incessant, deafening rattle while the smoke arose so thick we could scarcely see.

The generals seemed to have waked up at last and a courier came to say that we must hold on and the brigade would be up *after a while.* Carter, finding his left flank completely passed by a heavy column, and that he was about being flanked on the right ordered his men to retreat firing. This we did for about 300 yards after having fought for one hour against odds of four or five to one.

The brigade now coming to our support dismounted, we formed a longer line along a ridge in a dense piece of woods and here we lay and fired for three hours more incessantly.

Meanwhile the cavalry in our front had given place to the 5th U.S. Army Corps who fought us very heavily and at a distance between the skirmishers of about 40 yards and about 100 [yards] between the main lines. The [Federal] cavalry, meanwhile, hurried off across our right and striking the road from the Plank Road to Spottsylvania Court House, advanced toward the latter point. Our brigade was now withdrawn and

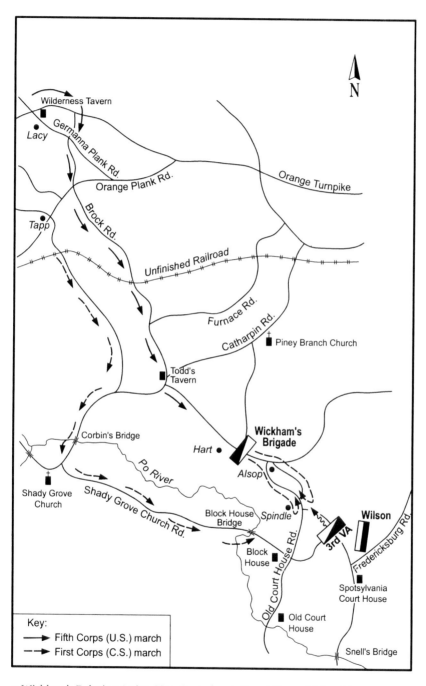

7. Wickham's Delaying Action, Near Spotsylvania Court House, 8 May 1864

relieved by Lomax' [brigade] (stationed a mile nearer the Court House), ordered to mount and our regiment hurried off at a gallop to the Court House.

Arriving there and turning the head of the column into the road the Yankees were on, we had two horses killed by a shell before we could dismount for they had planted a battery in sight of the Court House. They had dismounted skirmishers deployed and advancing, supported by heavy bodies of mounted men (at least a brigade in sight). Matthews squadron was deployed to the left of the road, dismounted, and I went with it on its extreme right. The rest of the regiment was on our left. We were vigorously shelled besides being under a heavy fire of small arms. As we were in an open field and the mounted men were preparing to charge us, we had to retreat across the road we came down, giving up the village temporarily. The Yankees now charged vigorously, capturing the greater part of the New Kent Company [Company F] of Matthews' squadron. The rest of us had to thank our legs for safety. Getting into some woods we now checked them somewhat.

The rest of the regiment and brigade were better off not having the brunt to bear so much. I and three others on the extreme right were rather cut off from the rest and, in attempting to get back, ran nearly upon a body of men who were taken by Sergeant Garrett[6] to be Yankees wherefrom we concealed ourselves and not being able to judge from the firing but that our men were driven back by the old court house, we set out after dark to get out of the enemy's lines (as we supposed), came near running upon several pickets, had a terrible walk through briars, bushes, swamps, and one creek thigh deep for eight miles.

Next morning we went to a house where they told us that Longstreet had gotten up about the time we were driven back at the Court House and retook the place and had held it since. So it seems we were in the midst of our own men that night. We then set out to join our regiment; about two o'clock after marching ten miles on foot, we learned that while our brigade was hotly engaged fighting infantry at the Court House, Major General P. Sheridan, with three divisions [of] cavalry, has passed the extreme right running off some pickets of the 5th Virginia Cavalry and was off for Richmond along the Telegraph Road and Stuart after him.

It was subsequently ascertained that our obstinate resistance to the 5th Corps on the 8th was of utmost importance; had we been driven off before Longstreet got up, Grant would have secured the road from Spottsylvania to Louisa Court House and, thus, cut off Lee from Richmond being himself between him and the latter point.

Indeed, our generals seemed aware of the importance of the struggle for they said we *must* hold our ground no matter *what the odds were against us.* And I have had several other opportunities of observing how generals, while *never approving* of a feeble resistance were nevertheless, at times, so far impressed with the old adage "a good run is better than a bad stand" that they were not utterly inconsolable on being repulsed whereas on other great occasions, like that I am now commenting on, they would recognize no choice, whatever, and say, "Soldiers, you must fight—this position must be held." And when they spoke thus, I noticed the soldiers fought with far greater desperation holding out in the face of losses that would otherwise have sufficed to cause a perfect stampede.

As we were withdrawing Sunday morning, General Fitz Lee riding by the "Old Brigade" said with great emotion, "Boys, you have made the most glorious fight you ever made, the noblest I ever saw." Our loss that day was quite heavy. Among the killed in the 3rd Regiment were [J. W.] Fitzgerald and J[ames D.] Vaughan, Company E, and Thomas Pride, Company G, the latter killed in a yard of me while lying on his belly behind a large tree by a diagonal musket shot that took effect in his right temple.[7]

General Fitzhugh Lee came up with Sheridan's rear guard at Mitchell's Shop some 10 or 15 miles from Massaponax Church and at once ordered the 4 regiments to commence a successive charge by squadrons.[8] I hadn't gotten up and therefore can't describe the fight accurately.

Captain Moss' Buckingham squadron was in front and in their front set of fours was my brother Edmund, whose health had prevented his joining the army till February of this year when he entered the Buckingham Company as a private.[9] So the charge was made down the road upon the Yankee rear [which] halted and prepared to receive it. A body of the latter [Federals] charged them on the flank separating the front set from the rest, the latter being thrown into disorder, thereby. My brother and three companions wheeling about found a party of 15 or 16 "Yanks" between them and their command, and demanded their surrender. Some of them [Federals] started to comply when others, seeing the confusion, etc, said, "Don't surrender to 4 damned rebels, kill them." Thereupon they commenced firing at very short range and our party of four only escaped by leaping the fence. My brother got a ball through his clothes and another through the belt holster of his pistol.

After some further delay and while [Fitz] Lee was trying to devise some scheme to fall upon the flank, Brigadier General Wickham, in pursuance of his instructions, rode up to Captain Matthews, commanding a squadron of the 3rd and ordered him to break through at all hazards, promising that he should have support.

At this time Sheridan had several regiments flanking the road on both sides ready to deliver a cross fire, a regiment drawn up in the road with a section of artillery unlimbered and shotted just behind them.

Matthews commanded forward and dashed away splendidly followed by his men. Getting under the cross fire, his men and horses began to fall and this, together with a number of dead horses of Captain Watkins' squadrons E and K which had made a partially successful charge before this and lost only about a dozen horses and no men, lying in the road constituted such an obstacle as to severe his columns, those in front, (about 25), keeping on at full speed cutting right and left and the enemy closing in behind them.

Matthews was shot down by a man just behind him while fighting one or two in front. 1st Lieutenant Palmore was wounded and unhorsed, Privates [Archer T.] McLaurine and [Rodophil] Jeter killed (also their horses) B[enjamin B.] Overton, mortally wounded, [John V.] Ryals badly [wounded] also [George B.] Mayo and [Powhatan J.] Ayers and 8 more captured. Two or three got out unharmed, the rest were thrown or had their horses killed.[10]

Other regiments suffered here, Lieutenant [Charles W.] Hubbard of the James City [Troop], 5th Virginia Cavalry, being killed.[11]

Having been repulsed in all of our efforts to penetrate Sheridan's column, we desisted from further attack but followed closely. I met with Reverend W[illiam] C. Meredith, chaplain of the 4th, who let me ride his horse till I got up with an ambulance on which I rode till overtaking the command shortly after the fight was over, when I got my horse again.[12]

Matthews was carried to a house nearby where he lingered, being shot through the liver, till the 13th, I think. I must here pay a brief tribute to his memory. He was the son of the Commonwealth's attorney of Cumberland, inherited from his father a great amount of talent but a reasonable share of sense and great force of character or *energy* which made

him appear better and accomplish far more than many greatly his superior in mere intellect. He had, by storekeeping, acquired a wonderful
knowledge of human nature and had studied the art of intrigue as a le-
gitimate and proper mode of self advancement. Hence, in all of his
intercourse with others, he was ever mindful of this one end, the grati-
fication of an intense ambition. He always advocated aspirants for office
in opposition to those already in for the reason that he might rather hope
to upset one insecure in his seat than one established by a repeated
choice.

He had, unfortunately, acquired too great a fondness for liquor and
sometimes drank too much. But I am happy to say that during the entire
campaign he was, as far as I know, *entirely abstemious,* even when around
Richmond and told me he had quit.

Now having, as in candor, pointed out his faults, I am happy to say
and believe they were all he had. Though, as I have previously stated, he
acted in the contest with me as I should not have done, yet I mentioned
it rather as an excuse for my poor run than as censure for my departed
rival (and friend, not withstanding). For what he did was not from un-
kindness to me but extreme solicitude for his own success.

George was a liberal, generous-hearted, good natured, jovial young
man who delighted to serve another a friendly turn when in his power.
Kind and charitable in the use of his money, honorable in regard to his
debts, full of respect and regard for the Christian religion, conscientious
in the discharge of his duty, conspicuous for his prompt obedience to
orders, bravery, and gallantry, being at the time of his death the best captain decidedly in the regiment. He always appeared much attached to me,
and doubtless was, for he consulted me, in preference to and more intimately than, anyone else in regard to management of his company and
other matters.

As a soldier he had "rather die than disobey" and accordingly charged
with the utmost enthusiasm into a position from which he must have
known he could not calculate upon coming out unhurt. To him is due
the meed of praise awarded to the bravest of the brave who fall in the
front rank of battle with the sweet words upon their lips, "Dulce et
decorum est pro patria mori."[13]

We marched all night the 9th and shelled the enemy's rear guard
while crossing the North Anna River. Crossing the 10th we followed to
Frederick's Hall, (I think it was), where the 1st and 2nd charged one or

two regiments and inflicted considerable loss. After this we only kept in sight of the rear guard. Sheridan went down the Mountain Road followed by Gordon's North Carolina Brigade. Wickham's and Lomax's brigades encamped at Hanover Junction.

The 11th, at 10 a.m., [we] attacked a detachment at their work of destruction along the railroad at Ashland and about to burn the place. We charged them and drove them off, killing and capturing six or eight.

At 12 noon we gained the head of Brook Turnpike at Yellow Tavern. Lomax's Brigade dismounted and formed across the mouth of and facing up the Mountain Road. Our brigade dismounted and formed at right angles to Lomax and on his right flank. In rear of each brigade 4 rifle guns were planted.

Dispatches were sent to General Bragg commanding Richmond to send us reinforcement and we could capture a large portion of the force, perhaps, but he didn't have any to send. Dispatches from Gordon said he was pressing their rear and skirmishing heavily.

In our three brigades we had something less than 3000. Sheridan's force was variously estimated at 10 to 12 thousand of which one brigade was mounted infantry.[14]

About 2 p.m. he appeared in our front and the action at once commenced. Leaving a small force to check Gordon, he brought up a very heavy force upon us. The first discharges of our artillery fell right among my regiment mortally wounding one trooper and crushing the arm of another, besides knocking down the small pines at a dreadful rate. This so disorganized the regiment that its efficiency was greatly impaired. But it was reformed, moved a little to the right, and made a handsome charge in conjunction with the 1st and 4th upon the flank of a column which was attacking Lomax heavily. [We] compelled the enemy to fall back in great disorder.

At length the enemy began to attack us all along the line very heavily, charging first one point then another on foot but being handsomely repulsed each time. We felt that the safety of the Capital depended on us. And, indeed, it did for the 2nd line of fortifications were not manned for several hours after we commenced the action and there were no troops on the outer lines, whatever, nor any on the inner line.

Finally, Lomax was so heavily pressed that the 1st Virginia had to go to his support. The 3rd took its place under heavy fire and the 2nd closed on the right of the 4th. I had just thrown forward a body of men under

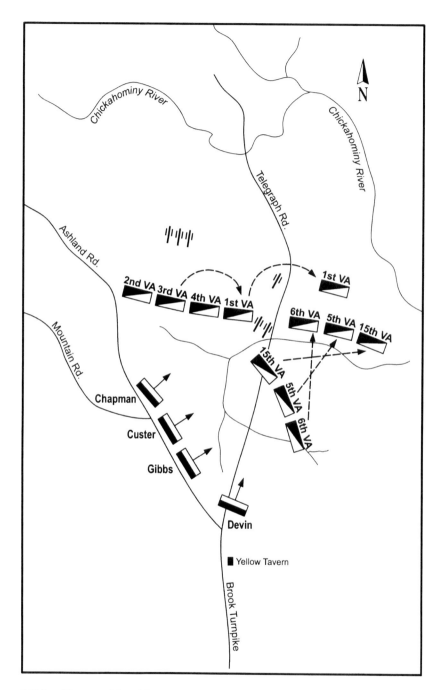

8. Yellow Tavern, 11 May 1864

a very heavy fire by command of the lieutenant colonel [Carter] commanding the 3rd Virginia Cavalry and, carbine in hand, was doing my best to pick off some of the rascals who were shooting at us, when I received orders to "Retreat in good order." Whereupon I brought off my command and, observing the line moving back rapidly and in disorder [and] hearing loud huzzahs and a fire of increased intensity from the enemy, I felt convinced that my worst fears were realized.

A few minutes before, a very large mounted body concealed from my view by the conformation of the ground, but evidently large from the loud tramping of the horses, had swept down like an avalanche upon Lomax and it was now evident that they had broken or run over his lines, that the day was lost, and the road towards the fortifications open.

I afterwards learned that at the critical moment Stuart ordered Colonel H. C. Pate of the 5th Virginia Cavalry to hold the enemy back at all hazards, to save the artillery, etc. that that officer replied he would [but] was shot dead in his track and many of his men killed when the rest fell back in confusion. Stuart, endeavoring by his own heroic doing, to rally this command and arouse the flagging spirits of his own old regiment, received his mortal wound and was borne from the field.

Those who know from experience anything of the bonds of union which common dangers, privations, and toils constitute between those who have shared them together can readily understand the enthusiasm with which the soldier speaks of his brave commander and his glorious leader. I have thought I might as well devote a brief space to the memory of [Major General James E. B. Stuart] that gallant chief who so long and so successfully commanded the cavalry of the Army of Northern Virginia. He, like others whose fame has excited envy and hatred has been slandered without stint and many have vainly thought to bury his hard earned and well deserved honors beneath a load of infamy.

He was born in southwestern Virginia in about 1832 and, inhaling the pure mountain air of that highland country, he grew up vigorous and strong in both body and mind. His power of endurance exceeded those of any one of my acquaintance in the army whilst he had a cheerfulness and elasticity of spirit that plainly showed bodily health and sociability and generosity of disposition. He was about 5 feet, 10 inches in height, about 160 pounds weight, had a light blue eye, light hair, beard, high cheek bones, a large and nearly straight nose. He graduated with distinction at West Point and became a captain in the 2nd, I think, U.S. Regiment of Cavalry.[15]

As soon as Virginia separated from the union, he resigned, came home, received from Governor John Letcher the commission of colonel of the 1st Virginia Cavalry and operated under General J. E. Johnston in the Valley. In autumn, 1861, he became a brigadier general, commanding the 1st Brigade, Virginia Cavalry near Centreville. In June, 1862, he distinguished himself greatly by passing around McClellan's army from right to left, taking a gunboat and destroying a great quantity of store at the White House of the Pamunkey, (McClellan's base).

About the 1st of July he was promoted major general for his valor, etc. with two brigades of cavalry, Hampton and Fitz Lee commanding. He rendered great service in the Maryland campaign of this year and especially in holding McClellan's army back by a week's incessant fighting so as to completely protect Lee's army and trains while retreating from Jefferson County to Culpeper Court House. Beginning at Aldie on the 31st of October, he fought at Philamont, November 1st, Union on the 2nd, and Middleburg and Upperville on the 3rd, Markham Station and Piedmont on the 4th, Barbee's Crossroad on the 5th, Warrenton on the 6th, and Waterloo Bridge etc., on the 7th. Here he displayed his greatest forte, strategy, admirably. McClellan hadn't any doubt that Lee's whole army was right behind Stuart while the truth was the nearest point by which the infantry were passing in their march was nearly 20 miles from us.

During the following winter as I have elsewhere shown, he was very active, as indeed at all times during the war.

In the early summer his command was increased by adding William H. F. Lee's and Robertson's brigades to about 8,000 men in the saddle. On the 9th of June the ball opened by Major General Pleasanton charging in his pickets and attacking him in his position near Brandy Station–Culpeper at daybreak with about 10,000 men. The fight raged with varying success till nearly sunset. Now the high tones of command were followed by the heavy tramp of a thousand horses. Now the shrill bugle rally was followed by the thunder like roar of the fatal artillery. Till at length, the Genius of War firing his whole soul, Stuart firmly resolved to close the scene, waved his battle blade, and every bugle pealing for "The Charge" dashed impetuously upon Pleasanton's command with his whole force. The enemy wavered, wheeled, and retreated across the Rappahannock leaving behind three guns, some half a dozen regimental colors, and several hundred killed and wounded.

On the 11th of June we broke camp and moved forward rapidly to Middleburg in Loudoun. Of the rest of this campaign I have given an account already. In September, 1863, Hampton, Fitzhugh Lee, and W. H. F. Lee were made major generals commanding 1st, 2nd, and 3rd Divisions of a Cavalry Corps of which Stuart was major general, commanding (Congress never having provided for a Lieutenant General of Cavalry). On the 11th May, 1864, at Yellow Tavern he was shot through the body, (the liver I believe), and died in about twelve hours.

He made his cavalry more completely and thoroughly be the "eyes and ears" of the army than any other officer I ever knew. Up to the time of his death, our cavalry had had only two or three pitched battles with the whole of the enemy's cavalry and therefore we had never had opportunity to thoroughly test his qualities as a cavalry commander in a heavy engagement. But for outpost duty, reconnaissances, scouts, raids, organizing efficient signal and detective corps, etc, etc, he hadn't his equal in the Southern army.

During his [Stuart's] life, Lee seemed to anticipate, as if by divination, every movement of the enemy. After his death there was always more or less of perplexity as to what Grant would do next and no positive knowledge of his plans or movements until they were actually being put into execution.

Stuart was a consistent member of a Christian church, devoted to his wife and children, very gallant to all ladies, (whence the tongues of malice invented some foul slanders), somewhat vain of the pomp and circumstance of war, delighted in a fine pageant such as a Grand Review of his Cavalry Corps, etc., was devoted to martial pursuits of exhaustless resources in a dangerous situation, never seemed to weary of marching or to care about loss of sleep, was a true patriot and as brave as Julius Caesar. His name will illumine the pages of the History of the "Grand Rebellion in the *so-called* Confederate States."

Lt. Robert T. Hubard, Jr., Company G
(Courtesy of Margery Henneman
Crowther)

Chellowe, Buckingham County, Virginia
(From the editor's collection)

General J. E. B. Stuart
(U.S. Army Military History Institute)

General Fitzhugh Lee
(U.S. Army Military History Institute)

General Williams C. Wickham
(Library of Congress)

Colonel Thomas T. Munford
(Library of Congress)

General Thomas L. Rosser
(Library of Congress)

Major James Breathed
(National Archives)

General George A. Custer
(Library of Congress)

Major John B. Hood
(Library of Congress)

Colonel Thomas F. Goode, Company A
(From *Yesterday When It Is Past*, 1957)

Colonel Thomas H. Owen, Company C
(From *Our Kin*, 1958)

Lieutenant Colonel John T. Thornton,
Company K
(From the editor's collection)

Major Jefferson C. Phillips, Company B
(From the Hampton History Museum)

Captain Jesse S. Jones, Company B
(Courtesy of Marion S. Davis)

Lieutenant Henry B. McClellan,
Company G
(Williams College Archives and
Special Collections)

Thomas Nelson Conrad, Chaplain
(From *The Confederate Spy*, 1892)

Captain Henry R. Johnson (*center*),
Company G
(From the editor's collection)

Captain William A. Perkins, Company G
(From the editor's collection)

Captain James D. Isbell, Company G
(From the editor's collection)

Captain George H. Matthews Jr.,
Company G
(From the editor's collection)

Private William Hill Smith, Company A
(Courtesy of Amelia Hough)

Private John W. Anderson, Company C
(Library of Congress)

General Roger A. Pryor, Company E
(Library of Congress)

Private William A. Pomfrey, Company F
(Courtesy of Captain Kenneth E.
Fisher, USAF)

Private Henry K. Adams, Company G
(From the editor's collection)

Sergeant Samuel F. Coleman, Company G
(From the editor's collection)

Private William C. Corson, Company G
(Courtesy of Miriam Corson Holland)

Private Christopher C. Waller,
Company H
(Courtesy of Douglas Waller Powell)

Private Flemming C. Watkins,
Company H
(Courtesy of Elizabeth Carr)

11

"A Furious Charge Was Made Upon Our Line"

We fell back to the Ashland Road and retreated over the Chickahominy across Half Sink Bridge, the retreat being covered by the 1st and 3rd Virginia Cavalry. Lomax's Brigade lost heavily and ours considerably. The former lost two or three guns, I forget which.[1] The gallant captain of artillery, [Major James] Breathed, was twice sabred that day but killed two or three Yankees and got off.[2]

The enemy, turning down Brook Turnpike crossed Brook Creek, (leaving us behind as unworthy of further notice) and entered the third, (or outer), line of fortifications going into camp on the farm of my most excellent friend, Mr. John Stewart—Brook Hill. *That night* two infantry brigades occupied the *second line* of fortifications which mounted a number of heavy guns.

This obstinate fight [Yellow Tavern] lasted until about 5 p.m. and considering the great disparity of numbers, was one of which we had no cause to feel ashamed. But its effect was very bad, demonstrating, as it did, to *the men* that our cavalry with its paucity of arms of improved patterns and half-starved horses couldn't hope to contend successfully with the larger, splendidly mounted and equipped command of Philip Sheridan, Major General. He had an entire brigade armed with Spencer's splendid breach-loading rifle which fired accurately 600 yards and seven successive shots without reloading. Many others had the Henry gun, a *sixteen-shooter* (firing 16 successive shots after one loading), and all the rest Sharpe's splendid single-shooter rifle. About half of our men had captured Sharpe's carbines or his barrels with a miserably made Richmond breach while the others either had muzzle loading Enfield rifles or only their pistols and sabres.

It was universally admitted that, though defeated in this fight, the time we gained General Bragg saved Richmond. In all previous campaigns the superior pluck and gallantry of our boys had more than balanced the weight and numbers and the great advantages the enemy had in regard to arms and horses. And on nearly every occasion the enemy's cavalry had been worsted, whatever odds he had, unless backed by infantry. Now, however, a dear bought experience, rigid discipline, constant drilling, and a more thorough organization and complete equipment of three divisions (of about 4,000 men each), gave Sheridan a decided superiority over three divisions, (averaging about 2,500 men).

For in addition to other causes, the spirits of our men were greatly depressed by continued disasters to our arms, increased hardships, and lessening prospects of either independence or speedy peace. Yet our dear private soldiery, noble men, whose families, many of them, were suffering for the very necessities of life, some were burnt out of house and home, braced themselves for another great endeavor and as the dangers thickened around the army's beloved Commander and "Father," resolved that they would make at least one other earnest endeavor to rise to the height of his sublime courage and fortitude.

Weary, hungry, wet, and despondent our little division sneaked off through the rain about 10 p.m. and stumbling along in the darkness turned aside into the woods about 12 midnight near Atlee's Station to rest ourselves and our jaded beasts. We kindled some indifferent fires, got a little corn for our horses, some tough, half-done bread for ourselves, rolled up in our wet blankets, and slept till daylight.

Day broke apparently sad and sorrowful and weeping for our defeat the day before. It was dripping, dripping all the time, the mud in the roads ankle deep and the fields almost a quagmire. We went down to Meadow Bridge, (that is, "the place where" the bridge had been), and got into a skirmish with the Yankees on the other side. Lieutenant Colonel Robert Randolph, commanding the 4th Virginia Cavalry, was shot through the head and killed instantly.[3]

We were lying or squatting behind the embankment of the Virginia Central Railroad popping away when, (about 12 noon), orders came to "double quick" to the horses, mount, and form at once. We did so and learned that one of Sheridan's brigades had gotten across a blind ford at Miss Crenshaw's and was moving down towards us.[4]

After getting "our boys" all together, the division took a road from which they could retreat to Hanover Court House or Old Church, as occasion might require. Circulating around for some time and finding the enemy had gone towards the Court House, we went into camp at Pole Green Church.

Next morning, 13th of May, we sallied out and started towards Mechanicsville. There came several couriers from [Major] General Hoke on the south side [of the James River] that there were three (3) regiments of Yankees "cut off" near Cold Harbor. As our generals always had a great itching for an opportunity to bag a lot of poor devils who were so unfortunate as to be *cut off,* so our own redoubtable Fitz mounted his steed and made haste to possess them, he and a mighty host with him, even the "Ould Brigade."

We demonstrated heavily for several hours and received a sufficient demonstration in return to leave no doubt on our minds that these poor unfortunates were old enough and strong enough to take care of themselves. We lost some very valuable men, about thirty altogether, and accomplished nothing. My brother, Edmund, while well out to the front skirmishing with the enemy, received a severe wound on his head just under the left ear from which he didn't recover for several months.

Sheridan went into camp near Old Church and got supplied from the White House to refresh and recruit his command, also some 2,000 fresh horses. We went across the Chickahominy and charged about nearly every day in the locality.

On the 21st May evening a select command from our division and Hampton's under Major General Fitz Lee started off for Charles City for the purpose of attacking and capturing, if possible, a garrison of Negro troops stationed on the banks of the James River at Fort Kennon.[5] They were represented to be unfortified and depending greatly on the people. We had about 800 men and two small guns. We found out afterwards that they had a formidable octagonal earthwork mounting six guns surrounded by a moat nine to twelve feet wide, fully six feet deep crossed by a drawbridge, surrounded by a formidable abatis [barrier of fallen trees] fifty feet through, the whole encircled at 400 yards distance by a deep ravine skirted by a dense growth of copse wood.

About 12 noon on the 23rd, we came in sight of an infantry picket of twenty-five men about 300 yards from the ravine. A squadron of the 1st Virginia Cavalry charged them. Though Negroes, they fell back firing and killed two men in the 1st Regiment and wounded several horses.[6] They sustained no loss and immediately a regiment in camp between the ravine and the fort were called to arms by the long-roll. A portion of our force dismounted and, charging across the ravine after a few volleys, drove this African regiment into the fort. Arrangements were now pretty soon made and our men charged the fort.[7] But owing to some mistake, the right half of the line didn't advance and the left, after getting in 200 yards of the fort, had to withdraw under a murderous fire.

One gunboat with two or three heavy guns was firing at us all the time but generally fired high. Another gunboat now came down with reinforcements from Fort Powhatan, increasing the force to about 1,500 men, (about 500 white men).[8]

Major General Lee was now informed that the right flank of the fort was very weak and could be, doubtless, carried with ease. The General, in his great anxiety to see for himself the character of the fort and the nature of the approaches, had been exposing himself and most heroically being followed by but one person, an orderly who was obliged to rely, in a great measure, upon the information from scouts and they proved, in this instance, wholly and fatally worthless.

Our little force was massed on the left of our line and at 3:30 p.m. the bugle sounded the charge. Bravely, desperately our boys pressed forward but getting into the abatis, they found it wholly impossible whilst the fire was most galling. Lieutenant [acting Captain Peachy Gilmer C.] Breckinridge, of the 2nd Virginia Cavalry, and many brave soldiers fell mortally wounded and General Wickham, finding advance impossible, ordered a retreat. It turned out that the flank was, if possible, stronger than any other portion of the fort.

We now abandoned all hope of success and withdrew, having lost about 150 men. We had scarcely rested ourselves before we were ordered out in another fight. Grant's army had come down to Hanover Court House, crossed the Pamunkey River there and at lower fords. He was believed to be advancing upon Cold Harbor via Hawes' Shop and to that point Major General Hampton, commanding Cavalry Corps, was ordered.

Wickham's Brigade, in front, came upon the enemy at 12 noon [28

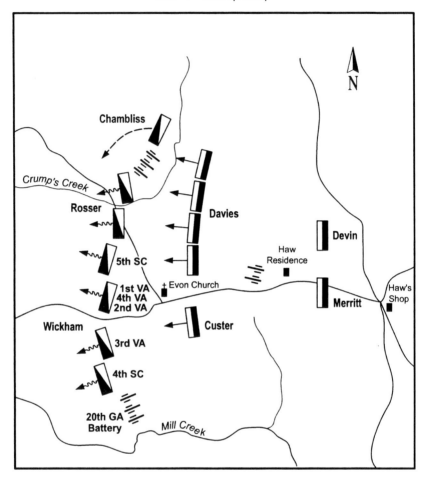

9. Haw's Shop, 28 May 1864

May], dismounted, deployed to the right and left, and advancing a little became hotly engaged at once. Rosser's Brigade went in on our left but had only a small force in their front. The woods were thick and we were tolerably well protected but our line was not straight, there being one considerable angle. In consequence of this, we were exposed to a cross fire. The fire was most incessant and tremendous. Captains [John A.] Chapell, [William] Collins, and myself were in this angle, the balls from our battery and the enemy's both passed directly over us three as we were exactly in the line between them. One percussion shell from the enemy,

(6-pounder), struck a tree, behind which Captain Chapell stood, only four feet above his head and remained stuck between a splinter and the body of the tree without exploding.

Charge after charge was made upon our brigade but to no purpose. For four mortal hours they stood their ground, a glorious band of Virginia patriots, and in all that time there was scarcely a moment in which some portion of the brigade was not resisting a heavy pressure.

Now they had massed their force (two divisions of cavalry) and a division of infantry had come up to their support followed closely by a corps of infantry. A grand charge was made against our whole front. On, on they came. We had only one thin line and they just swarmed right upon and through the line. Captain Collins and I discharged every barrel of our pistols at a batch of Yankees who got upon the line ten paces to our right and then withdrew.

At the point where the line was run over, the troops were badly disordered but a part held their own. Two squadrons of my regiment and the 2nd on their right held their ground. Two of our squadrons were overwhelmed, the 5th squadron and 4th and 1st Regiments fell back to restore the line. Old Wickham rode around waving his sabre and cursing "like a trooper," sure enough.

As we retired about 40 yards we met the [20th] Georgia Battalion going in to aid us. I saw the Lieutenant Colonel [John M. Millen], commanding, and tried to rally some men on his left and got four or five men moved forward a few feet. One was shot in the head and fell over dead, as I thought. Another, Embry [Emory] Coleman, Company C, was shot in the leg and I found I could do nothing just then.[9] But in a few minutes we got better order restored and I had the pleasure of going in again with the gallant Colonel [John Dunovant] commanding the 5th South Carolina. These two fresh regiments suffered terribly but filled the gap in the line. We repelled the partially successful attack.

Whilst the foe was preparing for another desperate assault, orders came to our commanders to withdraw, it having been definitely ascertained that Grant's army was certainly in our front. Our regiment lost one man in every five engaged. Captain Lamb—Company D, Captain Feild—Company I, and other officers and a number of men were badly wounded whilst a noble youth, Sergeant Frank [Francis W.] Guy of Company E and other fine fellows breathed their last on that hard fought field.[10] The loss in our command was about 600. The Federal Medical

Director told Mrs. William Newton, of Hanover, whose house is near the battlefield, that they had 1004 men killed and severely wounded.[11] This battle lasted four hours. Our troops withdrew at 4 p.m.

On the 31st of May we marched by Mechanicsville down the Chickahominy to support Butler's (Hampton's) Division on the Cold Harbor Road. Lomax's Brigade in front got into a heavy skirmish and sustained some loss. Our brigade supported and stood with sabres drawn ready to charge for some time but occasion didn't require it.

Grant was endeavoring to strike the Chickahominy at and secure McClellan's Bridge so as to make directly across to Malvern Hill. He was now pursuing the same policy adopted on the Rappahannock; that of lapping the right flank of the Army of Northern Virginia and thus passing it or forcing it back. Immortal honor is due General Robert E. Lee for this splendid campaign, beyond all question the most skillful retreat ever made. At Spottsylvania Court House, on the bank of the Po Creek, at the South Anna, and Hawes' Shop, General Grant had been met and successfully checked and his plans frustrated. Now he hoped, at last, to be successful and really "get around" his adversary but here, right in his path, stood Hampton's half-fed, half armed, half mounted, ill-disciplined, yet ubiquitous and resolute Cavalry Corps. And he knew them well enough to know that indifferent looking as they were, their presence meant *fight*.

The dust was suffocating and blinding whilst the whispering ball and whizzing shell were not atall soothing. Among the gallant men killed today [31st May] was Major Cabell [Edward] Flournoy, commanding the 6th Virginia Cavalry, (son of Honorable Stanhope Flournoy).[12]

Whilst sitting on my horse to the right of the 3rd and left of the 4th a half spent cannonball came bounding along, struck and broke the hind leg of a horse in the front rank of the 4th Virginia Cavalry and jumped over the heads of the men in the rear rank. About night we withdrew to go into camp leaving pickets out. Lomax and Butler were driven about 400 yards during the whole fight.[13]

Next morning, June 1st, our division took its position in General Lee's line of battle to the right of his infantry and stretching to the river about 200 yards above McClellan's Bridge and began with our sabres, a few old hoes, and spades to "dig dirt" and a portion of the men gathered timbers for earthworks. By 9 or 10 a.m. our works were about three feet high.

The enemy now appeared in small numbers along our whole front.[14] Our line made an angle of about 100 degrees with the infantry line and had a narrow bastion in the angle where 6 12-pounder Napoleons were mounted. Captain [Major] Breathed of our Horse Artillery had his 4 guns planted on a river bluff behind us 400 yards beautifully commanding McClellan's Bridge. Another battery of 4 guns was planted on a high hill 200 yards in rear of the bastion. Owing to the shape of our line, the men in some parts of it had to stand a fire both front and rear. There was a little knoll about 50 yards from McClellan's Bridge and between bridge and us.[15]

After their dismounted skirmishers had been popping away for an hour or more, a group of [Federal] officers collected on the knoll. A sharp cracking noise was heard. The dust at their horses' feet was thrown ten feet high and away they scampered. We knew at once what was to pay and turning towards our battery, saw the smoke wreath rising upward whilst the rammer was promptly wiping out his gun. In a few minutes more a section of U.S. flying artillery came dashing up the knoll and wheeled into position. Breathed was now in his glory.

Four shots in quick succession caused the flying artillery to go off faster than they came. Presently 800 or 1,000 horsemen appeared in front of the bastion at scarcely 300 yards distance and it was some minutes before the guns nearest could be lowered so as to bear upon them. Then, before we scarcely had time to get over this excitement, a rifle piece opened on us from the pines a little more to our right and at very close range. We at once returned an exceedingly rapid fire from 12 guns and knocked her all to pieces, horses and all, in five minutes.

Meanwhile the enemy was forming his lines of dismounted cavalry and pushing his infantry down by the left flank. His skirmishers, too, were getting nearer by degrees and evidently an assault was impending. Our cavalry had so long a line they were nothing more than skirmishers while our little three-foot bastion didn't protect the rear of the men.

About 3 p.m. Major General John C. Breckinridge's Division marched into our works and relieved us, General John Echols' Brigade in front. We crept out as "lowly" as possible but the enemy saw us and increased their fire by which some of our men were wounded.

In an hour or so after we left a very heavy charge was made, Echols' Brigade driven out of the bastion with the 6 guns captured. Another one of Breckinridge's brigades charged and retook the works and guns immediately after but the fighting was heavy till night and proved the line to be defective in formation. So it was altered and held afterward.[16]

We crossed at New Bridge and extended Lee's line to Breckinridge's. Here General Grant was foiled again and kept from crossing the river except at Long Bridge or some lower point, thus being compelled to make the elbow of the Chickahominy River.

The [3rd] of June we spent fortifying in front of the York [River] Railroad bridge in a drizzling rain and the [4th of June], likewise. The [5th] we marched down near White Oak Swamp and picketed the bridge across the Chickahominy there. While some of the boys were naked hauling a seine, the Yankees came down to the river and fired a few shots which caused the fishing frolic to be very suddenly terminated.[17]

On the 8th we set out for Ashland, why or wherefore we knew not. We arrived there that night and the 2nd night encamped at the "Forks of Hanover." Hampton's Division was in front of ours. Sheridan, with two divisions, about 8,000 men, had set out to destroy the Virginia Central Railroad and Orange & Alexandria [Rail]road and connect with Major General David Hunter who had marched up from New Creek via Lexington and Fincastle to Lynchburg. Jubal Early with his division went by the Southside Railroad.

General William E. Jones, a gallant officer was killed, in a desperate effort to retard Hunter before he got to Staunton, near the little village of Mt. Meridian, Augusta County, and his forces so demoralized that they offered little resistance afterwards with the exception that Brigadier General John McCausland was successful in some slight affairs among the mountain passes of Rockbridge and Botetourt counties.[18]

On the night of the 10th we encamped at Louisa Court House while Hampton's Division pushed on to occupy Gordonsville before Sheridan, whose column was marching on a road parallel with and to the right of ours.

At sunrise on June 11th, our division moved out due north from the Court House and in one mile charged Sheridan's pickets. Coming now upon a larger body, we deployed skirmishers, halted to reconnoiter, brought up and planted some two or three pieces of artillery [Shoemaker's Battery] and somehow or other lost two or three hours.

The clover in the field where we stood dismounted being fine, our horses were biting at it very vigorously and in this way Captain William

Boyd's "A" [company] and I, having gotten some twenty-five yards in front of the line, were reclining on the grass and allowing our horses to bait. Mine being white attracted the attention of a Yankee sharpshooter who could not have been nearer than 800 yards. He fired at times and the ball fell about five feet short but it was a line shot. On loading, he fired again, the ball this time striking the ground in about six inches of the hind feet of my horse. Our guns now opened upon their skirmishers who fell back somewhat.

Fitz Lee, apparently still doubtful whether they were in force in his front, the character of the ground concealed the fact, gave the command for his whole line of dismounted men to advance in quick time. This was done in fine order and revealed the fact that no force of consequence was upon our front.

The roar of distant artillery and the indistinct rattling of small arms convinced us that Hampton's Division was having no child's play. General Lee had his command mounted rapidly and moved at a trot towards the scene of the strife. Couriers presently met him with the report that the fight was heavy and Butler's Brigade had suffered heavily in men and horses and lost its train and artillery, (two guns).

We now pushed forward rapidly and Lomax's Brigade in front charged right upon a portion of Custar's Division at Trevillian's Station and was at once hotly engaged. Major Robert F. Mason of Fitz Lee's staff, commanding the 15th Virginia Cavalry, made a splendid charge and with Colonel Munford of the 2nd Virginia Cavalry captured three or four ambulances, (including Custar's headquarters containing a Negro wench), and several pieces of artillery but the guns were retaken by the enemy.

Our regiment was dismounted to support Lomax's Brigade, a portion of which was temporarily repulsed, and charged on foot up to and held a fence running south from the [Trevilian] Station. The 2nd and 1st Regiments were sent off to the left under Munford to close, as far as possible, the gap between our line,([running] north and south), and Hampton's which was northwest and southeast facing northeast and some six miles off. The 4th Virginia Cavalry took position on our right at the Station. Lomax's line extended the line on its right. With the enemy in our front we kept up a desultory fire but neither party charged the other.

Sheridan had a great advantage over us on this occasion as he had his two divisions supporting each other and between our two which were some six miles apart and, in numbers, at least 2,000 less than his.[19] For

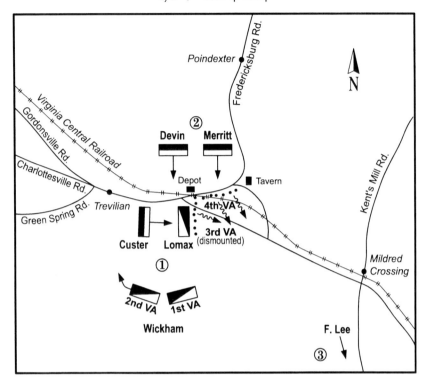

10. Trevilian Station, 11 June 1864

a long time our connection was broken so that Hampton couldn't communicate with Lee, nor Lee with him.

At about 12 noon General Custar, who was a very brave officer, though a contemptible man, placing himself at the head of his old brigade, charged Butler's Brigade, (which was in front), with so much intrepidity that he went right through in solid column and captured his trains, two guns, and about 700 cavalry horses.

Brigadier General Thomas S. Rosser, however, commanding Hampton's center, seeing the right completely broken, saved the day by one of those masterly exhibitions of promptness and heroism for which he was distinguished. Gathering such of his brigades as were mounted with a blast of the bugle they charged full upon Custar's flank and so magnificently that the latter column broke and fled precipitately, Custar with a few followers narrowly escaped capture by plunging into a dense thicket. Butler's horses and some of his wagons were retaken.

About 3 p.m. Sheridan, finding he could not do much with Hampton, massed his forces against us. Our regimental commander, Carter, had instructions if the 4th Regiment was driven back, he must throw his right back so as to face the flank of the advancing column and check it as much as possible. Our battery of four guns now opened on the enemy who were appearing in increased force immediately in front of my regiment. Their battery of two or four guns replied, the balls of both sides passing right over where we were lying at a height varying from six to fifteen feet above the ground.

Just beyond and parallel with the fence behind which we were was a road with a bank on the other side of about one foot. A shell struck this bank and exploded between it and my head coming in a direct line to me. I and young [Mellborne] Arvin[20] of Prince Edward were lying side by side and both were covered with dust, enveloped in smoke, and somewhat stunned. Taking advantage of a thicket in front of the 4th Regiment, the enemy concentrated there without being seen and suddenly a whole brigade armed with 7-shooters charged on foot in solid column of squadrons and companies. They were very near when they came in sight. The "Old 4th" stood their ground and poured a deadly fire into them but with no effect. On, on they came but the 4th, (as was true of the whole force), being in a single line with no support, fell back in disorder. The Yankees poured through the gap and pressed rapidly by our right which was being now hotly engaged in front. Our brave commander, Lieutenant Colonel Carter, while about giving the necessary order for swinging his line around, was shot in the right knee, several men being shot down at the same time, and their friends rushing up to them created confusion, and the right began to fall back in disorder. I was near the centre and, being ignorant of the fall of the commander, devoted my attention to trying to have the regiment withdrawn in an organized manner and as far as possible directed them to fire upon the charging column which was moving rapidly past us and had gotten to where our artillery had been.

The panic, (as is usual), was contagious, the men in their anxiety to save their horses got terribly scattered in getting through a piece of wood. There they found the enemy not pressing so vigorously, rallied and reconnected with the 4th and our good commander soon had his line all right again, though some 300 yards retired and his artillery all safe.

The road parallel with our front was at right angles to that leading to

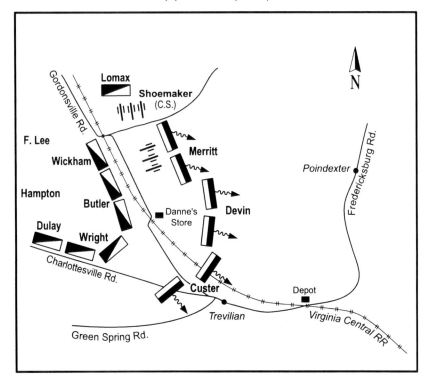

11. Trevilian Station, 12 June 1864

Gordonsville and its right prong afforded Sheridan the best mode of communication with Fredericksburg and the road he came. The 4th Regiment commanded the intersections of these roads and hence the determined charge, etc. which broke through it.

After dark we mounted and went into camp. Next morning [we] made a circuit to the left and stopped in the rich Green Spring country to get rations and forage, grazing for some hours. By some accident we were detained for some time before we could get corn. Couriers came up from Hampton that the enemy were preparing to attack and we must hurry up. We struck the Gordonsville Road and turning down towards Trevillian's Station moved rapidly on to Hampton's support.

Butler's Brigade, though fighting splendidly today, was being heavily pressed and suffering severely from small arms and artillery. Fitz Lee proposed to Hampton to let him take his two brigades and forming a right angle with his division, charge the enemy in flank. Hampton said

Butler must be strengthened at once and ordered Wickham to dismount and go right in while General Lee was directed to take Lomax's Brigade and make the flank movement.

It was now about 3 p.m. Butler's line formed an obtuse angle, vertex out, and it was the portion of the line on the left that we were to occupy so that his men might close in to the right and be stronger.

Marching through a large piece of woods and having several men shot going through, we came to an open field which was being ploughed beautifully by cannon and minnie balls. Munford being senior colonel usually claimed to have the right of the brigade for the 2nd; but on this occasion he not only didn't claim the position but positively refused when ordered to take it on the ground that the 3rd being in front of his regiment, too much time would be lost in bringing his by. Jesse Jones, Company B, commanding regiment, and I jumped over the fence into the field followed promptly by the noble boys who composed the 3rd, and formed the men rapidly in line of battle by "Front into line." Moving directly across the field we were enfiladed by a battery on the railroad firing at Butler's men to the right of the angle. One ricochet ball came bounding along down the line, struck in the track of one man just as he raised his foot, jumped over the back of Private [John B.] Phillips, Company "G," who squatted "to let it pass," struck the ground again right in front of the line, then jumped over in the woods on the left.[21] Halting behind a low fence on the line, three or four [cannon] shot in quick succession came right down the whole length of the line missing our heads [by] only one or two feet, bursting right at us but miraculously hurting nobody.

Getting over this fence, we jumped upon the railroad track when immediately a ball came right up the cut, just grazing us, as it were. Seeing the gun now plainly enfilading us and in full view, too, we got across the track and lay down in the bushes on the other side behind a yard railing where we were subjected to an incessant fire of small arms front and flank and the artillery all the while enfilading us.

When men were wounded, comrades hardly dared to take them off and two men in my regiment, [John E.] Young, Company "I" and [James H.] Ware, Company "D" lost their arms of flesh in this very way, the former trying to help off a wounded comrade, the latter assisting to take off the body of Lieutenant Berryman J. Hill, Company "I," who was killed by a ball passing in at one ear, out the other.[22]

I was struck in the right hip by a flank shot and but for my pistol breaking the force of the ball, would have been mortally wounded. Thinking from the force of the blow that I was seriously wounded, I got a friend to start off with me but soon, finding I could walk unsupported, sent him back. I found I had only a contusion though a very severe one which made me quite lame for two days and compelled me to go to hospital for the night.

Soon after I left, a furious charge was made upon our line but most gloriously repulsed. Another and another followed with like result. At length, about 5:30 p.m., everything being ready, Lomax's Brigade completely surprised the enemy's right by a sudden and vigorous charge which, being attended with a simultaneous charge of our whole line, the 2nd, 4th, and 1st Regiments were on our left, turned the tide of battle and gave us the victory. The enemy fell back rapidly and retreated entirely during the night leaving fifty dead and some one or two hundred wounded in our hands.

We were so much crippled by the two days fighting, having lost fully as many as the enemy and our poor horses, so exhausted, that we didn't press him but slept on the field. And next day the corps again marched nearly parallel, (Sheridan's some eight miles in front), on the same roads we respectively came, each endeavoring to join its main army.

This conflict was perhaps the most, or at least one of the most, important cavalry engagements of the war. Sheridan confidently expected to join Hunter at Lynchburg. Had he done so the war would have ended in three months or less.[23] Early got to Lynchburg in time to save the town and had every arrangement to attack at daybreak perfected but Hunter retreated precipitately during the night. Early's cavalry alone could overtake him but it worried him no little before he got to Salem. Early moved by Lexington to Winchester, thus compelling Hunter to leave Virginia.

About the 6th or 7th [1st] of June, Longstreet made a heavy demonstration upon Grant's right and took two lines of fortifications. But our troops suffered smartly. Wyatt's Battery of Charlottesville lost all of its horses and had some thirty men killed or wounded, among the former Captain [James W.] Wyatt and 1st Lieutenant Charles Rives of Albemarle.[24]

On the 8th or 10th [3 June] General Grant made a heavy assault upon Lee's whole line, charging four or five times. Our works were very good, our men calm and mowed down the enemy who were completely repulsed, losing 10,000 men placed hors de combat (Lee's estimate at the time confirmed by Butler's acknowledgement afterwards). Grant only reported a loss of 2,500. Our loss was only 500, the men being well protected by their works.[25]

Soon after, Grant pulled up his pegs and cut out for the Southside. But for the great skill of Beauregard, commanding on the Southside, Burnside [Butler] would have taken Petersburg. But he repulsed him and held his lines till Lee's whole army came up.[26]

Sheridan moved [from Trevilian Station] to Fredericksburg to get forage and rations and we marched to the North Anna River and down it some distance then by Mangohick Church in King William [County] then across the Pamunkey to Hanover Court House. The enemy moved down the left bank of the Mattaponi to West Point, thence to White House.

On the 20th of June, Major General Hampton, commanding Fitz Lee's and Butler's Divisions, opened on the fortifications at the White House with eight guns at about 12 noon. The fire was promptly returned by the fort, (which mounted four thirty-two-pounders and two field pieces) and a gunboat lying in the river. Our position was so elevated that their fire hurt us but little while we thought ours was quite effective. There was said to be two regiments of infantry and one of cavalry at the fort and Sheridan still on the other side of the river.

Hampton thought he ought to be able to dislodge this force. But while we "had the position," we were about 1 1/2 miles off and the intervening ground was dead level and perfectly free from all manner of obstruction to the sight. Everything was made ready and the troops were all dismounted and formed in line behind the bushes that skirted the plateau over which the charge was to be made and as we looked upon the formidable bastion fort with its ditch and high embankment and frowning guns, and as we remembered that we had no scaling ladders, our guns a good way off, we felt the conviction that a charge across a level plain about a mile upon such a fort by a single line numbering about 1,500 men must prove disastrous. Our two divisions had been smartly cut up and so many horses broken down that taking 1/4 to hold horses, we hadn't more than 1,500 in line. The very videttes in front of the fort seemed to mock us as they quietly picked blackberries almost in rifle-shot.

The remonstrances of General Lee prevailed, the assault was given up and we went into camp near St. Peter's Church, (the same in which Lieutenant General George Washington, 1st President of the United States, was married to Mrs. Custis).[27]

Next morning early, our pickets were driven in and we moved down the road towards the White House half mile and commenced obstructing the road. Butler began to be engaged sharply in the railroad and soon we were put in line of battle and advanced on foot.

Pretty soon we met a plenty of "blue-jackets" and a sharp "skrimmage," as the soldiers said, took place right away. Our regiment being commanded by an officer, I will not call his name, in whom the men had no confidence as an officer, though a very gentlemanly, well disposed man, they didn't fight well atall and a portion of them giving way, the commander couldn't rally his men atall and they fell back some distance before the subordinate officer and General Wickham rallied them and restored the line.[28] Two captains were put under arrest at the same time.

After a while, the regiment was again broken badly and again rallied by Colonel Munford, the captains, and myself. It seemed evident that they wouldn't fight under the officer in command atall. I never knew them to act so badly.

After a while, Hampton, finding that Sheridan was in front of him and not wishing to fight him, new[ly] supplied as he [Sheridan] was and reinforced by the garrison of the fort in that position, withdrew about one mile and a half to a strong position behind [St. Peters?] Creek.

Sheridan moved right on by Crump's Crossroads towards James River. We went via Bottom's bridge and White Oak Swamp into Charles City County. Gregg's U.S. Division marched out from Long Bridge to Nance's Shop to cover the movement of Sheridan's trains and thence to James River.

At 12 noon on the 24th June, Fitz Lee's and Butler's Division arrived at that point [Nance's Shop], formed dismounted line of battle, skirmishers advanced, and opened fire, etc. About 3 p.m. Butler's troops pushed forward beautifully to our left and somewhat in flank of Gregg.

Fitz Lee now ordered a charge by his division! We moved rapidly across a field of 400 yards under fire, dislodged the enemy from, and then charged through a piece of woods 200 yards and into an open field again.

Here we drew a galling fire from a battery in front 1/4 mile and a line of riflemen behind a fence to our right. Colonel Owen, commanding the 3rd Virginia Cavalry, finding himself smartly in advance of the other regiments and suffering smartly, directed his men to halt and lie down,

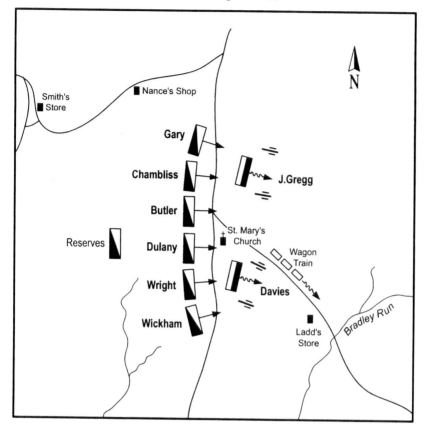

12. Nance's Shop, 14 June 1864

communicating with his right and left. As soon as the other regiments were well up we charged ahead over the rising ground and, dislodging the enemy from every position, pressed rapidly across a field of four to six hundred yards, Rosser's Brigade of Butler's Division, by their flank charge, forcing the battery to retire. Forming the two divisions in line, we now continued to drive the enemy for a mile or more, inflicting considerable loss upon him.

Night coming on, at length we went into camp and next day marched towards Richmond. Our two divisions lost in this fight about 300 out of 1,500 in killed and wounded.[29] We went into camp at Wilton near Richmond on June 26th.

The division of Major General W. H. F. Lee was all this time about 10 miles south of Petersburg in Dinwiddie County. Major General James H. Wilson (U.S.A.), with his division of Sheridan's Corps, was over there, too. And when the latter went to Louisa, Wilson went on a raid towards Burkeville Junction, etc. with from four to five thousand men.

"Rooney" Lee's horses being like ours, subject to "emptiness of stomach" and "weakness of knees," he could only muster some 1800 and with these he "followed Wilson around," never getting in sight of him after he left Dinwiddie Court House except once at Staunton River where the former [Wilson] was repulsed by the "melish" [militia] in a fight of several hours.

Returning via Lawrenceville, his camp at Saponi [Sapony] Church was charged at night by Wade Hampton at the head of Butler's Division, his [Wilson's] command badly whipped, and much of his plunder, (he'd taken two to three thousand Negroes, some 50 to 75 carriages, and robbed nearly every house along his route) retaken.

Hampton moved by Jarrett's Station, (on the Weldon Road), and placed himself between Wilson and Prince George Court House leaving videttes at that point to inform him of Wilson's approach. William Lee was gradually closing up behind him and [William] Mahone's Division of infantry stood ready at Reams' Station "to receive company."

Our division crossed James River at 12 noon on the 28th and went into camp seven miles from Petersburg without a mouthful of food for our horses. Next morning we started without feeding and arrived at Reams' Station at 12 noon just as Wilson had opened on Mahone's command. Lomax originally went in on Mahone's right, struck Wilson's raiders in flank and confused them smartly. The 1st and 2nd [Regiments] went in with Lomax.

Colonel Owen was now moved to the front with sabres drawn for a charge. We moved off at a trot, passing a hundred parked wagons already set on fire, eight or ten caissons, a hospital train of fifty carriages, and a good number of carriages full of wounded from which the horses had been taken, and crossing Stony Creek [Rowanty Creek?] came up with the rear guard.[30]

They fired right sharply upon and partially checked us but the Colonel, dashing to the front and calling to his men, was fully supported. The enemy retired rather sullenly until our sabres began to nock their caps off. They then fled precipitately exposing to view about 150 Negroes scampering across the fields, (of all sizes and sexes), with great bundles

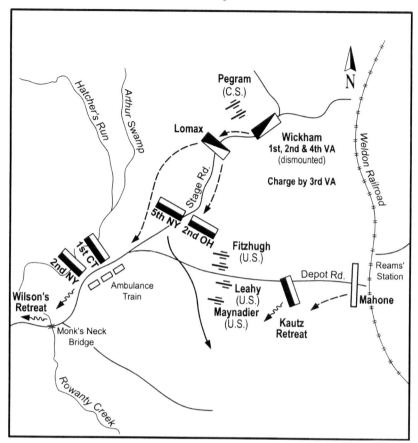

13. Reams' Station, 29 June 1864

of plunder stolen from their masters' houses, upon their backs. Some fell over, bundles and all, others were knocked over, one or two were shot, whilst a few died of fright, such screaming and yelling as they sent up Pandemonium itself could scarcely beat.[31]

The Yankee line was soon broken all to pieces, about a squadron made off through the fields to our right. Another turned to the left and we, passing on after those in our front, the latter squadron surrendered to the 4th Virginia Cavalry.

Colonel Owen, rushing upon a dismounted fellow, was shot in the left thigh and had his pants scorched, the muzzle of the carbine was so near. He wasn't much hurt and shot his antagonist dead with his pistol.

He now captured four fine wagons, (one General Wilson's headquarters wagon with the baggage of himself and his staff).

Whilst the Colonel was occupied with some of the retreating foe, a body of about 25 men were pointed out to me on our flank trying to make off with a gun. Our regiment, small at first, was now reduced almost to nothing by details sent back with prisoners, etc. I gathered about 8 sharpshooters and poured such a hot fire into the fellows that they cut out the horses and abandoned the gun, which we secured and found to be a fine brass piece. We also got three other guns while Mahone got six.

The Colonel, I, and such men as we had left pressed on and presently came upon a largely superior force who had apparently prepared to make a stand. We began skirmishing with them and sent back for reinforcements. Lomax coming up soon after, we charged right ahead and drove the enemy about a mile where he made another stand. Lomax's Brigade now coming up were put in front and we pressed ahead until the enemy reached [Stony Creek], not being able to get his [Wilson's] whole force over the bridge at once, Wilson formed line of battle and showed fight.[32]

Our whole division was now dismounted and formed a line of battle. One of the captured guns was now brought up and a captured sergeant and squad belonging to that battery were made to man it. Colonel Owen stood by and told the sergeant if he didn't "point her right," he'd cut his head off. The sergeant sighted his piece and commanded, "Ready, aim, fire!" As the ball struck right plumb among his comrades, the old fellow, forgetting where he was and being all a-glow with the excitement of practice, cried out, "That's it, boys. Now give them another right in the same place." After a few more shots, our bugles blew a charge and the whole line moved enthusiastically forward with that elasticity which sure victory can give. The enemy now crossed over the stream and fled in utter route. We followed until 10 o'clock at night and went into camp without any forage. There was, it is true, a patch of green oats near but most of the men were too tired to cut any for their horses.

At daylight we moved on in pursuit and crossing the Nottoway River found there two beautiful steel rifle guns thrown from the bridge into the river. These were the last Wilson had.

We marched on until we got to Jarrett's Station 35 miles from Reams' and 45 from Petersburg. *Here we got corn aplenty* and stayed all night. The pickets Hampton left here got drunk, failed to notify Hampton of

Wilson's approach. In fact, one man and all four horses were captured. So Hampton couldn't intercept him at the crossroads below and Wilson, finding out Hampton's whereabouts, made a circuit and avoided him.

Wilson carried off about 300 Negroes mounted. We retook about 1,500, captured (with Mahone's command) about 300 prisoners and arms, many horses, twelve guns, eight caissons, about 75 wagons, and 40 or 50 carriages and ambulances.

Our horses, it will be seen, were grazed a little on the morning of the 28th of June below Richmond and hadn't a mouthful of food afterwards until about 3 p.m., June 30th at Jarrett's Station, 65 miles from Richmond.

The gallant Captain, now Major, Breathed of Stuart's Horse Artillery was dangerously wounded in the abdomen, but being made of "heart-pine," got well in a few weeks.

As the 3rd Virginia Cavalry had first put Wilson in motion and given impetus to his retreat, Colonel Thomas H. Owen was the lion of the occasion. And on the 1st July, Major General Fitzhugh Lee had the four heavily loaded wagons drawn up in front of the headquarters of the 3rd Virginia Cavalry and sent a staff officer to the Colonel informing him that, (save the private baggage of Major General Wilson which would be sent through the lines to him according to military etiquette), their contents were at his disposal.

Amongst Wilson's papers was found an envelope full of cartes de visite, one of his sister, one of General Grant and other officers, and one of a young saucy looking *Negro woman* very finely dressed. I was one of the first who examined this envelope and reserved myself all the photographs except the "black one." A splendid shabraque [horse blanket] of blue broad cloth richly embroidered with gold lace and a gold eagle in each corner was presented by the Colonel to Brigadier General Williams C. Wickham. A nice artillery officer's sword was presented by him to the militia officer [B. L. Farinholt] who commanded so successfully at Staunton River Bridge.[33] Many preserves in sealed cans were sent to General Fitz Lee. Every officer and nearly every man in the regiment got a nice trophy. I got a good overcoat, gum cloth, and other small articles. July 2nd we went into camp on Stony Creek near Reams' Station.

12

"We're Off for the Valley"

The weather was now extremely hot. The drought which began about the middle of May still continued, causing the roads to be dusty in the extreme.[1] Wilson's raiders so damaged the Danville & Southside Railroads that Lee's army was for several weeks destitute of rations and our commands were subsisted on the coarsest corn-meal I ever saw. The rations were so short that when the meal was sifted it furnished only one repast for 24 hours.

The men were now attacked with dysentery, chills and fevers, etc. and some were threatened with scurvy. The abominable camp itch which had *prevailed* in the army for 2 years now broke out with greater violence than ever, the little pimples running together formed great ulcers 3 or 4 inches in circumference.[2]

To relieve the monotony, brigade drills and dress parades were instituted but the horses were so poor and had such sore backs that but few men turned out.

It was at this camp we received the sad intelligence of the death of Lieutenant Colonel William R. Carter which occurred at Gordonsville Hospital, July 8th, 1864. This officer, son of a Nottoway school master was by profession a lawyer, aged 33. [He] entered service as a private, Company "E," 3rd Virginia Cavalry, and was captured while on picket with two other troopers, (who made their escape), in front of Bethel the morning it was attacked and [he was] taken in charge by Lieutenant Judson Kilpatrick who in 1863 was brigadier general commanding a division of the U.S. Cavalry Corps, Army of the Potomac and is now Minister to Chile (1866).

In autumn of 1861 Carter was elected lieutenant of his company and in April, 1862, captain. He was a man of *great* energy of mind rather than of body, fond of study, a close and right accurate observer of men and things and a pretty good judge of human nature, though accounted stingy by many with his friends. He was extremely generous in heart and liberal in purse. Though a rigid disciplinarian, he was so very brave and obstinate a fighter that, if possible, the men rather preferred fighting under him than their Colonel [Owen], seeing that the latter, though as gallant as possible, was not so calm and un-excited in battle. But then Carter was very absent-minded which was fully as bad. He was regarded as one of the very best officers in our brigade and would almost certainly have risen to a colonel very soon.

He was something of a predestinarian for in *September, 1863,* he told me one day that he had a presentiment of which he had vainly sought to divest himself that he should be very badly wounded in one of his legs and either lose the limb or his life.

The Colonel [Owen] being wounded, he commanded the regiment with great distinction to himself and to it in nearly all the fights of that campaign. Refusing to listen to the advice of friends, he exposed himself in the most reckless and unnecessary manner saying if he was destined to be shot he would be and if not, he wouldn't. When wounded he was not, thus, as it were, "tempting the Lord" but merely doing his duty. Had his limb been amputated he would probably have recovered but like many others, he had the services of a surgeon who was indifferent in more respects than one. In his death the regiment lost an invaluable officer and I, a warm friend.

Our Major Henry Carrington, though a most estimable officer, had convinced Generals Lee and Wickham that he had no military capacity and that the men would not fight under him. So they declined to promote him.

The Colonel [Owen] told me of his preference for me and said if I thought there was any possibility of his recommendation being approved he would forward my name for the promotion. Thanking him for his kindness, I declined on two grounds: first, our laws were so very rigid in regard to promotion out of the line I knew that without political influence, (which was omnipotent at Richmond), I couldn't hope to be passed over all the captains and, second, my failing [to be promoted], which I knew was inevitable, would be uselessly and unavoidably injuring the well merited popularity of our colonel with his company officers. He determined on some promotion for me, however, and promoting the senior captain [William M. Feild], forwarded my name for captain of his company [Company I, Dinwiddie Troop]. General R. E. Lee thought the latter appointment couldn't be made until the 1st lieutenant of the company was first examined or designated. So it was postponed until March, 1865, and again strongly recommended and passed through to the War Department but not heard from before the surrender.

During this time Early, with 8,000 men, had gotten in two miles of Washington but didn't enter because he knew his little army would be hemmed in there by the forces that were being rapidly collected. He returned to Winchester.

On the 5th of August at 4 p.m., a four horse ambulance stood at our headquarters ready to take a party of young officers to a party at Mr. Thweatt's. I was just drawing on my gloves when a distant bugle (at division headquarters) sounded "boots and saddles." Then came men running and riding into camp with the rumor that "something's up, we're going off." The loud, clear notes of [Cyrus] Keister, (brigade bugler), pealed forth upon the summer air and immediately the bugles of the four regiments gaily responded.

All was now disappointment, hurry, and confusion. Up rides a courier, "Colonel, the general says mount and move out at the sound of the bugle following the —— Regiment along the road to Petersburg."

"What's up, Hill?"

"Well, we're off for the Valley, I believe, sir."

So it was. Kershaw's Division went by rail to Orange Court House and the design being to alarm Grant and, if possible, induce [him] to withdraw a large portion of his force from the Richmond front. Lieutenant General R[ichard] H. Anderson was sent in command of the column.

We passed through Richmond on the 7th, (in regular military array). On the 15th after a very pleasant, but uneventful, march, we arrived at Front Royal at 12 noon. Kershaw's Division was there in camp.

On the 17th afternoon, Wickham commanding division, Owen the brigade, Carrington our regiment, we moved out (our brigade) to take possession of Guard Hill which commanded the fords at the forks of the Shenandoah. An infantry brigade [William T. Wofford's] was sent across on our right to cooperate.

Colonel Owen, ordering the command to follow in column and sup-

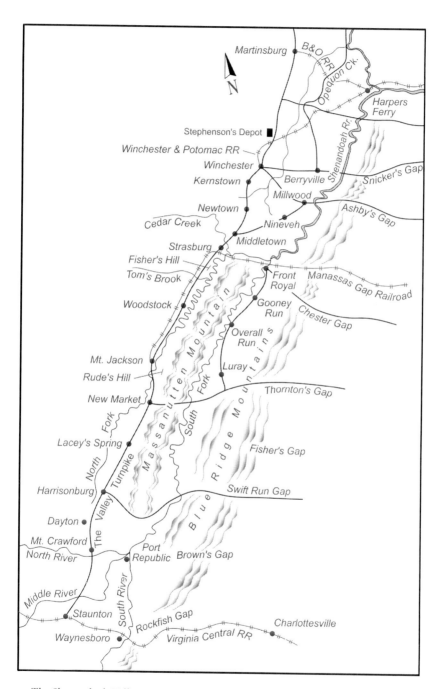

14. The Shenandoah Valley, 1864

port, charged across the river at the head of a squadron of 1st Virginia Cavalry and over the hill, driving in a picket of sixty or seventy. The latter, on ascending the next hill beyond a little creek with a bad crossing, made a stand and poured a hot fire into our men and so effective that of about ten men brought to the rear wounded, seven or eight were shot *through the breast,* a larger proportion than I ever saw elsewhere.[3]

The whole command now occupied Guard Hill filing off to the right and left and coming into line. Half the brigade were now dismounted while the 3rd and 4th Regiments stood still. Major Breathed soon brought two guns to bear from the highest position upon a division of Federal cavalry drawn up in line 1,000 yards or more distant. Immediately a battery of theirs, in rear on an eminence, responded to Breathed.[4]

Presently Wickham, with more courage than prudence, on seeing a line of dismounted skirmishers advancing ordered Colonel Owen to send the 3rd Regiment forward with orders to charge as far as possible and, if overpowered, to fall back. Owen came to where I was sitting, told me the orders and said, "You all will have a difficult job, Bob, to whip those fellows but see that the regiment does its duty and I'll try to be near you."

Away we dashed (numbering, all told, 117), charged through a storm of shell and small [arms fire] upon and repulsed the skirmish line. Lieutenant John Jordan, Company "C," riding near me tried his best to shoot their commander who was dressed in black colors, jacket and pants and light buck gauntlets, but not a shot took effect.[5] I fired at a group of skirmishers with my pistol when one of them replied, the ball wounding my mare in the neck and lodging in my saddle in 2 1/2 *inches* of my right thigh.

Three regiments now came forward with drawn sabres to the charge.[6] There we were 1/2 mile from supports, charged by a force of at least five to one. Of course, we beat a hasty retreat. One regiment followed us up so rapidly that some six or eight of their horses ran away and the riders getting among us were all killed or captured. One fellow dashing by me, I called out to those by me to "Shoot the scoundrel" and fired three shots myself, but he got off around a hill. My mare's fretting and prancing made it impossible to shoot well.

Reforming and blowing awhile, we were ordered in again to support the 4th which was charging. After getting about 200 yards from the branch, we met the 4th driven back in disorder. Colonel Owen, however,

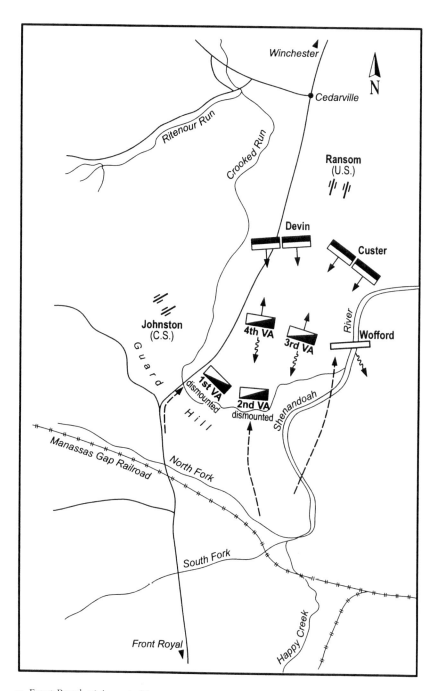

Winchester

Cedarville

Ritenour Run

Crooked Run

Ransom
(U.S.)

Devin

Custer

Johnston
(C.S.)

Guard

4th VA

3rd VA

River

Wofford

1st VA
dismounted

2nd VA
dismounted

Shenandoah

Hill

Manassas Gap Railroad

North Fork

South Fork

Front Royal

Happy Creek

N

15. Front Royal, 16 August 1864

being present, our men were not disorganized but moved forward and at the command dismounted and deployed to the front beautifully driving back a heavy line of dismounted who, under cover of the hills to the right, were trying to get to the branch.

Custar's own staff color was now plainly seen in 75 yards of us as he rode along encouraging his men.[7] Not having dismounted myself, I rode up to the left of our line and saw a heavy body of horse again driving back the 4th which had made a [second] charge. Rushing among the latter I, with Adjutant [James] Keith of the 4th tried to halt some of the men for I knew my regiment on foot would be flanked and feared many would be captured. Two or three stopped with us. We stayed long enough to fire one or two shots a piece into the head of their column which was checked with grape by our artillery.

Being cut off from the ford, we plunged into the stream below. My poor steed was thrown by a rock and pitched me into the water. I sprung up in a minute, found her too much excited to enable me to mount her again and leading her across, [I] clambered up the almost precipitous sides of Guard Hill. Just as I got across a less fortunate Confederate was captured very near the other bank by a mounted Yankee and carried off on the side of the Yankee next to me so I was prevented from firing on the latter. Just below me our "led horses" got across.

Our gallant Colonel bringing up the rear, galloped up to them just in time to save Corporal [James] Baker of "K," Prince Edward.[8] A Yankee had given him a stunning blow and was rising in his saddle for a second when a tremendous right cut from the Colonel across the villains face felled him to the earth. A second [blow] as he was falling, the Colonel and Baker thought, finished him. The latter was leading three horses and hence couldn't defend himself.

Major Carrington and ten or twelve men were cut off and lay in a briar thicket while Yankee squadrons road all around them cussing and swearing. The infantry brigade, by the same foolish process of sending a single regiment into the fight unsupported a quarter of a mile to our right, had about two hundred men cut off and captured.

Lieutenant General Anderson, Major General Kershaw and acting Major General Wickham all witnessed and were together responsible for the stupid, bungling way in which this fight was directed. And to them is to be ascribed the great skill displayed in sending out one regiment of cavalry (117 men) and one of infantry (500 men) to charge [Alfred T. A.] Torbert's and Custar's Divisions![9]

It is related of Wickham that just as we were repulsed the second time, he came galloping in among the members of the 4th calling out, "Halt, men, halt! Where the h——l are you going to? Rally around your General." The words were scarcely out of his mouth when someone warned him that a Federal regiment was already between him and the ford and he was off in a twinkling. I mention this not to detract from his courage, however, for he acted well on the field, but only as an amusing incident going to show that in a fight, the "rallying point" isn't always *stationary*! Though repulsed in our charges, we accomplished the object of the day which was to secure the fords for next day's crossing.

Our loss altogether was about three hundred men, among them Captain [Charles] Palmore, Company "G," Lieutenant T[homas H.] Hall, Company "C," and some ten men of the 3rd Virginia Cavalry captured.[10]

Next morning early we moved forward. The enemy retreated before day and as he marched on, burned every barn, wheat stack, hay rick, and straw pile for miles on both sides of the road and even burnt several fields of *timothy* and *blue grass* dried by the drought which he thought *might* afford some little nourishment to our horses.[11]

But thanks to a kind Providence and a nobly generous, self-sacrificing, patriotic people, we were met by the citizens of Clarke [County] with every exhibition of joy and with the assurance that with all the meanness and vandalism of the infernal Yankees, they hadn't succeeded in destroying everything and of what was left, if it pleased God, we should have fullshare. So we rested our weary limbs and fed on good rations ourselves, and our horses on good hay not far from Millwood.

Next day passing through Berryville we encamped not far from Charlestown and the next night on the road to Smithfield.

Early's line now faced north, his left at Bunker Hill and his right at Charlestown. On the 22nd, (I think), General Fitz Lee was sent with his division and Lomax's, (just promoted to command Imboden's, McCausland's, and Bradley Johnson's brigades), to make a feint of crossing at Williamsport while Early did the like at Sheppardstown. Breckinridge's Division, going down to Sheppardstown, met the Federal Cavalry Corps just coming out to reconnoitre. Being reinforced, he drove them across the river after quite a heavy "affair" in which each side lost several hundred. Among ours was my poor friend, Joseph K. Irving, who was acting as Signal Officer for Breckinridge, who was mortally wounded and died after several weary months at Staunton. He was always a warm friend of mine and I felt disposed always to draw the veil of charity over his faults and remember only his virtues.[12]

The lapse of a week found us back at our camp between Smithfield and Charlestown. General Sheridan, having accumulated a very large force, showed a decided disposition to advance and after some days our right was withdrawn beyond the Opecan [sic] so that it formed nearly a right angle with our left. About the 10th our cavalry had a sharp skirmish and drove the enemy from the Opecan to and through Berryville to Charlestown across the Opecan.

About the 12th a Federal column moved off from Berryville aiming to gain our rear towards Strasburg. Our cavalry marched off to New-town, headed them there, then to Strasburg, remained a day or two and returned.

Early meanwhile crossed the Opecan and tried for a second time to provoke Sheridan into a fight but the latter retreated again to Charles-town. We now went into camp in sight of Winchester and there re-mained until the memorable fight of the 19th of September.

Early's command was on a line from Bunker Hill to the Opecan at Brucetown then up it [the river] to the Berryville Pike where we pick-eted. [Stephen D.] Ramseur's Division was encamped one mile east of Winchester.

Scarcely two consecutive days of quiet in camp had we known from the time we reached the Valley. Our horses fared badly getting only lim-ited supplies of hay. We had beef and flour and quantities of apples.

13
"Tattered Flags Sporting in the Breeze"

The morning was clear and cool, the booming of artillery at day-break was our only reveille. Without food for man or beast we saddled, mounted, formed, and moved off to Winchester by sunrise. Passing through town, we took the northeastern road towards Jordan's Springs and dismounted on the hill beyond Mill Creek where our four-gun battery was placed so as to bear upon the Berryville Pike along which the enemy was advancing.[1]

Ramseur skirmished heavily but saw nothing in his front but cavalry for several hours. Early hastened up from Bunker Hill with Rodes' and Gordon's Divisions ordering Breckinridge's Division at Brucetown to follow and Lomax's cavalry to move in rear towards Winchester from Brucetown and beyond Bunker Hill towards Winchester.

About 9 a.m. when Ramseur had been fighting with artillery quite warmly and was now putting his skirmishers in seriously, the head of Early's column arrived. Rodes and Gordon had barely time to face into line and unlimber their guns before they were compelled to throw out skirmishers to meet the advancing enemy and five minutes after to meet a furious charge.

I got a better view of the enemy's column than any other on the occasion. They charged at double-quick firing rapidly across an open field some hundred yards wide and through a body of woods driving back our skirmishers upon the main line. Our battery did some execution as they went across the field but couldn't break them. Our infantry and artillery now opened a murderous fire under which they recoiled and retreated. Our horse battery now poured it into them again. A second line came up rapidly and in splendid order; the retreating troops passed through and by without demoralizing them.

Our four-gun battery now did beautiful work putting six or eight shots right among them. Rhodes and Gordon now charged and carried everything before them through the woods, across the field and away out of sight in the woods beyond. The artillery limbered up and galloped to the front and our line was thus advanced half a mile.

The fight now raged furiously but being in the woods nothing much could be seen of it.

About 1 p.m. Major General Torbert began to threaten our right flank with two cavalry divisions. Our division and [William] Jackson's Brigade of Lomax's Division went over there. Fitz Lee was on the field commanding all the cavalry, acted with great gallantry, and was severely wounded later in the day, his horse being killed under him at the same time, his own favorite mare having been shot earlier in the action.[2]

Lomax was now drawing back Johnson's Brigade from Bunker Hill. Breckinridge's Division had arrived and taken our place on the left. Imboden's and McCausland's cavalry brigades still skirmished with Averell's Division near Brucetown.

About 3 p.m. just as Torbert seemed about to advance upon us and we sat with sabres drawn ready for a charge, an excited courier galloped up and brought orders for our regiment and 1st and 2nd to hurry to the left, that Averell had run Imboden and McCausland into Winchester and turned our left just as Early had Sheridan's infantry in retreat and the day almost ours.

This was awful. We went off at a gallop, all was excitement, crowds of infantry were straggling from the field "to the rear" without arms, cavalrymen scampering about, and batteries of artillery galloping off from the left to avoid capture.

Breckinridge's Division, quite small, was deployed into a mere skirmish line and that, with the 62nd Virginia Cavalry, Imboden's Brigade, held Averell in check with his 4,000 splendidly equipped dragoons. One of his regiments already occupied the 3rd height from Winchester and a group of fifteen or twenty occupied Fort Jackson which stood upon the 2nd height 1/2 mile from town.

Up this 2nd we charged at full speed under fire with glittering blades and the resolution of despair. We occupied it, the 1st and 2nd [Virginia] dismounted and got into the fortification. Our regiment stood mounted

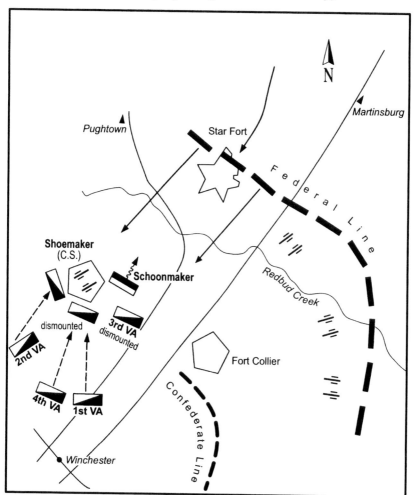

16. Winchester, 19 September 1864

in a depression on the eastern slope just below the summit. Here we could see all below and sad it was to see.

Our line, now attenuated by loss, and struggling to a small skirmish line, semi-circular in shape, seemed to be rapidly *melting* away. Here and there were to be seen ambulances and batteries galloping off while two or three guns kept up a sullen fire. The Valley Turnpike was filled with the retiring multitude of men, guns, wagons, etc., and away off to the southeast Torbert, from a high hill, was "pouring the hot shot" into them with his artillery. (Why he didn't charge and capture everything I could never understand.)

One of Averell's brigades now came forward "en eschelon". The front regiment charged and broke through the 62nd, which fled, and then galloped off to the left to pick up prisoners. The second rushed full upon the scattered infantrymen and broke them. The villains in our front, (on the hill), now set up a tremendous *huzza*! and set out full-tilt to scatter *us*. Our dismounted men let them get in range and gave them a volley which emptied several saddles and sent them back faster than they came.

Two two-gun batteries were now advanced into the plain below and, as all our other forces were now (about 4 p.m.) well gone, they opened upon us for we had our gun in the fort popping away at them.[3] Though our elevation must have been 200 feet or more, they fired with great accuracy. Our little gun couldn't do much and it was sent off after our retreating column. We held our own until sunset under a damaging artillery fire and saw the dark blue line after line of the enemy's great force closing in upon Winchester. We fell back behind the range of hills west of town, our rear guard skirmishing sharply.

At Milltown we started towards the "pike" but were charged in front and, after repulsing them, we deemed it best to continue west of the hills and got off safely, passing across the "pike" at Middletown 12 miles from Winchester about 1 a.m. on our way to Front Royal, Early following back to Strasburg and Fisher's Hill.

But for our poor, half-armed cavalry, (they had long muzzle loading muskets and nothing else), having been defeated, we would have gained a great victory. As it was, Early was routed but the enemy didn't know it. Sheridan had in the fight about 35,000 infantry, 11,000 cavalry, and artillery to correspond. His loss was over 8,000 killed and wounded. Early had 8,000 muskets and about 2,600 artillery and cavalry. His loss was from 800 to 1,200 men and I *believe* a few pieces of artillery. This looks like great disparity of loss but I am satisfied from facts obtained from both sides that it is about correct.[4]

September 20th General Fitz Lee's Division crossed at Front Royal and, leaving the 4th Virginia there on picket, moved on the road to Luray about six miles and went into camp about 4 p.m. [We] moved out at 10 a.m., 21st September, toward Front Royal to relieve 4th Virginia, then heavily pressed and falling back in disorder. [We] took position, through

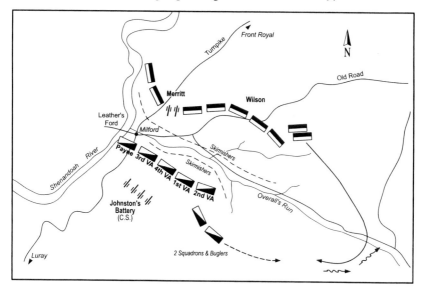

17. Milford, 21 September 1864

up some fortifications as, without spades and picks, we were availing ourselves of rails, fallen trees, large rocks, etc. In [the] afternoon had [a] sharp artillery duel with the enemy who didn't attempt to venture to assault our position.

At midnight we fell back behind a creek [Overall Run] and took position on the hills beyond Milford. Here without implements we formed a line and piled up dirt and rock knee high at a position halfway down the slope of the hill in order to command the creek which was still some 200 yards off.

At sun-rise the enemy charged in our picket across the creek and rushed pell-mell to the bridge. A murderous volley then caused them to recoil and beat a hasty retreat to the protection of the hills beyond. Our battery [Johnston's] was planted on the eminence behind us which commanded the heights in our front.

The force in front soon proved to be Major General Torbert commanding 1st (Merritt's) and 3rd (Custar's) Divisions, Cavalry of the Army of the Potomac.[5] Having deployed a heavy line of skirmishers, well supported by a heavy line of battle, (dismounted), with mounted regiments in reserve and wheeling his artillery into position, he gave us battle. The range was too long for small arms to be effective but his shells annoyed us greatly. 2nd Lieutenant Edgar Crump, Company "F," 3rd Virginia, was half covered and seriously wounded by the rock from the work in front of him being thrown on him by an exploding shell. Several other portions of the line were knocked down and some valuable men killed in our regiment and some others. It was almost impossible to carry our wounded up the hill to the rear, so good was the practice of their sharpshooters.

Torbert vainly endeavored to silence our battery which, under the daring Breathed, poured such hot shot into his artillery that the latter was completely knocked to pieces and driven.[6]

About 5 p.m. a brigade turned our right flank which was unprotected, owing to the great inferiority of our force, and moving around a little mountain seriously threatened our rear. Colonel Thomas T. Munford, with two dismounted squadrons and some 4 buglers, however, being sent there, [he] got into the mountain and by high [voice] command to the officer commanding the other "brigade" to move directly upon the enemy's led-horses, while he engaged their dismounted brigades and the oft re-echoed blasts of the four bugles sounding the charge, so completely deceived and terrified the enemy that they hastened to their horses and fell back leaving him master of the situation.

Every effort to cross in our front having failed, his flank movement defeated, his artillery crippled, his adjutant general having lost a leg, many officers and men being killed and wounded, Torbert confessed to a citizen that he couldn't "*carry that position*" and retreated.[7]

Feeling no little elated at thus having whipped more than two-to-one and so soon, too, after the disastrous battle of Winchester, imagine our surprise while picketing on South Branch of the Shenandoah about 12 noon on the 23rd at seeing a sergeant and two privates of an artillery company of Gordon's Division coming up, red and exhausted with heat and fatigue and announcing the awful catastrophe of Fisher's Hill the day before.[8] Soon we marched off and encamped that night just south of Luray, Page County.

Next morning Colonel Payne of the 4th Virginia, but commanding Lomax's Brigade, was sent back through Luray to hold any enemy in check that might appear while our brigade took the direct road to New Market over the Massanutten Mountain.

My horse being bare-foot, I obtained leave to get her shod and went to a shop hard by the camp. [I] was detained some time, heard no noise, and riding along towards the mountain, saw some eighteen to twenty bare-headed men enter the road in front of me by a road from the right. [I] soon guessed that "Mr." Payne had met with "an accident." [I] galloped up and learned that he had encountered what he thought a small force, dismounted half his force, formed line of battle, and advanced, whereupon he was suddenly attacked on front and flanks by overwhelming odds and completely "squelched." [He] had half his wagons captured, one or two abandoned and the others rattled off towards Port Republic.[9]

Coming up with Colonel [Reuben B.] Boston of the 5th Virginia, he told me that the brigade was worsted but was rallying and would push off towards Port Republic.

Bidding him adieu I now pushed forward [and] soon came upon two fellows loaded down with hoe-cakes for their regiments. [I] told them the road was open [unguarded] behind them [and] that "half a loaf was better than no bread" and they had better jog along even at the risk of "wasting a little."

Crossing the Shenandoah, I found one brigade with its wagon train halted half way up the mountain to [New Market Gap], rather the head of the column was on top, the end at the foot of the mountain. [I] inquired the cause and learned that two couriers from Early had arrived [and] one ordering us to march to his assistance as fast as possible, the other to "save our trains and move forthwith to Port Republic by the New Market and Gordonsville and the Port Republic Turnpike." Neither courier could tell which left Early last nor did the dispatches show this. In three miles of Luray with a rough mountain road along the banks of the river to [White House?] Bridge where the Luray Road ran into ours, a point equi-distant from us and from Luray, we were in a quandry. Early's line of battle was being constantly forced back and was there, not over two miles north of New Market, while his trains had all passed there [through New Market]. Finally, the enemy were reported to have moved through Luray and appeared about taking [the] Port Republic Road.

Our regiment and the 1st were sent off at a gallop to get possession of this bridge about three miles [away], got there in time, threw out a picket towards Luray and "fortified." No enemy appeared and we passed on safely and went into camp about 11 p.m.

Next day marched to [Conrad's Store?] in Rockingham [County], fed horses, and rested some hours, marched all night and reached Port Republic just before day. Next day the army came in, followed up closely by the enemy. Kershaw's Division ordered from Gordonsville came down through Brown's Gap the next day, about 2,000 strong.

The day after we had a heavy skirmish in a field near the gap which threatened to be serious. But the enemy only showed cavalry and they were driven off.[10]

The army was so demoralized that nothing but the perfect security of the mountain fastnesses in which it had found shelter saved it from going to pieces. Next morning [27 September] we moved with Gordon's Division to attack and, if possible cut off, a detached Yankee [Powell's] cavalry division at Wier's [Weyer's] Cave. All our movements seemed about to be crowned with success when the zeal of some officer ordered a battery to open too soon and gave the alarm and allowed the rascals to get off.[11] Basil Gildersleeve, [of the] University [of Virginia], was badly wounded here [but] casualties [were] not many.[12]

Hearing that the enemy's cavalry had gone up to Staunton and commenced tearing up the railroad, our brigade was dispatched to Waynesboro marching over all sorts of mountain roads. We arrived at the tunnel late in the afternoon of [28 September] and found the Yankees between there and town.

[The next morning] our regiment being in rear was kept with the artillery, the 4th followed by the 1st and 2nd charged magnificently and immediately, surprising the Yankees completely and driving them across the river and through town. But they rallied behind the hills, charged in turn and inflicted considerable loss on the front squadron of the 4th which had gone a little too far, perhaps, and was not sufficiently supported. Captain Moss, commanding, was seriously wounded in two places, Lieutenant [N. D.] Morris slightly and a number of non-commissioned and privates. Among the latter, my brother Edmund received a very severe and painful wound across the top of his left hip bone and was borne, disabled, from the field.

About night we carried the hills, a flank demonstration having been made by Colonel Payne and General Gordon between Waynesboro and Staunton.[13]

I got comfortable quarters for Edmund, had his wound dressed, and sent him by train to Charlottesville, then went on to Staunton and joined my command near town. We stayed about there till next day when Early, having advanced again, moved along what is called the Mountain Road, left of the Valley Turnpike towards [New Market]. Found the enemy had retreated so precipitately that we did not come up with him until the evening of the 3rd of October, I believe, at [Bridgewater] where we had quite a lively skirmish but failed to accomplish much.[14]

I was now completely disabled from following my command in consequence of large boils caused by that filthy and malignant disorder known as "camp itch" which for two years had prevailed as an epidemic in the army and to which, notwithstanding every possible precaution, I had at last fallen victim. Next day I was sent to Charlottesville Hospital by our surgeon and did not rejoin the command again till November 3rd at Moore's farm near Mt. Jackson.[15]

Meanwhile, under Major General T. L. Rosser, a brave but indifferent officer, our glorious brigade that had never been defeated was subjected to the humiliation and shame of a most disastrous defeat along with that officer's whole command on the 9th of October on upper Cedar Creek. He rushed headlong upon the retreating enemy, some twenty miles ahead of the infantry, leaving his flanks exposed in the most stupid and reckless manner. Our brigade was hemmed in, its *entire hospital captured a mile in its rear* while it was fighting in the front and this sad news spreading among the men, they broke and fled in confusion. This, indeed, proved their only means of escape, almost. Rosser lost nine guns and some fifteen to twenty ambulances and wagons. Never was inordinate vanity and conceit more thoroughly punished than in [the] case of this peacock on that occasion.[16]

This man Rosser is son of a defaulting sheriff of Campbell County who went to Texas. R[osser] himself had married a Miss Winston near Hanover Court House, a charming lady who, however, was fool enough to say she only wanted the war to last long enough for "Colonel Rosser to become a Major General." Her wish was gratified.

When he reached the Valley, he found the wagon trains of our brigade some ten miles in rear of the command and he said, "Order those wagons up. *I am in the Valley now.*" His brigade had just arrived from Petersburg where it had gained distinction by splendid fighting. And he, luckily for him, was promoted Major General *before* the 9th of October.[17]

The brigade, however, did splendid work under our gallant Colonel Thomas Owen's lead in the night attack at Cedar Creek on October 19th driving a brigade of infantry out of their camp, routing them, capturing a number and doing very well the entire day.[18]

I have said but little of the brilliant victory lost in the moment of its fruition at Cedar Creek on the 19th October because [I was] not present at the time.

On the 8th November we moved down the Mountain Road towards Winchester, Early's army advancing along the Turnpike, encountered the enemy on a line running through Newtown on the 10th and had a heavy skirmish. Rosser again left our flank entirely exposed though a brigade of Yankees were on our left and rear not over 1 mile beyond a ridge. And, indeed, one regiment of them reconnoitered our rear that evening capturing one of a foraging party from our regiment. We encamped on the ground. Next morning early Rosser's Brigade took position to our left confronting the brigade just mentioned. We held the road on which we came and Payne was sent to the front of Early on the Pike while Lomax's Division on Early's right covered all roads in that direction.

Payne, after fighting smartly for some hours drove the enemy in a beautiful charge through and half a mile beyond Newtown. We lay quiet till noon when our skirmishers, being driven in, a vigorous attack was made on us. Rosser's Brigade had been skirmishing for some two hours and had fallen back about 1 1/2 miles behind a position parallel with us. Notwithstanding this and the fact that the 4th Virginia and [half of] the 1st had been carried off by Rosser to flank the rascals who were chasing his brigade so, the old 3rd, when the bugle blast sounded, on the gale rushed yelling to the front with a resolute charge that ensured success and for 1 mile swept everything before it.

Our left being charged meanwhile by a flanking column, the 2nd Virginia met and repulsed it beautifully and drove it over the ridge. Rosser's brigade had been routed and, though Captain [Mordecai W.] Strother, commanding the 4th Virginia, had been eminently successful in his flank, its effects were merely temporary and the gathering masses of "blue-bellies" plainly demonstrated the necessity of falling back to "restore the line." So we soon received orders to join the rest of the command (some 2 1/2 miles in our rear now) and there, to our relief, saw Lomax marching up with half his division. He had been fighting some on the right.

At nightfall Early retired to Strasburg and we to a parallel point and bivouacked. We then fell back again to Mt. Jackson and New Market.

I always understood this movement to have been a "reconnasaince in force" to alarm Sheridan and prevent his reinforcing Grant at Petersburg.

We now lay quiet in camp til the 17th of November. The evening before we heard that a division of Federal cavalry had gone into camp some 3 miles beyond Edinburg where a squadron of 3rd Virginia were on picket. Next morning the 4th [Virginia] having come to relieve us at Mt. Jackson and a squadron gone to relieve ours on outpost, our regiment returned to camp two miles above Mt. Jackson on the east side of the Shenandoah just opposite Rood's [sic] Hill on Moore's farm.

We had just dismounted when the foaming horse of an excited courier heralded the rapid advance of Major General Torbert's formidable division. Another courier was sent off at headlong speed to hurry up the infantry beyond New Market. The 1st Virginia Cavalry went off across the river at a rapid trot to occupy Rood's Hill, the 2nd and 3rd moved down the railroad some 200 yards and formed line of battle, the 4th Virginia having fallen back nearly to camp and then skirmishing heavily. Their picket squadron was driven headlong through the town and across the river and river flats by Major General Custar's Division at a charge.[19]

Early's veteran infantry regiments were now distinctly seen with their tattered flags sporting in the breeze pressing rapidly forward while his 6- and 12-pounder field pieces went thundering along the turnpike toward the scene of action. Our tents were rapidly struck by the quartermaster's department, wagons loaded, and shoved off. All was excitement and hurry that bracing but raw and cloudy November morning.

Presently Custar's entire division formed in battle array on Meem's low grounds. Another division formed a second line across our front and their left lapping Custar's rear. Another division or brigade was halted on the other side of town. Rosser's and Lomax's brigades were higher up the Valley foraging.

At length, one of Early's batteries being in position and a line of infantry skirmishers thrown forward, (both, however, concealed from the enemy in the flat), one of Custar's regiments at a bugle blast dashed off to charge the hill. The 1st Virginia Cavalry, as though retiring, wheeled to the left and disappeared down a ravine. On the Yankees rushed as if sure of success when three shells in quick succession went whizzing through the air from our guns, followed by a volley and a forward movement of our skirmishers.

To increase the confusion, the 1st Virginia now turned the foot of the

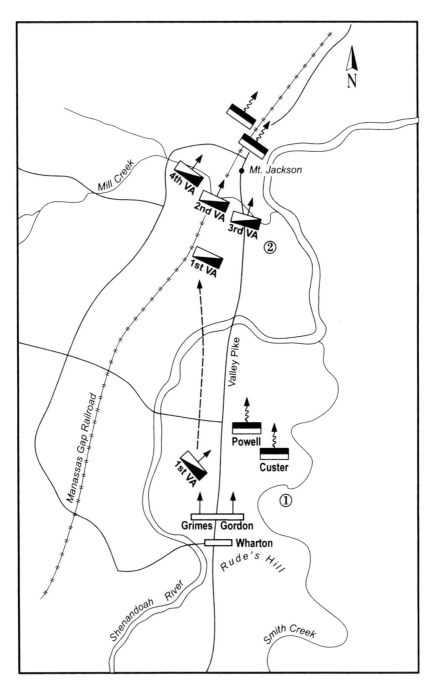

18. Mt. Jackson, 22 November 1864

hill and fell suddenly upon the flank of the charging regiment which fell back upon its supports followed closely by the 1st Virginia into the mid-flats. Here a sharp skirmish took place, Major Charles Irving deploying his regiment for the purpose. But our infantry advancing well out, Custar began to withdraw.

Just then "Forward" rung along our lines and we trotted off some distance, half dismounted and under the lead of Thomas Munford, commanding brigade. [We] soon dislodged a strong force from a thick wood. The sharp crack of the rifles, the one-sided artillery fire on the right showed that the infantry were making progress. Our mounted and dismounted men soon came up in full view of town.

As we on the left came out upon the open field, Major General Rosser ordered the two mounted squadrons of my regiment, with which I was supported on the left by two [squadrons] of the 2nd and having one squadron of the 1st in front as skirmishers, to move steadily forward and be ready to charge when near enough.

On a hill to the left of town stood four regiments of mounted Yankees in line fronting us and we moved directly towards these. As we got in 250 yards of them one whole regiment fired a volley right into us as we ascended a slope but most of the shot fell short. Two or three horses were hit. Our men pressed forward now under their continued fire for a few yards when finding it impossible to make a direct front attack, we wheeled to the right by fours, galloped to the turnpike, and wheeling by the left into column, we charged through town amid the waving of handkerchiefs and deafening cheers of the people.

The Yankees on the hill to our left, being flanked, thought of nothing but safety and galloped off. But in a hundred yards or so driving one part before us, we came upon a brigade drawn up to meet us with only a little depression of sixty yards intervening. We halted for a moment for support. Our commander, Lieutenant Colonel Feild, seemed undecided what to do and we had several men and horse shot in a minute. The 1st Virginia came up at a charge but finding the column too strong, likewise halted.

Just then we made another flank movement to the left by Colonel Munford's command, placed a wood between us and the enemy's brigade and, having an infantry column entering Mt. Jackson and already popping away a little, we soon dislodged these men.

We now, however came upon a force of three regiments which seemed disposed to show fight. We charged them but would, I believe, have been repulsed had not a portion of the 4th [Virginia] charged in flank and broke the enemy. The latter now only attempted to retard our pursuit and fell back rapidly beyond Edinburg. Our brigade lost some sixty or seventy killed and wounded, the infantry some eight or ten only, I believe.

On the 4th or 5th December my boy, Mike, had tied my black mare "Bet's" halter rein to her ankle while she was grazing on Meem's low grounds in order that he might catch her again. In that condition she ran into swimming water and was drowned. I bought in New Market on the 7th December a very strong, likely Morgan 4-year-old horse for $2500 cash Confederate money.

We now held our camp without molestation until the 7th December when we marched through Brock's Gap on a cattle, sheep and horse stealing (impressing) expedition into Hardy, Pendleton, Pocahontas, etc. counties whence we returned on the 20th of December to Swoop's Depot, 10 miles west of Staunton.[20]

About the 20th a Yankee cavalry column advanced on Gordonsville which was covered by Lomax's Division and we marched to reinforce him on the night of the 21st, encamping at Ivy Depot, Albemarle County, on the 23rd and 24th, at Greenwood on the 25th, thence marched on the 27th to Nelson. [We] passed through Tye River Gap January 3rd, thence again to Swoop's Depot, thence in about two days to Barboursville, Orange County, thence about the 1st of March to Richmond, encamping 1 mile from Mechanicsville to the northeast.[21]

Correspondence, 1864

Hd Qrs, 3rd Va. Cav.
3 Miles east of Richmond
Monday evening, May 16, '64
My Dear Brother,

I wrote a hasty note to Pa some few days ago and have had no time to write since. Yesterday we crossed to the Richmond side of Chickahominy and went into camp. I had the good fortune to get hold of some clean clothes and take a bath which I very much enjoyed. We left camp early this morning and came across here to the "Darby Road" leading to Charles City and about five miles from Chaffin's farm. The Yankee cavalry corps is on this side of the Chickahominy and had videttes about Malvern Hill. We are now grazing our horses having nothing else to feed on; and I am using my bible as writing desk.[1]

Edmund has, I hope, gotten off home before this. I saw him started to Richmond last Friday. He was wounded by a rifle ball about two inches behind the left ear, the ball coming out on the face one inch in front of the ear. The wound is not dangerous but will trouble him some. I felt so grateful at his not losing a limb or being killed that I could not feel much disturbed about the wound such as it was.

We had heavier fighting on three of the days than I have ever participated in before. One day our line of battle withstood an infantry line twice as strong for 1 1/2 hours in a wood (Sunday, 8th). Edmund has acted with great gallantry from all I can learn and gained for himself quite a reputation in his company. He deserves to be very much petted by you all now and you must not be sparing with your favors. My duties here prevented me from going to Richmond to see whether he got off or not.

Captain Matthews, poor fellow, died of his wounds on the 13th and his body has been brought to Richmond. The casualties in our regiment were to be published in today's Examiner. I haven't seen it but suppose they are out.

Dr. Lewis Randolph was at Spottsylvania Court House attending our wounded when we had to fall back rather suddenly Sunday morning and he, staying behind, was taken off by the Yankees; but released after they had carried him about two miles.[2] They kept his horse, blankets, etc., but not his instruments. Dr. Leigh, Brigade Surgeon, says he is now with some of our wounded at or near Bumpa's [Bumpass] Station, [Virginia] Central Railroad.

I have not been wounded atall yet but am astonished at it for the fire through which we have passed has been terrible. The 15th [Virginia Cavalry] Regiment gave way on our left Saturday, 7th and, thus, a large number of Yankees got behind our 5th squadron with which I was fighting on foot. Two of them came up behind in twenty feet of me. One raised his gun when I fired at and, I think, killed him. The other ran off. We then got off and fell back to the line.

We hear this evening that Butler is falling back, we having captured a whole brigade and commander.[3]

Send me a fresh horse to Richmond if either is fat. Mail about leaving.

Fresh and glorious news. Beauregard whipping them. L. Polk gone to Lee. Breckinridge whipped Seigel [sic].[4]

Love to all, R. T. Hubard, Jr.

～

Hd. Qrs. 3rd Va. Cav.
July 20th, 1864
Col. J. S. Hubard
Dear Brother,

Availing myself of an opportunity afforded by McKinney's Tom of sending a letter home, I write a few lines by way of informing you how I am. I wrote to Lou only a few days ago and have but little to write about.

Two of the young ladies to whom I sent Yankee photographs have responded in very sweet notes which were highly entertaining and revived many pleasant recollections.[5] As to who they were, I leave you to guess. I know you had greatly rather find out in this way than any other.

I received a very cheerful letter from William last evening indicating great buoyancy of spirit at the prospect of marrying some congenial fair one who he insists for the present be *inconnue* [unknown]. William is old enough to make his own matches and I think it best for us all to leave him to make his own selection and, having made it, to receive him and his bride with all the cordiality that is due him. I haven't *an idea* as to the sort of a match he is about to make. I'm completely befogged and hope he will do well.

The bearer of this will take home for me my captured blue Yankee overcoat and cape. I want the lining taken out of the cape and, if likely to be injured by dying, the buttons taken off coat and cape, I then desire the coat and cape to be dyed as nicely as possible some dark color. I had rather not have it black if any other color (than blue) can be given it. And as aunt Sarah has paid much attention to such matters, I wish Lou would either advise with her about dying the coat or send Ursula over to Saratoga and request aunt Sarah to superintend it's dying by Ursula as a special favor to me.[6] Pa would say, I know, that Ursula could do it well enough and aunt Sarah ought not to be troubled. But overcoats are now worth $800 to $1000 and I want this coat fixed as nicely as possible. Besides, people are sometimes glad to have an opportunity to go to a little trouble for friends and I am sure this would be aunt Sarah's feeling in this instance. At all events, I desire Lou to ask her if she could have it dyed some pretty and suitable color. Remember, I want the *lining* of *the cape* to remain *red* and therefore to be taken out before the latter is dyed. The coat lining needn't be taken out.

Col. Owen has just forwarded a communication for Captain Feild's promotion to Lieutenant Colonel and mine to Captain of his company (Dinwiddie Troop). He has been assured that it will be favorably and strongly endorsed at Brigade and Division Headquarters and I think there is but little doubt of its going through. Yet, the Secretary of War is sometimes very particular and I wish to be on the safe side. I wish you would get Edmund to write to Mr. Seddon to this effect—that without any solicitation on my part or that of any of my friends, my

colonel has forwarded a recommendation for my promotion to captaincy of Feild's company, in case of his promotion, on the grounds of
capacity, efficiency, gallant conduct on the field and that he would be
gratified if he would use his influence by having the opportunity
made by the President without delay. (turn over) (continued from
margin on other page) Mr. Seddon proposed to Uncle E. his great
willingness to aid me. He has now a chance to put this appointment
through almost without an effort. For the company will have no com-
missioned officer left to claim promotion, there being but one other
who *is to be retired from the service* and the choice is between *me* and
the *Non-Commissioned Officers* of that company.

    All the grease spots, etc., should be washed out of the overcoat
before it is dyed.

[no signature]

Year 5
1865

14
"A Spectacle of Monstrous Absurdity!"

I am already quite weary of my task. Each succeeding day makes it more sad and painful to dwell upon the scenes, particularly the closing scene of our grand, noble but, alas, fatally unsuccessful struggle against powerful human odds and Divine destiny. It was God's will that all which we held sacred and dear should, for the time at least, be lost to us.

As our glorious flag, stained with the blood of many a hard fought field, torn by many a whizzing bullet drooped despondingly about its staff, so our army, worn with labors and fatigues and campaigns more arduous, more terrible than mortal man had ever endured, became moody, despondent, sad as it saw our country's fall written in the future and felt that crushed and shattered as it was, the power was no longer left it to protect and defend. Yes! They felt that their lives so nobly offered, their bodies so cheerfully interposed would no longer prove a bulwark to stay the tide that now bore so heavily upon us. Upon every face was engraved in words of fire: "*Lost—All is lost.*"

With this conviction deep-seated upon their hearts, with starvation, nakedness, slavery, and wretchedness staring them in the face, the noble remnant of the Army of the South under the gallant Johnston fell back from Georgia to Columbia, to Charlotte, to its place of final surrender. The Army of the Trans-Mississippi, unable to come to our aid, stood mute and motionless and quietly waited the course of inexorable fate. Robert E. Lee, his noble form still erect amid the gathering elements which he foresaw would sweep him and his army from the field and carry away the last hopes of his country was still resolute, still brave, still true. And the immortal Army of Northern Virginia, loving him more dearly than ever, gathered closely around him and renewed their pledge to be true to their country and their professions of willing to confide their fortunes to his judgment.

The question: he had said give me 50,000 fresh troops or I cannot hold the Capital. Whence were they to come? The energies of the Conscription Bureau were exhausted. The old and young, sick and well were in the service of the country. Enroll the Negroes said many and Lee said give them to me, I will make soldiers of them. But, alas, it was too late. Time did not permit their proper drilling and discipline and, besides, they were the only laboring class left in the country.[1]

No, we had reached that point beyond which human nature cannot go. The physical and financial resources of the country had been taxed to their utmost and beyond that they could not be carried. While our soldiers were fighting and freezing in the damp, cold rifle pits, their wives and children were *naked* and *starving* at home. It was impossible to do more. All that statesmanship could do, all that bravery could accomplish, all that patriotic, self-sacrificing manhood could endure, all that ever-faithful, patient, constant women could sacrifice and suffer had been done, endured, and sacrificed.[2] We have, at least, the consolation that never on earth has greater wisdom, energy, bravery, fortitude, self-denial, faith, patriotism been shown by any people than by our dear, beloved heart-stricken and ruined Southern men and women!

On the 31st March, 1865,[3] Major General [George E.] Pickett, with about 4,500 infantry, Fitz Lee's, William H. F. Lee's, and Rosser's cavalry divisions, about 4,500 cavalry, stood in a heavy rain at 9 a.m. on a position known as Five Forks, where a road running due south from the Southside Railroad towards the Boydton Plank Road intersects a road running southwest from Petersburg and from which intersection a road runs direct to Dinwiddie Court House five miles off.

Our cavalry got there the day before and checked the advance of Major General Philip Sheridan who, at the head of 12,000 cavalry, (estimated at the time), was trying to pass [R. E.] Lee's right and compel him to fall back to save his communications with the interior. We had a sharp skirmish and held the ground.

Every arrangement being at last completed, our line being formed, Fitz Lee moved forward along the Court House Road.[4] William Lee took the left hand road to gain the Plank Road followed by Rosser who soon made a detour to the left so as to occupy the center. The whole infantry force followed the right centre and right flank.

At noon, William ["Rooney"] Lee carried the ford across [Chamberlain's Bed] Creek at the head of his division, one brigade have been previously repulsed with great loss. Rosser soon became fully occupied while only an occasional shot along our front relieved the monotony. By 1:30 p.m. the incessant, terrific rattle of musketry and irregular rumbling of artillery told but too plainly that awful carnage was taking place on the right.

At length it slackened a little and then came the long awaited courier with, "We have turned their flank with great slaughter and now the General says you must go right ahead and, if possible, reach the Court House." Through the mud and mire, (for though the rain was over the mud was ankle deep), we trotted rapidly driving the hostile skirmishers like chaff before the wind. In a mile and a half we came up with their battle line, dismounted, formed a thick skirmish line and, with deafening cheers, charged to the front. The firing was brisk but we were assured of victory and halted not.

Through the pines on the right came galloping the enthusiastic Rosser on his bobtail black, "Forward, boys, forward! My men are on your right. Our line is perfect and we are driving them everywhere." The enthusiasm was now unbounded and the woods rung with the wild yells of the still brave soldiers of the Old Division—God help the noble band!

Lieutenant [Charles C.] Croxton fell, pierced through the forehead with a minie ball. Hearing a sigh as they passed him, his comrades of the 4th pressed bravely on. I passed the dead body of Lieutenant Ed. Garrett, a brave, manly officer of Cumberland but [I] hadn't time to see that his forehead had been likewise pierced.

Then Lieutenant Colonel Feild and his horse fell to the ground.[5] Motioning two soldiers to his aid, I rushed onward with our noble boys to dislodge the villains who were concealed in a wood and picking our offi cers down. We charged across an open field right straight upon them and they fled. And now we halted in obedience to orders in about 1 1/2 miles of the Court House.

A brisk cannonade had been opened upon our lines by quite a number of guns in position behind a strong redoubt that had been thrown up about the Court House. Such was the condition of the roads and so very

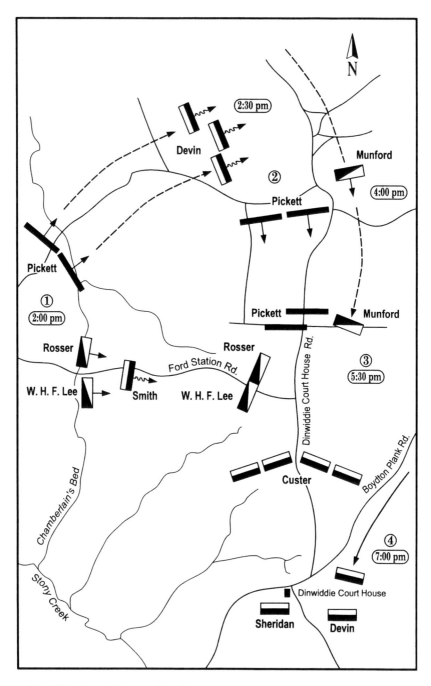

19. Dinwiddie Court House, 31 March 1865

soggy were the fields that it had proven utterly impractical for us to bring up a single gun. So night having set in, we being without artillery and a heavy infantry force to back him, we gave up the contest and went into camp.[6]

During the day Lieutenant General [Richard H.] Anderson, commanding from our left along Hatcher's Run to Lieutenant General A. P. Hill's right near Petersburg, had had some heavy fighting. On the morning of the 1st April, we lay quiet and undisturbed in camp. At dawn we commenced falling back to our original position on the line of Five Forks.

General Pickett having given general directions to the division and brigade commanders as to resuming their places, etc. rode off with General Fitz Lee to a farm house some three miles from the Forks to enjoy a sumptuous dinner and be treated as the hero of the day before. The liquor flowed freely and soon he was in that condition in which a man little recks of what goes on around him.[7]

Fitz Lee's Division passed the forks and went into camp 1/2 mile on the road thence to the Southside Railroad and fed their horses. Rosser was on our left connecting with Anderson. His command in camp had only a picket on its front. Our command had a picket of forty men forming a link in the line between Rosser and Pickett's infantry on our right and William Lee's cavalry were on the extreme right.

All along our march that morning the enemy's cavalry had pressed our rear guard very closely and by 12 noon deployed in force along the infantry front where we opened a brisk cannonade. By 2 o'clock a heavy fight was in progress yet our division lay *sunning* themselves 1/2 mile in rear of the line with horses unbridled! I inquired anxiously what this meant, fearing that wise counsels were not prevailing but could get no information.

About 2 p.m. an army corps about 10,000 strong emerged from the woods in front of our mounted picket of forty men, among them were the Buckingham Troop and my two brothers, James and Edmund.[8] [The infantry was] in two lines of battle with a heavy skirmish line in front. Another corps of equal size appeared in front of Pickett's infantry. Their cavalry, now about 10,000 moved off to the front and right flank of W. H. F. Lee's cavalry. Our forty skirmishers were ordered "to fall back firing." A spectacle of monstrous absurdity!

About 2 p.m. we were mounted and galloped off a few yards, then

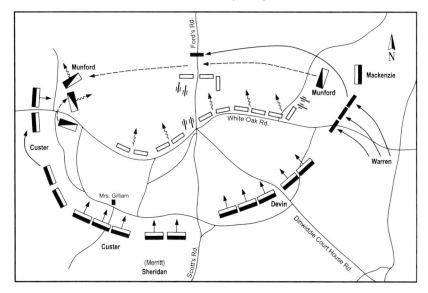

20. Five Forks, 1 April 1865

dismounted and galloped off *to their support*! A farce, of course, this was. As our regiment, commanded by Captain Jesse S. Jones, Company "B," faced into line, we had no orders and knew not exactly what was expected of us. He and I held a consultation and the result was to dispatch two couriers in opposite direction to try to find a brigade or division commander and get some instructions. (These couriers never returned during the fight.)

Meanwhile, seeing a heavy column of infantry passing from right to left across our front some 200 yards, we opened fire and thought we were doing some execution when triumphant huzzahs and rapidly receding firing on our left told too plainly that we "were flanked." In attempting now to fall back and keep connected as well as possible with the troops on right and left, the latter doubling back towards our rear, it happened that the irregularity of the country, the bogs, and the suddenness of the movement divided our regiment in half; the left half with which I was and the Captain commanding soon fell back to the road on which we had camped and about halfway between the camp and the Forks.

Between us and the camp the enemy were now in the road in force and a portion of their force had gone 1/4 mile west of it, (this road [on which we were] ran north), and they swung around forming a line facing south whilst William Lee's right having been turned, the Federal Cavalry Corps formed facing north on his front occupying thus, three sides of a square, leaving only the western one open to us.

The 11th Virginia Infantry, Major [James Risque] Hutter commanding, came down to the place we were at and one fragment of a regiment formed on their right and we faced north confronting the left flanking column of Federals with our right resting on the road.

The critical situation, the complication of matters, the absence of Pickett, etc. had so demoralized the troops that as soon as the Yankees opened a hot fire at a distance of 100 yards, our line gave way. Captain Jesse Jones, Captain Carrington, Captain Boyd, all of my regiment and myself by great exertions restored the line. We were tolerably sheltered by a thicket of young pines. In trying to turn back a stout infantryman, he told me, "I'll stop if my captain will but there he goes ahead of me."

I went up to the captain and told him we must hold on so that our centre could fall back, or they would all be taken, and he must return to his position and keep his men in place. Thus I got them both back.[9]

Taking my place in line and bending on one knee to see what the enemy's position was, I was shot down by a scalp wound over my right temple with a musket ball. Finding myself not much stunned, I rose to my feet with blood gushing down my right cheek in a stream. I retired to the rear of our centre accompanied by Sergeant Brown, Company "A".[10] Here I met Private [Joe T.] Spencer, Company "K," 4th Virginia Cavalry, from Buckingham, with a captured horse which he would insist on my mounting immediately and going out. Finding expostulation vain, I mounted bareback with the sergeant behind me and wandering through bushes and bogs for about three miles, reached the hospital of William Lee's cavalry on the Southside Railroad and was directed by the surgeon to get aboard the train for the wounded which came along.

Before we started, (about dark), I learned that just after I left, (sunset), our whole force was driven back in confusion with the loss of all the guns and very much disorganized, that Pickett was so drunk he knew not what to do, and but for his staff, would have fled on the train I was on.

Our force only numbered about 8,000, (having lost about 1,000 the day before and the enemy [lost] about 1,500), while the Federals had two infantry corps, (each 20,000 men), and 10,000 cavalry in the fight.[11]

General R. E. Lee, during the night, weakened A. P. Hill and Anderson greatly to save his right flank. The enemy discovered the movement and poured over his works on the morning of the 2nd of April in a perfect torrent. A. P. Hill was killed and the city taken. That night at 12 or 1 a.m., Richmond was evacuated. And thus expired the last hopes of the Confederacy.

I got to Farmville at 9 a.m. Sunday morning, the 2nd, was taken in charge by old Mr. Bruce, the Scotch bar keeper, who had a surgeon brought to dress my wound, provided a fine breakfast and a nice toddy. Staying with him some hours, I went, at Dr. Lyle's earnest solicitation, to his house and remained till the next day, enjoying the sympathy of himself, his wife, and lovely daughter, Miss Anna, and their kind ministrations to my comfort.[12]

On Monday I got home feeling miscrably depressed but with my wound kindly healing by "the first intention." The next Sunday [9 April], the Yankees being in the neighborhood, their main army being then at Appomattox Court House and not wishing to be captured until I knew the fate of the Army of Northern Virginia, I mounted my horse and left. Slept that night in a stable loft near the Buckingham Institute, (Flippin's), and went next evening to George Nicholas' on James River.

Tuesday morning Major Mason of Fitz Lee's staff, Henry Nicholas, Company "G," 3rd Virginia Cavalry, and others arrived and reported the surrender.[13] I then went to Uncle Robert Bolling's, met Reverend W. C. Meredith and brother Edmund, who had been by home on Friday to get a fresh horse and hadn't been able to get to his regiment again. We three got home Thursday night and found all well and rejoiced to see us.

Bolling had returned from the Institute before I left Chellow and had all the horses hid in a wood near Moses Smith's, (some 19 [horses] with 3 or 4 Negroes).

Eleven Yankees came Tuesday morning to "Chellow," cursed father, one drew a sword over his head to frighten him into telling where his horses were, made him give them some liquor, took Philip's and Reuben's pistols away from them, got a Negro guide, went after, found, and carried off all the horses to the Court House and about seven Negroes with them. [They] gave them the horses they were riding and separated. The Negroes brought home and delivered the horses they had.

Finis

December 3, 1866—I now close my journal or record of the war of 1861–1865. It is, of course, very imperfect but will serve its purpose of preserving for future reference the little incidents in my humble military career. And these may in after years be interesting to me or to those who come after me.

I will add here that brother James was captured at Deep Creek in Amelia on the 4th or 5th of April, marched on foot to Amelia Court House, and thence immediately to City Point without stopping one hour to rest. There with blistered feet, empty stomach, and dropping spirits he went aboard a steamer and was carried to Point Lookout and confined about 6 weeks and finally released at the solicitation of friends on his parole. During all this time we knew not whether he was dead or alive.[1]

By superior force and wealth and the active sympathies of all the earth and the permission of Jehovah, they (the North) finally succeeded in crushing our armies and our finances. Some wise purpose which we cannot discern moved the Most High to permit these things so to be. He does all things for the best. Though we can't see *now, why* these things should have been permitted, yet since they have been, we must, as a matter of faith, believe that "God is wise in *all His ways* and good in all His works."

[signed] R. T. Hubard, Jr.

Correspondence, 1865

Chellow
April 18th, 1865
My Dear Sister [Isaetta],

Your brother Lewis arrived this evening. Father being quite unwell and having written a good deal today, I have insisted on writing this letter for him. So you must not feel slighted at his not writing. I will do my best to represent him. I have feared that you might feel strongly of our not writing to you and attribute it to a want of regard for you—though I felt satisfied that if you would reflect a moment about the matter, you would make proper allowances. We would have sent days ago but we could gather nothing and to start a negro off to Albemarle would have been useless up to within 48 hours as parties of Yankees and stragglers from our army were running all over the county north of us and would have been certain to take any horse they met.

Last night and today we have heard this much only—Ursula's son Tom says a Yankee officer by the name of Howard was passing by "Whispering" and asked whose land it was. When told, he said, "that very man was captured between Petersburg and Farmville with some others who were cut off by being unable to cross a creek and sent to Richmond."

Hudson ("Rosny" negro) says he saw three or four men, two of whom were members of the 44th Regiment and they told him brother James was taken prisoner and not hurt as some of them saw him *after he was captured* and that he was sent to Richmond.

Mr. Wilson Call told Edmund he saw two soldiers who said they knew the fact that brother James was captured and not hurt. But he didn't remember whether they said they *saw* him after he was taken or not.

Now, whether to put any reliance in these statements or not, I can't say. But I am inclined to think there must be some truth in them for though coming from different sources, they are all *confirmatory* of *each other* and agree throughout.

I understand that the prisoners captured near Richmond and Petersburg were sent to Fortress Monroe or north and this is reasonable for the Yankees did not then know that they would capture Lee's army. We have felt so certain that brother James was unhurt that we confidently expected he was in Albemarle by this time. And, indeed, I would not be surprised if he gets there before this letter now.

Everything has been so unsettled that it was impracticable to send one of the little boys or negroes to Amelia to make inquiries and Edmund and I only surrendered and got our paroles yesterday [April 17]. He was talking today about going down to see if he could learn anything.

Now the prisoners sent north will certainly be paroled, I think. But as the parole of the Army of Northern Virginia was in pursuance of terms obtained by General Lee, it does not necessarily follow that prisoners previously captured will be immediately paroled. I *think* they will be but they *may* not for some weeks or months.

So you must not be alarmed if you fail to hear from your husband immediately. He told Edmund he had no idea of trying to cross the creek with his weak horse, and if he met with the Yankees, they certainly wouldn't have shot him by himself.

Whilst it is painful for you and all of us to be kept in suspense about him, and whilst it is true that anxiety is almost sure to produce apprehension, I cannot but think that there is scarcely a *single valid reason* for *any* other belief than that brother was not hurt but simply captured. You may be assured that the moment any reliable intelligence of him is received here it will be sent to you. And you must always feel assured that we all feel as much love for you and interest in all that concerns you as if you were one of us by birth instead of marriage.

We received letters from William and his wife today. They were well and at Watt's house.

The Yankees came here, drew a sword over Pa to make him tell where the horses were, which he didn't do. Took all his liquor, Philip's shoes, some meat and left. They found the horses and took them all but gave the negroes back some. They took none of brother James' but his mule.

The negroes have all been deranged declaring they were free and didn't hit a lick of work from Tuesday last til today. Harrison, John, John Deane, Leonard and Edward from "Rosny" are gone. Several still absent at their wives' houses and the rest scarcely willing to do anything. Many of them are talking about working for wages, etc, etc. Today they went to work and planted a little corn. The Yankees in Farmville threatened to whip them if they didn't quit coming there. What will be the upshot of it I don't know. While I write there is not a negro man or boy on the plantation, all having gone off since sunset except Isham who stays here closely. I suppose the others will return here tomorrow though, this, of course, is mere conjecture.

I am getting well of my wound. Lou is complaining right much of a sore throat. Pa is quite unwell though going about. The rest are well. Pa asks me to say that your letter by Lewis with that by Colonel Smith are all he has received. All unite with me in love to you, your children, parents, and brother Robert.

Your Affectionate brother, R. T. Hubard Jr.

Postwar Correspondence

205 Harrison St.
Lynchburg, VA
Oct. 26th, 1909

Adjutant Robert T. Hubard
My Dear Adjutant,

I am sure the pleasure would have been mine to have met any of my old comrades of the 3rd Va. Cavalry who were kind enough to have hunted for me at the (Burton Hotel, Danville) at the last reunion. I had been quite sick before leaving home and was induced to enjoy the hospitality of a friend in a private home &, hence, was cut off from *mixing* with many old comrades I would have loved to meet again.

I thank you very much for sending a copy of a letter my great grandfather, Colonel Robert Munford to your paternal grandfather, Major Wm. Hubard of Charlotte. Those old *cronies* were friends *indeed* and *in need* and stood together as we friends did in our Civil War. My paternal great grandfather was with General Washington and Colonel Bland in Braddock's retreat. And Major Anthony Singleton, my grandmother's father (maternal) was shot through the lungs at Eutaw & lost his guns in that battle. Those old patriots transmitted their blood & love of country to their descendants & we should all feel proud of any of them as their connections.

I am not as *clear* on *genealogy* as I would like to be; have quite a collection of family history but fear I will never find it *convenient* to untangle its intricacies. I am greatly obliged for the paper. I always remember your good services with pleasure & pride; know as a soldier you reflected credit upon our arms and your command!

With my best wishes for you & my old comrades & sincere thanks,

Thomas T. Munford

～

June 5, 1910

Dear Robert [Robert Thruston Hubard III, Hubard's fourth child],

The Daughters of the Confederacy of Farmville invited me to address them at their annual dinner given the Veterans June 3rd. Fortunately I got well enough to go; and took as my general theme the bloody character of the battles the fourth campaign,—but specially the battle of 8th May, 1864 on the Brock Road 1-1/2 miles west of Spottsylvania Court House between Fitz Lee's Brigade on one side about 2200 officers and men and on the other side General Wesley Merritt's Cavalry Divisions "Reserved [sic] Brigade"—five regiments supported by General Warren's 5th Corps Infantry 25000 men. Our men fought on foot in the brush and mostly on elbows and knees for four hours without yielding an inch, lines about seventy yards apart.

Merritt opened the attack at 4 a.m. on our 3rd Virginia Cavalry on picket at the barricade and after both our flanks had been turned we received orders to fall back and form on the brigade 1st, 2nd, and 4th Regiments and General Warren's infantry relieved Merritt's men then, 6 a.m., and his rifle-men closed in, to seventy yards, on our line.

A 3rd Regiment boy killed a Yankee, close up to our lines, and crawled to him and brought in his knapsack, to where I was posted. I saw it; with big brass letters "5th Corps" on it.

Among our boys killed while resting on elbows and behind trees, were "Tom Pride" of Cumberland, in about four feet of me. I heard the "thuymp" of the ball, as it pierced his temple and saw his head drop on its face, dead! I spoke to men nearby to take the brave boy's body to the rear.

Our Lieutenant Colonel, in all that fight, stood pistol in hand, in middle of a narrow road straight to the enemy. I saw two fellows crouched behind the bushes trying to pick him off and went to him and urged him to take a less exposed position. "No," said he, "I will stand here, to encourage the men *to stand firm*." Result, General Warren had orders to occupy Spottsylvania Court House at 8 o'clock that morning! On the contrary, *we* had him *busy* in our front on that hour, and Longstreet's Corps marched in to the place we had "kept open" for them, and at once began fortifying.

So that instead of Grant keeping Lee out, Lee got in and kept Grant out, till the 12th May when the bloody angle was taken. General A. A. Humphreys Chief of Staff Army of the Potomac in his book "Virginia Campaigns 1864 & 5" said: General Warren's headquarters were to occupy Spottsylvania Court House with his corps by day break (8 a.m.) May 8th, '64; "and would have been [there], *but for the presence of Fitz Lee on the Brock road*." top p. 69 (underscoring mine).

No southern author has ever given our cavalry any credit for this fight, in which our small force fired at least 80,000 rounds at the enemy; this tremendous fire in a brush wood, gave the impression there were 10,000 men. At Farmville on June 3rd were Buckingham, Cumberland, and Prince Edward Cavalry (of the Brigade) all delighted that I was there to vindicate their right to commendation for saving the "vantage" for General Lee's army that day, and I never was so complimented and so gratified myself.

But now you must not be disheartened for Colonel R. B. Berkeley, Jr., said to me, "I must in candor tell you I am feeling more interest in the "classic" speech of R. T., Jr, on the 15th than the "War speech" of R. T., Sr., on this 3rd inst."

Every seat in the Academy of Music was full and among the audience was Judge Hundley, Dr. English, his daughter, Zaida, and Mr. Hill.[1]

I am expecting to meet [daughter] Marian and the boys tomorrow. It is raining now, 1 p.m., but not heavily.

Rev. L[yttleton] E. Hubard and lady and, I believe, Philip are well. Your Ma is not very well from indigestion. P[ocahontas] B. is well.

Things generally, crops, garden, and poultry in good shape. Mutton and lambs in good order.

R. K. Brock is making fair progress on my a/c from September 1885 to November 10th 1894. I shall if possible get up to November 10th 1901. (Practically the close of my a/c) by July Court.

Affectionately, Robert T. Hubard

Afterword

Sent to receive medical care at Farmville, then onward to his father's Buckingham County plantation north of that town, Robert Hubard enjoyed the rare luxury of recovering in his own house in a region of Virginia that had been spared the hard hand of war. According to Hubard's concluding paragraph, his war memoirs were completed on 3 December 1866, a year and one-half after the conclusion of the war. It is easy to imagine that during this healing period Hubard spent hours reviewing the war letters he had sent to his family from the campaigns in Virginia, Maryland, and Pennsylvania. Using a ledger as a journal, he transcribed in an easily read hand the account of his departure from the University of Virginia in 1861, the course of the war as he experienced it, and his homecoming in 1865.

With the war over in Virginia and his slaves emancipated, Robert Hubard, Sr., with the help of his recovering son, struggled to keep the family plantations profitable. Contracts were signed with the freedmen who remained at Chellowe. Wages were paid to some, and shares of crops were paid to others. During these adjustments, Robert, Jr., became a licensed attorney and started a law practice in December 1865.[1]

As Virginia tobacco conditions and prices slowly declined in the postwar years, the Hubards found it more and more difficult to remain solvent. Competition from North Carolina, South Carolina, Kentucky, Ohio, and Missouri tobacco crops cut into the Virginia market to the extent that by the time of Robert Hubard, Sr.'s, death in 1871, Robert, Jr., was the only one of the Hubard siblings who was not in debt. According to one study of the Hubard postwar fortunes, "As early as 1872, [brother]

James had written to Robert, 'We have all come to the conclusion that you are one of the "getting-along" Hubards.' Indeed, Robert had started in the late sixties to make small but careful investments and as a lawyer in the 1870s he made sure to become directly involved in the settlement of the huge estates of Cabell and Randolph [families]."[2]

Robert's fortunes in romance also blossomed in the postwar years. "It was the custom in those days for those who could afford it to spend the summer months at some of the resorts in the western portion of the State, or in Monroe and Greenbrier counties West Virginia. . . . Thither they drove in their carriages. The subject of this sketch [Hubard], young and tall and handsome, trained both in College and on the battlefields of the South, was at 'The Spring' [White Sulpher Springs] early on the morning after their arrival, and a very beautiful young lady, daughter of John R. Edmunds, educated in Baltimore, Sallie by name, came down to drink at the spring before breakfast and the young gentleman gallantly handed her a glass of water. This was the beginning of a romance that led to the union in marriage of these two."[3] Sallie and Robert were married in Halifax County, Virginia, on 27 October 1870.

Eight children (Marion, Salley, John, Robert, Philip, Lyttleton, Louise, and Pocahontas) were born to the couple from 1871 to 1884. An 1887 *Richmond Times-Dispatch* article noted that "the Colonel and Mrs. Hubard and their daughters are keeping up the reputation for hospitality of this handsome old country place, so well known in antebellum days. . . . Cards, tennis, driving, and mountain excursion are some of the amusements of the guests. The Colonel with his courteous gallantry and Mrs. Hubard with her gracious manner and unfailing attention to her guests leave little to be desired in the role of host and hostess."[4]

Having realized the futility of Chellowe's dependence on tobacco as a cash crop, Hubard redoubled his efforts as an attorney by opening an office in Richmond to augment his Buckingham-Cumberland-Prince Edward counties practice. As his practice grew, Robert Hubard invested in several nonagricultural pursuits. A local slate quarry was purchased and then leased out as a more economical expedient. The quarry enterprise was followed by the development of a railroad spur line and the Buckingham Construction Company, both of which were to support yet another Hubard industry, the Whispering Valley Lumber Company. "In 1891 Robert and his wife transferred all the capital invested in [the] construction [company] to stock in the lumber company itself, at the time about $10,000. This lumber business would lay the basis for Robert's wealth for the next twenty years."[5]

Public service also claimed Hubard's attention, with two terms spent in the Virginia House of Delegates for the 1875–1877 sessions. Although his decision to join the Republican Party in 1880 may have stifled Hubard's later congressional candidacies, he was popular enough to be called on to serve the commonwealth on the staff of Governor William E. Cameron (1882–1886) as a presidential elector (1884) and as commissioner of the census (1900).

Within the community, Robert Hubard was as highly respected for his legal expertise and political activities as he was for his successful business and agricultural enterprises. He was active in the Episcopal Church and the Buckingham Masonic Lodge No. 242. As a Confederate veteran, Hubard was frequently called on to speak to local civic groups, and as a veteran and a Mason, he was a featured speaker at the laying of the cornerstone of the Confederate monument at Buckingham Court House on 30 June 1908.

But he was, perhaps, most affectionately regarded during his lifetime and afterward as the beau ideal of a Virginia gentleman of the old days. According to one memorialist, Robert "was a stately man whom nearly every one honored and loved. . . . He was handsome, familiar in manners with a personality naturally obliging and accommodating with not a particle of selfishness ever influencing his actions. In a company of a hundred he would be noticed without effort. He was six feet tall, weighing about 175 pounds, well proportioned and healthy. Reared in the lap of luxury with none of its frailties or sins, he was the model gentleman of his day and time. . . . He was a splendid man, devoted to his family and friends, the soul of honor in every hour of his life."[6]

Although he possessed a strong constitution throughout an active life, Robert Hubard's health began to deteriorate shortly after the death of his wife, Sallie, in June 1918. Restricted in his activities for several years, Hubard lived the life of an invalid until contracting pneumonia in September 1921. He died at Chellowe on 28 September 1921 and was laid to rest in the family burying ground "under the shadow of Willis Mountain, behind which he had so often loved to see the sun go down and within the sound of Whispering Creek, whose murmur it had always been his delight to hear."[7]

Appendix A

Eyewitness Accounts of Bagley Shooting Incident

According to Samuel Burney, a soldier in Cobb's Legion, "I will tell you of a most melancholy occurrence which took place last Wednesday, November 13. Tuesday night at 12 o'clock we were ordered out on a secret expedition. . . .

We marched about six miles to a dark swamp and remained deathly still 'till about daybreak. We then went on further 'till we had gone three or four miles and then halted. This distance we marched in mud and water over ankle deep. We halted, as I said, and were told to load our guns quickly and quietly as we were in two miles of Newport's News and were two miles lower down than we intended to come. The guide led us in the wrong road.

We had loaded but a few moments when two pickets of ours rode up and inquired of us who we were. We told them we were Cobb's Legion and asked them who they were. They said they were Cumberland Cavalry, and, thinking all was right, they wheeled on their horses to leave. Just then someone said, 'They are Yankees! Mark, fire on them!' And the infantry companies fired, those on the right first.

We were on the left and thought we were in an ambush when we heard the right-hand companies fire. The boys got behind trees. I squatted in a tree top. Lieutenant Colonel Garnett and Major Bagley and Captain Morris of Burke County were out in front of the battalion. Major Bagley was killed and fell from his horse. Colonel Garnett's horse was crippled, and Captain Morris's hand was shot and his horse killed. Captain Morris had one of his men shot in the leg, which was amputated. There were no Yankees there, but our men thought so and fired on the above men."

Another, more vitriolic, version of the same incident was recorded by Georgian, J. W. Rheney: "While we were down on this voyage, we aroused one night and our legion of infantry was sent one way and the cavalry another. The infantry were to march to a certain place near a bridge and lie in ambush until morning to catch some Yankee scouts. But our guide, who undertook to carry us a near route, got lost and carried us about two miles too low down and through a very bad swamp in which we were liable to be cut off.

Well, after so long a route, we were drawn up in a line of battle, the guide telling us to hurry in cooking, that they were not far off. Our officers were in the road and the guide also.

We were scarcely drawn up in line of battle when guide says, 'Here they come!' which a little excited the men. Two men came riding up the road, who, having our badge around their hats, they were supposed to be our pickets and which they were. Lieutenant [Colonel] Garnett beckoned them to come up, which they did very briefly. They were Virginia pickets. Our guide was then asked by Major Bagley if he knew these two pickets. He said he did not, which was a lie. The picket said 'We're Virginia pickets.' The guide says, 'It's a damned lie!' And he—the guide—being frightened, hollowing out 'Fire!', and a goodly part of the battalion fired, our officers still being in front.

One of our noted officers, Major Bagley, was shot dead. Captain Morris shot in the hand, but not a bad wound. The guide hollowing out to shoot and telling a lie, denying to know the pickets, the whole blame is laid on him. These two pickets were badly wounded but not killed. They say that they are personally acquainted with our guide who caused the mischief. There are many sad hearts for the loss of the Major, but I believe it is a general wish that it had been the guide who got shot instead of the Major!

I would not write a thing about this scrape, but I know it has been written by a good many others and by some who I know would try to give a description of it who could not, for I cannot do it myself. The amount of it is that we fired at our own pickets, through misunderstanding."[1]

Appendix B

Carter Account of Chambersburg Raid

Oct. 14th   The portion of the regiment detailed to go with Gen. Stuart into Md. & Penn. returned this morning with horses very much jaded & broken down from hard service. This expedition taken from the different brigades was composed of 1800 cavalry & two guns. They rendezvoused at Darksville, Berkeley Co., on the 9th Oct. & marched one mile beyond Hedgesville where they encamped for the night.

Early next morning they took up their line of march about sunrise & crossed the Potomac at a very rocky ford, capturing some ten or fifteen prisoners on the other side of the river, which prisoners were sent back under guard. Here they learned that a division of the enemy, 10,000 strong, had just marched along the same road. But Gen. Stuart proceeded towards Chambersburg, Penn., giving orders to have details sent out as soon as they passed the line, to capture all horses that were serviceable for artillery or cavalry.

He reached Chambersburg & found the Home Guards prepared to make resistance, but sending them word that if they did not submit unconditionally & at once, he would shell the town; the commanding officer in the place very soon surrendered & the Gen. spent the night in the town with most of the command outside. This was a very rainy & disagreeable night, but such was the fear of the inhabitants that they readily furnished the soldiers, or "rebels," as they called them, everything they needed or wished to eat.

On the morning of Oct. 11th they set out early with the horses & other things they had taken—after destroying a large lot of sabres & such pistols as they could not bring away—towards Emmetsburg. Here our men met with a very cordial reception & were loudly applauded by the citizens of that place.

They marched through Liberty & New Market & proceeded towards the Potomac without making any halt since leaving Chambersburg. They went by Hyattstown and, cutting a new road to the river, struck it at White's Ford. Here they found some cavalry on picket & charged, capturing some ten or fifteen of them. After shelling the woods & such parties of the enemy as dared to show themselves, the whole command crossed the river & camped for the night & returned the next morning to camp, crossing the Shenandoah at Snicker's Ford & proceeding by way of Berryville & Smithfield.

This extraordinary expedition around McClellan's whole army, which was spread all along the Potomac River, was accomplished without loss of any consequence. Not a man was killed and none were lost save a few drunken stragglers who lost their commands & were then left behind. It carried terror into the enemy's lines and it is said on good authority that the citizens of Philadelphia were frightened lest they too might be visited by the rebels.

Some 1200 horses were captured & several wagons; but in a material point of view it is extremely doubtful whether anything was gained as it is more than probable that the horses broken down & permanently injured would more than counterbalance those captured.

This expedition conclusively showed that almost anything is possible to a brave & determined leader at the head of good troops. It may not be improper to mention the high compliments, paid by our enemies, to the orderly and gentlemanly conduct of our troops, who respected private property under the extraordinary provocations of having their own homes devastated and female relations insulted by these same enemies.

Notes

PREFACE

The epigraph to the preface is from William B. Hubard to James L. Hubard, 1 August 1861, Randolph-Hubard Papers, Box 1, No. 4717, University of Virginia Special Collections, Charlottesville.

1. William Stebbins Hubard, *Hubards of North America* (Roanoke, Va.: William Stebbins Hubard, 1998).

2. John Burdick, "From Virtue to Fitness: The Accommodation of a Planter Family to Postbellum Virginia," *Virginia Magazine of History and Biography* 93, no. 1 (January 1985): 16; Percial Moses Thomas, "Plantations in Transition: A Study of Four Virginia Plantations, 1860–1870" (PhD diss., University of Virginia, 1979), 91.

3. Thomas, "Plantations in Transition," 118.

4. Douglas S. Freeman, *Lee's Lieutenants: A Study in Command,* vol. 3, *Gettysburg to Appomattox* (New York: Charles Scribner's Sons, 1942), 214–15.

5. Thomas, "Plantations in Transition," 172.

6. According to a 3rd Virginia trooper, "I found the Command encamped near Middle-Brook in Augusta County. The horses were starving to death and the men on the eve of mutiny. . . . If the cavalry is not disbanded, Wickham's Brigade will not have two hundred men for duty in the Spring. A large majority of men who go home on details now come back without horses. They say they will not bring horses here to be starved. . . . We have only 12 men for duty in my company." William Clark Corson, *My Dear Jennie,* edited by Blake W. Corson, Jr. (Richmond, Va.: Dietz Press, 1982), 134–35.

7. William W. Blackford, *War Years with Jeb Stuart* (New York: Charles Scribner's Sons, 1946), xiii.

INTRODUCTION

1. Estimates of the manpower, losses, and cost of the Civil War vary according to the sources consulted. According to one authoritative source, the Federal army

probably enlisted just over two million men for varying terms of service. The Confederate army is even more difficult to count, but 750,000 may be a reasonable estimate. Federal deaths from all causes numbered 360,222. Confederate deaths from battle wounds and disease have been estimated at 258,000. The financial cost of the war for the Federal government was $3,027,791,000. Estimates of the cost to the Confederate government are nearly impossible, considering the devaluation of their money as the war progressed. As of October 1863, however, Confederate reports show total war expenditures of nearly $2,100,000,000. See E. B. Long, *The Civil War Day by Day: An Almanac, 1861–1865* (Garden City, N.Y.: Doubleday and Co. 1971), 705, 710–11, 726–27.

2. In the late summer and fall of 1864, General Philip H. Sheridan was ordered to clear the Shenandoah Valley of Confederate troop concentrations. He was also directed to destroy mills, granaries, barns, and livestock capable of yielding food to the Confederate cause. Although Sheridan's troops did great damage to property along the Valley Pike, they left many more farms and mills untouched in the bottoms and back-road regions. Thus, in October 1864, Sheridan's cavalry leaders reported far less destruction than either Sheridan or Hubard believed had been caused: 43 flour mills and 347 barns destroyed, in addition to 30,000 bushels of grain burned and 2,000 head of livestock shot or driven from farms. See Michael G. Mahon, *The Shenandoah Valley: 1861–1865* (Mechanicsburg, Pa.: Stackpole Books, 1999), 124.

3. Hubard quoted or paraphrased from several famous antebellum speeches here, including Henry Clay's 1848 "no North no South" Missouri Compromise speech, Daniel Webster's 1830 "one and inseparable" debate remark, William Seward's "irrepressible conflict" speech of 1858, and Abraham Lincoln's "all free or all slave states" remarks in his 1858 "house divided" speech.

1. "THREE CHEERS FOR THE SOUTHERN FLAG!"

1. "Only 30 unconditional secessionists had been elected among 152 members, and by a vote of more than two to one the voters of Virginia required that any findings of the commission must be submitted for a plebiscite." Allan Nevins, *The War for the Union: The Improvised War, 1861–1862* (New York: Charles Scribner's Sons, 1959), 46.

2. Ruffin did not fire the first shot at Fort Sumter. That honor has been accorded Lieutenant Henry S. Farley. Ruffin may have fired an early shot from "the ironclad battery" where he was stationed, but that unit did not fire the opening, or signal, shot of the bombardment. See Patricia L. Faust, ed., *Historical Times Illustrated Encyclopedia of the Civil War* (New York: Harper and Row, 1986), 260.

3. The Virginia ordinance of secession passed by a vote of 88 to 55 but did not take the commonwealth out of the Union. It provided for a popular referendum on 23 May 1861. Long, *Civil War Day by Day*, 60.

4. A similar "flag raising," perhaps the same incident but said to have occurred in February, was described by another Virginia student as more of a schoolboy prank than a political statement. See Armistead C. Gordon, *Memories and Memorials of William Gordon McCabe* (Richmond, Va.: Old Dominion Press, 1925), 72–74.

5. In addition to raising a Confederate flag over the Virginia state capitol, state troops also occupied the U.S. Custom House and the Post Office in Richmond on 18 April. Long, *Civil War Day by Day*, 61.

6. Henry Robert Johnson (1827–1878) was thirty-three years old when the Cumberland Light Dragoons were mustered for service in 1861. He resigned his commission as captain of Company G in September 1861. After the war Johnson moved to Indian Territory (Oklahoma). See "Compiled Service Records of Confederate Soldiers Who Served in Organizations from the State of Virginia, Rolls 1–200," record group 109 (microfilm collection no. 324A, Virginia), 1961, 3rd Virginia Cavalry (previously 2nd Virginia Cavalry), rolls 25–37, National Archives and Records Administration, Washington, D.C. (hereafter referred to as CSR, 3rd Va. Cav.). Thomas F. Willson also resigned his commission in September 1861, but subsequently received a commission as major in the Confederate States Army. CSR, 3rd Va. Cav. William A. Perkins was promoted to captain of Company G on Captain H. R. Johnson's resignation. He served until March 1862, when he resigned due to family hardship: "Wife and eight children left with no support on sudden death of my father." CSR, 3rd Va. Cav. Benjamin J. Allen, thirty-five years old at the time of his commission as a lieutenant in Company G, served until an injury to his left arm forced his retirement from military service in March 1862. CSR, 3rd Va. Cav.

7. Robert Hall Chilton (1815–1879) was a graduate of the U.S. Military Academy (1837), captain (and brevet major) of dragoons and a Mexican War veteran. He resigned as major paymaster from the U.S. Army on 29 April 1861 in order to accept a commission in the Regular Confederate Army. Ezra J. Warner, *Generals in Gray* (Baton Rouge: Louisiana State University Press, 1959), 49. Ashland is located about fifteen miles north of Richmond's 1861 city limits. At the time of the Civil War, it was known as a health and recreation resort, hence the availability of the horseracing course and stables for use by Confederate cavalry recruits. Virginia Work Projects Administration, Writers' Program, *Virginia: A Guide to the Old Dominion* (New York: Oxford University Press, 1940), 354–55.

8. The Amelia Troop was to become Company G, 1st Virginia Cavalry. Lee Wallace, *A Guide to Virginia Military Organizations: 1861–1865* (Lynchburg, Va.: H. E. Howard, Inc., 1986), 40.

9. John Thruston Thornton (1829–1862) was a lawyer from Farmville, Virginia. He led the Prince Edward Troop (Company K) until elected lieutenant colonel in April 1862. CSR, 3rd Va. Cav. Thomas Francis Goode (1825–1905) left his law practice in Boydton, Virginia, to lead the Mecklenburg Dragoons (Company A). A thirty-five-year-old, Goode was promoted to major in August 1861 and to lieutenant colonel in October 1861 and then was elected colonel in April 1862. He resigned his commission due to ill health and subsequently accepted a seat in the Virginia legislature in 1863. CSR, 3rd Va. Cav. William Henry Fitzhugh Lee (1837–1891) was the second of General Robert E. Lee's three sons. Known by his nickname, "Rooney," he attended Harvard but left school to accept a commission in the U.S. Army in 1857. He resigned two years later to engage in farming but joined the Confederate army at the outbreak of hostilities. His unit became Company E, 5th Virginia Cavalry. Warner, *Generals*

in Gray, 184; Wallace, *Guide,* 45. Charles William Field (1828–1892) was a West Point graduate (1849) from Kentucky. He resigned from the U.S. Army in April 1861 and began the war as colonel of the 6th Virginia Cavalry before attaining higher rank. Warner, *Generals in Gray,* 87.

10. Considered to be a battle of note at the time, the Battle of Big Bethel was nothing more than a skirmish between raw troops. More significant were the first losses in the first land battle of the war; Private Henry L. Wyatt of North Carolina was the only Confederate soldier to be killed in the fight, and Lieutenant John T. Grebel became the first Regular U.S. Army officer to be killed in the war. U.S. War Department, *The War of the Rebellion: A Compilation of the Official Records of the War of the Union and Confederate Armies,* 128 vols. (Washington, D.C.: Government Printing Office, 1880–1901) (hereinafter cited as *O.R.*), ser. 1, vol. 2, pp. 77–104; William C. Davis, *First Blood: Fort Sumter to Bull Run* (Alexandria, Va.: Time-Life Books, 1983), 78–84, 86.

11. "Major" Theodore Winthrop (1828–1861) was General Benjamin Butler's military secretary (his rank may well have been one of courtesy) as well as an adventurer and promising author. His literary success was, unfortunately, spurred by his dramatic death at Big Bethel, as all of his prewar novels and travel narratives appeared posthumously.

12. On Lieutenant Hood's arrival on the Peninsula to train Magruder's cavalry companies, reportedly he was rebuffed by the company captains because they ranked him. When he returned from consulting with Magruder as a freshly promoted captain, he was told that his date of rank still left him junior to all the company captains. Magruder promoted Hood to major the same day, thus breaking the impasse caused by rank and seniority. John B. Hood, *Advance and Retreat* (New Orleans: Hood Orphan Memorial Fund, 1880), 17–18.

13. The troops were 7th New York Infantry Regiment. *O.R.,* ser. 1, vol. 2, pp. 296–98.

14. James D. Isbell enlisted as a private in the Cumberland Light Dragoons in May 1861 and, following further promotion to captain, died of disease in August 1862. CSR, 3rd Va. Cav. Charles R. Palmore, a thirty-one-year-old physician, enlisted in the Cumberland Light Dragoons in May 1861. Palmore served as a trooper, officer, and surgeon, once being left behind on a raid to care for wounded soldiers of both armies. He was wounded at Mitchell's Shop, Virginia, in May 1864 and was captured at Front Royal, Virginia, in August of the same year. He was paroled from the prisoner-of-war compound at Fort Delaware in June 1865. CSR, 3rd Va. Cav.

15. Robert Johnston (1830–1902) was a graduate of the U.S. Military Academy (1850) and had served as a lieutenant in the U.S. Cavalry until nominated a captain in the Confederate army in March 1861. He received his appointment as colonel in the 3rd Virginia Cavalry on 20 June 1861, sometimes adopting the title "Commander in Chief of Cavalry, Army of the Peninsula." Robert K. Krick, *Lee's Colonels* (Dayton, Ohio: Morningside House, 1992), 212.

16. Jefferson C. Phillips (1821–1910) was a thirty-nine-year-old Hampton farmer

when he helped to organize the Old Dominion Dragoons. He was promoted to major of the regiment in October 1861 but transferred to the 12th Virginia Cavalry in July 1862 with a promotion to lieutenant colonel. CSR, 3rd Va. Cav. Telemachus Taylor (1833–1888?)was twenty-eight years old at the time of his enlistment at New Kent Court House in June 1861. Mustered in as a lieutenant, Taylor was promoted to captain in February 1862 on the death of Captain Melville Vaiden. Taylor resigned in November 1862 due to chronic dysentery. CSR, 3rd Va. Cav. Robert Douthat (1820–1894?) was a Charles City County farmer, forty years old, and the first captain of Company D, the Charles City Light Dragoons. Douthat led the company until some time in the late summer or early autumn of 1862, when he resigned in 1864 on the death of his wife. He was taken into custody for a time by Federal troops when General U.S. Grant's engineers anchored an immense pontoon bridge on the James River at Upper Weyanoke, Douthat's plantation. CSR, 3rd Va. Cav. William A. Adams was a thirty-four-year-old engineer and surveyor from Dinwiddie County. In the reorganization of the regiment in April 1862, he lost the election for the captaincy of Company I, claimed fraud, and resigned his commission. CSR, 3rd Va. Cav. Thomas Howerton Owen was a graduate of Virginia Military Institute (1856) and engaged in farming and civil engineering in Halifax County. He lost the inaugural captaincy of Company C, the Black Walnut Dragoons, to William H. Easley in a bloodless fencing match. Easley, twenty-nine years old and an 1856 V.M.I. graduate as well, subsequently died of typhoid fever in December 1861. Owen was promoted to captain vice Adams and then to lieutenant colonel in September 1862. CSR, 3rd Va. Cav.; "Stories Are Part of County's History, Heritage," news clippings, Book No. 3, Kenneth Cook Scrapbook Collection, 24 vols., South Boston, Virginia, Public Library, South Boston. William Collins, Jr., was elected the first captain of the Catawba Troop, Company H, lost his office in the elections of April 1862, and was appointed captain in March 1863. He died of typhoid fever in December 1864. CSR, 3rd Va. Cav. John Jones was a twenty-five-year-old volunteer at the enlistment of the Nottoway Troop (Company E) on 27 May 1861. He led the company for exactly four months, resigning on 26 September 1861. CSR, 3rd Va. Cav.

17. William H. Jones was a forty-one-year-old farmer from Mecklenburg County. He enlisted in Company A, Mecklenburg Dragoons, in May 1861 and was promoted from private to captain on T. F. Goode's promotion in September 1861. He resigned in October 1864 in order to recover from tonsillitis and bronchitis. CSR, 3rd Va. Cav. William R. Vaughan was a thirty-three-year-old physician from Hampton. He enlisted as a lieutenant in May 1861 and was promoted to captain, succeeding J. C. Phillips, in April 1862. He resigned two months later and was detailed in July 1862 to perform duties more befitting his training, army surgeon. CSR, 3rd Va. Cav.

CORRESPONDENCE, 1861

1. Isaetta Carter Randolph Hubard was the wife of Robert T. Hubard, Jr.'s, oldest brother, Lt. Colonel James L. Hubard.

2. According to reports, the regiment's most recent engagement had been on

12 July when the Confederate troopers captured eleven soldiers from the 7th New York Infantry.

3. Isaetta's parents were Benjamin Franklin Randolph, M.D., and Sarah Champe Carter Randolph of "Round Top," Albemarle County, Virginia. Robert Mann Randolph was Isaetta's younger brother.

4. General John Buchanan Floyd, former governor of Virginia (1848–1852) and Federal secretary of state (1857–1861), led a Confederate brigade in the western Virginia campaign of autumn 1861. Lawrence L. Hewitt, "John Buchanan Floyd," in *The Confederate General*, vol. 2, edited by William C. Davis (Harrisburg, Pa.: National Historical Society, 1991), 132–33.

5. Elijah H. Grigg was twenty-five years old at the time of enlistment in May 1865. He was captured near Williamsburg on 4 May 1862 and exchanged in August 1862. He was detailed to the Signal Corps during the summer of 1864 and signed his parole in Farmville in April 1865. CSR, 3rd Va. Cav.

6. Thomas O. Towles enlisted at Cumberland Court House in May 1861. He was twenty-one years old at the time and served as a private until detailed as a hospital clerk from March through August 1864. He signed his parole in Farmville in April 1865. CSR, 3rd Va. Cav. John Prosser Woodson enlisted in May 1861 and served until discharged on a surgeon's certificate in October 1861. CSR, 3rd Va. Cav. James Madison Blanton, Jr., was a thirty-four-year-old physician when he joined Company G in May 1861. During the war, no date given, Blanton was discharged to his home to practice medicine. He died in Buckingham County on 5 February 1900. CSR, 3rd Va. Cav. Virginius B. Jeffries, thirty years old, enlisted with Company G in May 1861 as a sergeant. He was demoted to private in July 1863 and detailed as a hospital steward in the same month. He transferred to a clerk position in Richmond from February until August 1864. Jeffries was retired to the Invalid Corps in October 1864 and signed his parole at Farmville in April 1865. CSR, 3rd Va. Cav. George H. Matthews, Jr., twenty-four years old, joined the Cumberland Light Dragoons as a private in May 1861 and became a sergeant in February 1862. CSR, 3rd Va. Cav. Although Hubard's vote counts differ somewhat from the official company records, the result was, indeed, a tie vote.

7. The four companies of Georgia cavalry were the mounted units from Cobb's Georgia Legion. According to one member of the unit, "Our first service was on the peninsular below Yorktown under the general command of Gen. J. Bankhead Magruder. In March, 1862, the Legion was ordered across the James river at old Jamestown, first to Suffolk, Va., and then to Goldsboro, N. C." Wiley C. Howard, *Sketch of Cobb Legion Cavalry and Some Incidents and Scenes Remembered* (Atlanta, Ga., 1901), 1.

8. Lelia Skipwith was probably the daughter of Humberston and Lelia (Skipwith Robertson) Skipwith, who lived at Elm Hill near Clarksville, Mecklenburg County. Kenneth M. Stampp, *Records of Ante-Bellum Southern Plantations from the Revolution through the Civil War*, series L: Selections from the Earl Gregg Swem Li-

brary, College of William and Mary, part 3: Skipwith Family Papers, 1760–1977, http://www.lexisnexis.com/academic/guides/southern_hist/plantations/plantl3.asp, 3.

9. Thomas R. R. Cobb raised a combined regiment of infantry (six hundred), cavalry (three hundred), and artillery (one hundred) in Georgia at the outbreak of hostilities. The unit remained together until April 1863, when it was broken up and the components were assigned as separate infantry and cavalry units recruited to regimental strengths and given individual unit identities. Faust, *Historical Times Illustrated,* 147.

10. Magruder was held in low regard by a number of his troops, including his ranking subordinate, General Lafayette McLaws. His excited manner, some called it irrational behavior, in times of stress eventually resulted in Magruder's transfer from Virginia to Texas. Robert K. Krick, "John Bankhead Magruder," in *The Confederate General,* vol. 4, edited by William C. Davis (Harrisburg, Pa.: National Historical Society, 1991), 140–41.

11. The British blockade runner *Bermuda,* an iron-hulled screw merchantman out of Liverpool, arrived at Savannah, Georgia, on 18 September 1861 with a large cargo of arms and ammunition. Blockade running did not begin out of New Orleans until November 1861. Stephen R. Wise, *Lifeline of the Confederacy* (Columbia: University of South Carolina Press, 1988), 50–51, 77.

12. Samuel F. Booker joined the Cumberland Troop in May 1861. He was a farmer, thirty-six years old, six feet in height, with gray hair and blue eyes. He was discharged from the service in January 1862 in order to become commissioner of revenue for Cumberland County. CSR, 3rd Va. Cav. Henry Brainerd McClellan, a Pennsylvanian by birth and cousin of Federal general George B. McClellan, graduated from Williams College in 1858 at seventeen years of age and was teaching school on the William Perkins plantation in Cumberland County, Virginia, at the outbreak of the war. He joined the ranks of the Cumberland Light Dragoons in June 1861 and was promoted to a lieutenancy as adjutant of the 3rd Virginia Cavalry in May 1862. Robert J. Trout, *They Followed the Plume* (Mechanicsburg, Pa.: Stackpole Books, 1993), 200–201.

13. Probably a minor engagement near Sewell Mountain—Greenbrier River, western Virginia, on 3 October 1861. *O.R.,* ser. 1, vol. 5, pp. 224–30.

14. Brandon and Lower Brandon are plantations in Prince George County on the west side of the James River. Both were owned by the Harrison family. Isabella Ritchie Harrison, widow of George Evelyn Harrison, presided at Brandon during the Civil War. Her daughter, Isabella ("Belle"), never married, assisting her mother with estate business until Mrs. Harrison's death in 1898. Lower Brandon was the home of William Byrd Harrison, whose three sons in the Confederate service included Captain Benjamin H. Harrison, Charles City Light Dragoons, Company D, 3rd Virginia Cavalry. Emmie Ferguson Farrar, *Old Virginia Houses* (New York: Bonanza Books, 1957), 129, 136.

15. Morton Davis Blanton was twenty-one years old at the time of his enlistment

in May 1861. Blanton was detailed to a clerkship in Richmond from August 1863 through February 1864 and was one of the few members of the 3rd Virginia Cavalry to be paroled at Appomattox Court House in April 1865. He died in Scottsburg, Virginia, on 10 November 1908. CSR, 3rd Va. Cav.

16. Benjamin W. Leigh Blanton was a May 1861 enlistee at the time of this shooting incident. He spent five months in the hospital recovering and then offered to ride for the Commissary Department in April 1862. He was carried on sick rolls until August 1864. No further records are available. CSR, 3rd Va. Cav. Thomas N. French enlisted at Ashland in June 1861 and served until discharged in August 1862 due to paralysis. CSR, 3rd Va. Cav.

17. At this early date in the war, when military clothing was still far from uniform in color and design, colored armbands and hatbands were sometimes adopted by troops to distinguish friend from foe.

18. This incident is noted briefly in *O.R.*, ser. 1, vol. 4, p. 598. Major Edward F. Bagley had served in the U.S. Army as a lieutenant of infantry from 1847 to 1848 and then again as a lieutenant of artillery from 1856 until 1861. He entered the Civil War as a major in Cobb's Legion and was, indeed, mistakenly killed by his own men near Yorktown on 12 November 1861. Krick, *Lee's Colonels*, 42. Two interesting eyewitness accounts by members of Cobb's infantry unit are noted in appendix A.

19. "The Fifth Louisiana Infantry [was] under the command of Colonel Theodore G. Hunt. This outfit was full of New Orleans gamblers and sporting men. Late in the afternoon of 23 December 1861, Lieutenant Jones of the Fifth Louisiana was writing a report as night drew near and needed more light to finish that night, so he detailed an orderly to go to a sutler to procure candles. (Henry Carter [Richmond Howitzers] recalled that the sutler's name was Mr. Forward.) Upon the orderly's return, Lt. Jones found that the candles would not burn. Upon closer examination he found that they did not have wicks. This discovery threw Lt. Jones into a rage and he sent an insulting letter to the sutler, accusing him of dishonesty. The sutler's reply was equally insulting. Lt. Jones then challenged the sutler to a duel, which was promptly accepted to everyone's amazement because sutlers were not generally thought to be fighting men. The duel took place on 24 December 1861 at Young's Farm; the weapons were Mississippi rifles at 40 paces. A bottle was placed on a support equidistant between the two participants, each aimed at the bottle, and fired upon the proper command. Both men were hit in the groin area and both died almost instantly. White recalled seeing the bodies loaded onto a steamboat for the trip up the James River to Richmond." *Richmond (Va.) Evening Journal,* 1 December 1908, as documented by Donald W. Price, www.petuniapress.com/ml/20010321.txt.

20. Judah Philip Benjamin was the Confederate secretary of war at the time of this correspondence. Benjamin had previously served as the Confederate attorney general and finished the war as secretary of state.

21. According to company records, Thomas F. Willson resigned his 2nd lieutenancy on 26 September 1861 in order to accept a promotion to major in the Confederate States Army. He may have been the unnamed officer mentioned in this passage.

Henry B. McClellan, *The Life and Campaigns of Major-General J. E. B. Stuart* (Boston: Houghton Mifflin, 1885), 454; CSR, 3rd Va. Cav.

2. "THE RAPID DECLINE OF MARTIAL SPIRIT"

1. Benjamin H. Harrison was a thirty-three-year-old farmer from Charles City County. He enlisted as a lieutenant in May 1861 and was detailed to quartermaster duties for the regiment until promoted to captain in January 1862. Captain Harrison was killed at Malvern Hill on 3 July 1862 while escorting General Magruder during the battle. CSR, 3rd Va. Cav.

2. This archaic reference is to the system of wires or strings used to operate puppets, hence political slang for one who can direct the actions of others to his own benefit.

3. Samuel E. Garrett was a twenty-six-year-old volunteer in May 1861. He was promoted from private to lieutenant in August 1862 and then was detailed in October 1863 to command the company of sharpshooters raised from among the troopers to support the mounted force. He was wounded at the battle of Haw's Shop in May 1864. CSR, 3rd Va. Cav. Peyton R. Browne enlisted in Company G at Ashland in June 1861, was brevetted lieutenant in April 1862, and was paroled at Farmville in April 1865. CSR, 3rd Va. Cav.

4. The Federal garrison at Fort Monroe and troops in the surrounding army camps were hardly driven out by the CSS *Virginia*'s successes. Riflemen from the 20th Indiana Infantry Regiment, 1st New York Mounted Rifles, and artillerymen at three rifled cannon on the Newport News beach spent the latter half of the naval battle firing at Confederate sailors and ships. Captain Franklin Buchanan, commander of the *Virginia,* was wounded in the thigh while personally returning small-arms fire with a rifled musket. William C. Davis, *Duel between the First Ironclads* (Garden City, N.Y.: Doubleday, 1975), 103.

5. The commanding officer of the USS *Cumberland* during the fight with the *Virginia* was Lieutenant George U. Morris. He survived the battle unscathed. Casualties aboard the *Cumberland* were 121 killed and 29 wounded, out of a crew of 376. The commander of the USS *Congress,* Lieutenant Joseph Smith, Jr., was, in fact, killed during the battle with the *Virginia.* Hubard was probably referring to him in this passage. Casualties on the *Congress* were 110 killed or missing and 26 wounded, out of a crew of 434. Davis, *Duel,* 99, 109; R. W. Daly, *How the Merrimac Won* (New York: Thomas Y. Crowell Co., 1957), 184.

6. The Confederate Conscription Act of 16 April 1862 predated a Federal draft act by nearly a year. It affected every male from eighteen to thirty-five years of age and, as important, extended all short-term enlistments by two years or the duration of the war, if shorter than two years. Not uncommon to citizens in the North and South was the fear of dishonor at being conscripted into an otherwise all-volunteer army, thus driving many hesitant recruits into the ranks. Nevins, *War for the Union,* 89–90.

7. Edward W. Grigg, twenty-nine, and James A Grigg, thirty-four, served to-

gether until February 1864, when Edward became ill and was sent to a military hospital. His health remained fragile throughout the spring, and he finally succumbed to typhoid fever on 5 June 1864. James survived the war and was paroled in Farmville on 25 April 1866. CSR, 3rd Va. Cav.

8. Major James M. Goggin began the war as major of the 32nd Virginia Infantry, a unit he helped to recruit and then transferred to the staff of General Lafayette McLaws to serve as McLaws's adjutant. William C. Davis, "James Monroe Goggin," in *The Confederate General*, vol. 2, edited by William C. Davis (Harrisburg, Pa.: National Historical Society, 1991), 202.

3. "OUR LITTLE PENINSULA WORLD"

1. Many Confederates, and not a few Federal troops, were armed with antique smoothbore muskets in the first year of the war. The effective range with good powder and ball in dry weather was about one hundred yards, and, as Ulysses S. Grant observed of these weapons during his Mexican War days, "At the distance of a few hundred yards, a man might fire at you all day without you finding out." Ulysses S. Grant, *Personal Memoirs of U.S. Grant* (New York: Charles L. Webster and Co., 1885), 95.

2. George B. McClellan had approximately one hundred thousand men on the Peninsula at this time, whereas John B. Magruder's command is estimated to have been, at its largest, nineteen thousand men. McClellan's general report: *O.R.*, ser. 1, vol. 11, pt. 1, pp. 5–105; Magruder's reports: ibid., 403–11; Earl C. Hastings, Jr., and David Hastings, *A Pitiless Rain: The Battle of Williamsburg* (Shippensburg, Pa.: White Mane Publishing Co., 1997), 8, 16.

3. Henry W. Halleck was not named commander-in-chief of the U.S. Army until 11 July 1862. Long, *Civil War Day by Day*, 238.

4. The role controversies faced by the Federal cavalry early in the Civil War have been documented by historians including Stephen Z. Starr in *The Union Cavalry in the Civil War* (Baton Rouge: Louisiana State University Press, 1979–1985), 1:234–41. Far less has been written about the use and abuse of the Southern troopers on the Peninsula. Confined to a swampy and overgrown theater of operations and parceled out among infantry regiments, the Virginia and Georgia cavalry units had neither the opportunities nor the topography with which J. E. B. Stuart's men were blessed early in the war.

5. Stuart arrived at Yorktown in command of a brigade consisting of the 1st and 4th Virginia Cavalry, Wise Legion, Jeff Davis Legion, and the Stuart Horse Artillery. The 3rd Virginia Cavalry was assigned to Stuart's command soon after his arrival. *O.R.*, ser. 1, vol. 12, p. 570.

6. George Thomas Anderson (1824–1901), nicknamed "Tige" or "Tiger," had been elected colonel of the 11th Georgia Infantry at the war's start. At Yorktown, still a colonel, he commanded a brigade composed of four Georgia infantry regiments (7th, 8th, 9th, and 11th) and the 1st Kentucky Infantry. Anderson was not promoted to brigadier general until November 1862. Richard J. Sommers, "George Thomas

Anderson," in *The Confederate General*, vol. 1, edited by William C. Davis (Harrisburg, Pa.: National Historical Society, 1991), 20–21. Robert M. McKinney (1835–1862) was a native of Lynchburg, Virginia and a V.M.I graduate (1856) and had served as a professor at the North Carolina Military Institute. On the outbreak of hostilities, he was elected captain of a company in the 6th North Carolina Infantry (May 1861) and then won promotion to colonel of the 15th North Carolina (June 1861), which he was leading at Yorktown. Krick, *Lee's Colonels*, 254.

7. The engagement at Dam No. 1, also called Lee's Mill or Burnt Chimneys, actually occurred a day earlier, 16 April 1862. Long, *Civil War Day by Day*, 200.

8. The attack was made by companies from the 3rd, 4th, and 6th Vermont Infantry Regiments. *O.R.*, ser. 1, vol. 12, pp. 372–73.

9. General Benjamin Huger evacuated Norfolk on 9 May 1862 only after the Confederate army at Yorktown had retreated to Richmond. Long, *Civil War Day by Day*, 209.

10. The Confederates retreated on the night of 3 May, and Federal troops entered the siege works on the morning of 4 May 1862. Long, *Civil War Day by Day*, 206–7; Faust, *Historical Times Illustrated*, 847.

11. Improvised land mines, or torpedoes, were developed and employed for the first time in the Civil War at Yorktown by General Gabriel J. Rains. Federal commanders were outraged at this breach of military ethics, and several of Rains's peers in the Confederate service, including General James Longstreet, joined in the criticism of the unorthodox antipersonnel tactics. Warner, *Generals in Gray*, pp. 249–50; *O.R.*, ser. 1, vol. 11, pt. 1, pp. 349–50.

12. Colonel James Lucius Davis commanded the Wise Legion, designated later in May 1862 as the 10th Virginia Cavalry. Wallace, *Guide*, 51–52.

13. The road to Grove Wharf traced across the Peninsula to the James River shore. The Yorktown-Williamsburg Road ran more or less up the middle of the Peninsula.

14. Colonel Thomas F. Goode and a portion of the 3rd Virginia Cavalry were assigned flank duty as Stuart withdrew his cavalry column toward Williamsburg via Grove Wharf. Goode's command ran head-on into Colonel William W. Averell's 3rd Pennsylvania Cavalry on a wooded lane. The confused skirmish resulted in four Confederates wounded and approximately eight Federal casualties. The 3rd Virginia Cavalry also claimed a captured enemy flag, among the first of the Peninsular Campaign. *O.R.*, ser. 1, vol. 11, pt. 1, pp. 435, 445; McClellan, *Life and Campaigns*, 49.

15. William Richard Carter enlisted in Company E at Nottoway Court House on 27 May 1861 as a private. The twenty-seven-year-old lawyer owned the dubious distinction of becoming one of the earliest prisoners of war when he was captured at his vidette post near Big Bethel on 10 June 1861. He was exchanged at the request of General Magruder and on the order of General Benjamin Butler. Carter was promoted to captain in January 1862, to major in September 1862, and to lieutenant colonel in November 1862. He was seriously wounded on the first day's fight at Trevilian Station (11 June 1864) and died at Gordonsville on 8 July 1864. He was bur-

ied in Nottoway County. CSR, 3rd Va. Cav. Lieutenant George D. White enlisted as a sergeant in the Mecklenburg Troop (Company A) on 14 May 1861. He was promoted to lieutenant in the 25 April 1862 regimental elections and to captain on 21 October 1862. He was wounded in the foot at Gettysburg on 3 July 1863. White retired to the Invalid Corps on 9 June 1864. CSR, 3rd Va. Cav.

16. Stuart's captain of horse artillery was the West Point–trained Alabamian John Pelham.

17. Colonels Lee and Chambliss were evidently referring to Fitz Lee (1st Virginia Cavalry) and John Chambliss (13th Virginia Cavalry). Chambliss was not promoted to that position until July 1862, however, and the 13th Virginia was not yet part of Stuart's command. Arthur W. Bergeron, Jr., "John Randolph Chambliss, Jr.," in *The Confederate General,* vol. 1, edited by William C. Davis (Harrisburg, Pa.: National Historical Society, 1991), 172.

18. Joseph Hooker led the 2nd Division of the III Corps, which was commanded by Samuel P. Heintzelman. Although Hooker's troops did not arrive until the close of fighting on 4 May, Hubard's phrasing may have been meant to indicate that Hooker's aggressive tactics at Williamsburg on 5 May drew the rest of Heintzelman's III Corps into the fight. *O.R.,* ser. 1, vol. 11, pt. 1, pp. 464–70. Near Williamsburg, Colonel Williams C. Wickham led the 4th Virginia Cavalry in a charge that captured two Federal wagons and a howitzer battery. A sabre charge by the 6th U.S. Cavalry stopped the Virginians. Wickham was wounded by a sabre thrust in the side, and the 4th Virginia lost a battle flag. While wounded, Wickham was taken prisoner at his home in Hanover County during McClellan's advance. He was exchanged by special cartel for his wife's kinsman, Lieutenant Colonel Thomas L. Kane of the Pennsylvania Bucktails. Kenneth L. Stiles, *4th Virginia Cavalry* (Lynchburg, Va.: H. E. Howard, Inc., 1985), 10; *O.R.,* ser. 1, vol. 11, pt. 1, pp. 443, 445; Jedediah Hotchkiss, *Virginia,* vol. 3, pt. 2, *Confederate Military History,* edited by Clement Anselm Evans (Atlanta: Confederate Publishing Co., 1899), 686.

19. The sun probably did not shine much at the battle of Williamsburg because it rained in torrents throughout the fight. *O.R.,* ser. 1, vol. 11, pt. 1, 457–59; Hastings and Hastings, *Pitiless Rain,* 63.

20. Robert Thomas Page (1808–1886) was, at fifty-three years of age, one of the elders the 3rd Virginia Cavalry. He served as a courier for General James Longstreet during the spring of 1862, returned to regular duty after the Peninsular Campaign, and was promoted to corporal in July 1862. He fought in the major campaigns of the war and was promoted to sergeant in July 1864 and then to lieutenant in December 1864. He was paroled at Farmville, Virginia, in April 1865. CSR, 3rd Va. Cav.

21. Although there were actually five Confederate regiments involved in the action against Hancock's Federal brigade, the regiments to which Hubard refers in this passage were the 24th Virginia and the 5th North Carolina infantry regiments, which lost 190 of 500 men and 252 of 460 men, respectively, in the half-hour action. *O.R.,* ser. 1, vol. 11, pt. 1, pp. 606–11; Hastings and Hastings, *Pitiless Rain,* 111–12.

22. Losses at Williamsburg among the estimated 12,000 Federal troops as re-

ported by General McClellan were 2,239: 456 killed, 1,410 wounded and 373 missing. Confederate casualties from among about 9,000 participants totaled 1,503. Hastings and Hastings, *Pitiless Rain*, 117; *O.R.*, ser. 1, vol. 11, pt. 1, pp. 450, 569.

4. "THE ENEMY WERE WORSTED"

1. There is no evident explanation for Hubard's reference to this date. The evacuation of Williamsburg was completed on 6 May, and the Confederate army arrived at Richmond on 9 May 1862.

2. The fight at Eltham's Landing, Virginia, was also known as Barhamsville or West Point and occurred on 7 May 1862. A Federal division under William B. Franklin that had landed from river transports was blocked and forced to retreat by Confederates of William H. C. Whiting's division. *O.R.*, ser. 1, vol. 11, pt. 1, pp. 613–33; Faust, *Historical Times Illustrated*, 241–42.

3. The skirmish at Slatersville on 9 May 1862 involved the 1st Virginia Cavalry contesting the advance of a mixed force of Federal troops including squadrons of the 6th U.S. Cavalry, the 2nd Rhode Island, and 98th Pennsylvania infantry regiments and Battery L, 2nd U.S. Artillery. Casualties totaled three killed and six wounded among the Virginians and four killed and three wounded among the Federals. Robert J. Driver, *First Virginia Cavalry* (Lynchburg, Va.: H. E. Howard, Inc., 1991), 34; *O.R.*, ser. 1, vol. 11, pt. 2, pp. 246–47.

4. Compared to recent scholarly works, Hubard's estimates are a little inflated for both armies. According to one analysis of the Richmond front in May 1862, Johnston had fifty thousand men fit for duty and was able to count on Huger's Norfolk garrison for twelve thousand additional troops. McClellan's Army of the Potomac, minus casualties and detachments, probably numbered just over one hundred thousand. Steven H. Newton, *Joseph E. Johnston and the Defense of Richmond* (Lawrence: University Press of Kansas, 1998), 151.

5. There was, indeed, a terrible thunderstorm and downpour the night before the Battle of Seven Pines. In one Confederate camp, four soldiers were killed by a lightning strike. Huger's other difficulty, tactfully glossed over by Hubard, was the fact that Huger and his entire division had marched into position at 3 a.m. and overslept on the morning of 31 May. In addition, Huger learned that a battle was to be fought that morning only after an argument over troop movements with General James Longstreet. Stephen W. Sears, *To the Gates of Richmond: The Peninsula Campaign* (New York: Ticknor and Fields, 1992), 120, 123.

6. John B. Magruder did not participate in the Battle of Seven Pines. According to his biographer, he was either sick or otherwise indisposed during the two-day battle. Neither did his troops contribute any significant support to the Confederate left wing during the battle. Paul D. Casdorph, *Prince John Magruder: His Life and Campaigns* (New York: John Wiley and Sons, 1996), 161.

7. Confederate casualties amounted to 6,134, and Federal losses numbered 5,031. Each army fielded approximately forty-two thousand troops. Long, *Civil War Day by Day*, 220.

8. Stuart's cavalry command when he was promoted to major general on 25 July 1862 consisted of Wade Hampton's Brigade (1st North Carolina, Cobb's Legion, Jeff Davis Legion, Hampton's Legion, and 10th Virginia) and Fitz Lee's Brigade (1st, 3rd, 4th, 5th, and 9th Virginia regiments). McClellan, *Life and Campaigns*, 86.

9. Crump's Crossroads was also known as Baltimore Cross Roads and is now called Quinton.

10. Hubard's opinion of Stuart's famous circuit around McClellan's army in June 1862 runs contrary to most but raises an interesting question about Stuart's daring ride: was it a military necessity? According to Stuart's adjutant and biographer H. B. McClellan, Stuart's purpose for the expedition was, in fact, accomplished when he reached Old Church, approximately twenty miles from the Winston farm where the day's ride began. Yet a return to Confederate lines by the same road held the chance of confronting a Federal roadblock and the possibility of capture. Hence, Stuart decided to do the unexpected, to complete the ride of nearly one hundred miles around the Army of the Potomac. Stuart biographer John Thomason took a more critical view, suggesting that Stuart could have found a route back the way he had come if he had made an effort but yielded to the spirit of adventure. Furthermore, Thomason raised the possibility that Stuart's ride may have caused McClellan to fear for his lines of communication and supply, thus hastening the Federal commander's "change of base" to the James River in time to save his army during the Seven Days' battles. Stuart's report: *O.R.*, ser. 1, vol. 11, pt. 1, pp. 1036–40; McClellan, *Life and Campaigns*, 57–58; John W. Thomason, Jr., *Jeb Stuart* (New York: Charles Scribner's Sons, 1930), 153–55.

11. Cary A. Allen had enlisted the previous December at Yorktown. He continued in the service of the 3rd Virginia Cavalry until September 1863, when he was detailed as a conscript agent. He returned to the regiment in August 1864 and was paroled by Federal forces in April 1865. CSR, 3rd Va. Cav.

12. The battle to which Hubard refers here is probably Glendale or White Oak Swamp, fought on 30 June. Not only were Huger and Magruder found wanting on the day but also Jackson was so exhausted from the exertions of his spring campaign in the Shenandoah Valley and at Richmond that he was overcome by exhaustion and fell asleep in the middle of the day. Sears, *To the Gates of Richmond*, 288–89.

13. Stories of Magruder's drinking were not uncommon. A recent Magruder biographer, however, cites one source that holds Magruder may have been suffering from medication containing morphine. Casdorph, *Prince John Magruder*, 156, 181–82.

14. General Charles S. Winder had been selected by General Thomas J. Jackson to lead the "Stonewall" Brigade on Jackson's promotion. Winder was mortally wounded by an artillery shell at Cedar Mountain. Faust, *Historical Times Illustrated*, 835–36.

15. The battle Hubard described here is Cedar Mountain, fought on 9 August 1862 between Jackson's force of twenty-two thousand Confederates and Banks's Federal II Corps of twelve thousand men. Robert K. Krick, "Cedar Mountain," in *The Civil War Battlefield Guide*, 2nd ed., edited by Frances H. Kennedy (Boston: Houghton Mifflin Co. 1998), 105–7.

16. Longstreet's promotion to lieutenant general was dated 9 October 1862, and Jackson's was dated a day later, 10 October. Warner, *Generals in Gray*, 152, 192.

17. Stuart's command attacked and captured Federal general John Pope's supply depot at Catlett's Station on the night of 22 August 1862. Because Pope's cavalry had earlier in the month captured some of Stuart's personal effects, most notably his hat, Stuart's capture of Pope's uniform, dispatch book, and other personal baggage more than evened the score. McClellan, *Life and Campaigns*, 94–95; Stuart's report: *O.R.*, ser. 1, vol. 12, pt. 2, pp. 729–33.

18. Pope actually led a separate command called the Army of Virginia. Elements of McClellan's Army of the Potomac returning from the James River were directed to cooperate with Pope. McClellan's efforts at supporting Pope are generally acknowledged to have been halfhearted at best. Long, *Civil War Day by Day*, 257.

19. Federal casualties at 2nd Manassas amounted to sixteen thousand out of sixty thousand engaged, and Confederate losses totaled ninety-two hundred out of fifty thousand engaged. Faust, *Historical Times Illustrated*, 93.

20. During the 2nd Manassas campaign, Jackson's three divisions were led by W. B. Taliaferro, A. P. Hill, and A. R. Lawton, who replaced the wounded Richard S. Ewell after the battle of Groveton on 28 August 1862. Longstreet's five divisions were led by R. H. Anderson, D. R. Jones, C. M. Wilcox, J. B. Hood, and J. L. Kemper. John J. Hennessy, *Return to Bull Run* (New York: Simon and Schuster, 1993), 561–66.

21. In addition to the earlier noted Confederate conscription act of 1862, the Confederate Furlough and Bounty Act of 1861 allowed individual soldiers to transfer to other branches of service and allowed all southern regiments to hold elections to retain or replace officers of all ranks. According to one Confederate officer, "The majority re-enlisted but often in new commands; some did not re-enlist at all, others did much later. Many of the regiments reorganized with new officers. The general effect was to break up very much the organization of the army." Freeman, *Lee's Lieutenants*, 1:172; John Cheves Haskell, *The Haskell Memoirs*, edited by G. E. Govan and J. W. Livingood (New York: G. P. Putnam's Sons, 1960), 28, 141.

22. All of the following information is from CSR, 3rd Va. Cav.; names are italicized to enhance ease of reading. *John A. Palmer* was a twenty-seven-year-old Halifax County farmer on enlistment as a private in May 1861. He was promoted to sergeant major and detailed to regimental quartermaster duties in July 1861. He was promoted to acting assistant quartermaster in August 1861 and to assistant quartermaster in June 1862. In September 1863 Palmer was detailed to brigade quartermaster duties. He was present in February 1865, but no further records exist after that date. *Leroy Marion Wilson* enlisted in Company A in Mecklenburg County on 20 August 1861. He was immediately detailed as a company clerk until March 1862. Wilson was promoted to assistant commissary sergeant in June 1862. He was present for duty in January 1865, but no further records exist for his service. *John Randolph Leigh* enlisted with Company A (Mecklenburg Dragoons) in May 1862 as a surgeon. He was promoted to brigade surgeon in May 1864. Leigh signed his parole on 13 May 1865. *Alexander T. Bell* enlisted as an assistant surgeon (no date of enlistment noted

in his records) and served with the regiment until July 1863, when he transferred to Moorman's Battery, Horse Artillery. He died 24 February 1913 in the Confederate Home in Pikesville, Maryland, and was buried in the Episcopal Cemetery in Norfolk, Virginia. *John McClelland* enlisted as a chaplain in September 1862. He resigned in June 1863 both because of ill health and because of the need to support his family. *Tyree Goode Finch* enlisted in Mecklenburg County in May 1861 as a private. He was promoted to quartermaster sergeant in January 1862. Finch was last reported present for duty in August 1864. He died in 1886. *James T. Harriss* enlisted in Company A (Mecklenburg) in July 1861 as a private. He was promoted to corporal in October 1861 and to commissary sergeant in January 1862. He was detailed to horse procurement duty for the Horse Artillery in February 1863. He was last reported present for duty in August 1864. *John James Crowder* was a twenty-three-year-old private in Company A at the time of his enlistment in May 1861. He was subsequently promoted to orderly sergeant. He was last listed as present for duty in August 1864. Crowder died on 14 May 1914 and was buried in Bluestone Baptist Cemetery, Chase City, Virginia. *Robert F. Sturtivant* enlisted in Company A at Ashland on 27 May 1861 as a lieutenant. He was detailed as an adjutant at the request of Thomas F. Goode. He resigned on 11 September 1862. Sturtivant is buried in the Boydton Presbyterian Cemetery. *William Townes Boyd* was one of seven Boyds from Boydton enlisted in Company A. The twenty-three-year-old enlisted on 14 May 1861 as a private but was elected to a lieutenancy in July 1861. Boyd was wounded at Gettysburg on 3 July 1863. He was promoted to captain in June 1864. Few of his records exist after that date. Boyd survived the war and died in Covington, Tennessee, on 8 August 1916. *Jesse Simkins Jones* enlisted with Company B on the Peninsula on 29 June 1861. He was elected lieutenant in April 1862 and was promoted to captain on 2 July 1862. Jones remained a captain throughout the war but led the regiment in the absence of ranking officers on several occasions. There is no record of his parole date or location. Jones died on 24 January 1929 and was buried in St. John's Cemetery in Hampton, Virginia. *John Wray* was thirty-one years old when he enlisted as a sergeant in Company B at Hampton in May 1861. He was a promoted to lieutenant in August 1861. Wray was captured on 1 October 1863 and was sent to prison at Johnson's Island near Sandusky, Ohio. He was paroled on 12 June 1865. Wray died in 1904 and was buried in St. John's Cemetery, Hampton, Virginia. *Nathaniel Randolph Gammel,* born in July 1823, enlisted in Company B in September 1861 as a private. Gammel was promoted to lieutenant in October 1862 but resigned a month later due to a kidney infection. Resignation notwithstanding, Gammel was captured by Federal troops in Isle of Wight County on 14 August 1864 and spent the remainder of the war at Point Lookout Prison in Maryland. He was paroled in 1865. Gammel died on 25 July 1900 and was buried in St. John's Cemetery in Hampton, Virginia. *William T. Smith* was a twenty-seven-year-old farmer who enlisted in Company B at Hampton on 14 May 1861. Smith began his military career as a sergeant and was promoted to lieutenant in December 1862. Smith was wounded at Aldie on 17 June 1863. He survived the war and signed a parole on 24 April 1865 in Richmond. *John A. Chappell* enlisted in Company C at Black Walnut, Halifax County, on 20 May 1861 as a lieutenant. He was promoted to captain in October 1862 and led his company until mortally wounded in the left thigh at Winchester on 19 September 1864. Chappell died on 24 September and was buried in Oak Ridge Cemetery in South Boston, Virginia. *James William Hall* was a twenty-four-year-old teacher from Halifax County. He enlisted on 20 May 1861 at Black Walnut as a lieutenant. He was wounded in the left arm at Kelly's Ford on 17 March 1863. Hall was disabled by the wound, but no further records exist until he was paroled in May 1865. *Samuel H. Ragland* was a thirty-two-year-old farmer who enlisted in Company C on 20 May 1862 as a sergeant. He was wounded in the hand at Boonsboro, Maryland, and was promoted to lieutenant in October 1862. Ragland resigned in April 1863 due to his wound. *Franklin Guy* enlisted in Company D at Charles City Court House on 18 May 1861 as a thirty-year-old private. He was promoted to lieutenant in February 1862 and to captain in July 1862. He fought in the 3rd Virginia Cavalry until retiring on 30 April 1864 due to chronic diarrhea and dyspepsia. *John Lamb* was a twenty-year-old Charles City County farmer when he enlisted in Company D on 18 May 1861. He was captured near Charlestown, western Virginia, on 29 September 1862 but was exchanged within ten days. Lamb was promoted to lieutenant in September 1863 and to captain at the end of April 1864. He was wounded in the left thigh at Haw's Shop on 28 May 1864. Lamb survived the war and died in Richmond on 21 November 1924. *Bernard Hill Carter, Jr.,* of the Shirley plantation in Charles City County was related to Robert E. Lee, whose mother, the former Ann Hill Carter, was born and raised at Shirley. Carter, a twenty-five-year-old farmer, enlisted in Company D on 18 May 1861 as a private. He was promoted to corporal in January 1862 and to lieutenant later that spring. He was wounded and captured at Boonsboro, Maryland, on 15 September 1862. Carter was paroled and then exchanged on 3 October and 2 November 1862, respectively. He was killed in action at Chancellorsville on 1 May 1863. *William Hill Harwood, Jr.,* left his constable position in Charles City County to enlist as a corporal on 18 May 1861. The twenty-six-year-old was promoted to sergeant in July 1861 and to second lieutenant in August 1862. He was promoted to first lieutenant in May 1863 after B. H. Carter's death. Harwood was killed by artillery two days before the end of hostilities on 7 April 1865 near Farmville, Virginia. *John K. Jones,* twenty-four years old, enlisted in Company E at Warwick Court House on 26 November 1861 as a private. He was elected to be a lieutenant in the April 1862 reorganization of the army and was promoted to captain in October 1862. Jones was captured at Aldie and was held as a prisoner of war at Johnson's Island in August–September 1863. He was exchanged on 4 October 1864 in very ill health with typhoid fever, diarrhea, and rheumatism. Jones was paroled in May 1865. *Alexander Baxter Jones* was a twenty-one-year-old farmer-turned corporal on his enlistment in Nottoway County on 27 May 1861. He was promoted to third lieutenant in April 1862, to second lieutenant in July 1862 and to first lieutenant in October 1862. Jones served for the remainder of the war and was paroled on 6 May 1865. *Patrick Henry Fitzgerald* enlisted at Nottoway Court House on 27 May 1861 as a twenty-three-year-old private. He was promoted to sergeant in April 1862 and to lieutenant in October 1863. Fitzgerald was captured at Raccoon Ford on 11 October 1863 and was a prisoner of war at Johnson's Island (November 1863–April 1864) and at Point Lookout (April 1864–August 1864) and was exchanged at Fort Delaware on 30 September 1864 due to illness. He was paroled on 15 April 1865. *William Edmund Clopton* was an elder of Company F (New Kent) as a forty-one-year-old third lieutenant in May 1861. He was promoted to second lieutenant in September 1861 and to first lieutenant on 6 February 1862, but ill health and morale problems forced Clopton to resign on 24 October 1862. Clopton was captured on 1 July 1863 near White House, New Kent County, although Federal officers noted his proof of resignation from Confederate service. He was a prisoner at Fort Delaware and Johnson's Island from 18 July 1863 until 9 February 1864. Clopton was exchanged at Point Lookout on 27 April 1864. He was drafted and reenrolled in the 3rd Virginia Cavalry on 6 June 1864 as a private. *James Christian* enlisted in the New Kent Light Dragoons as a private on 28 June 1861. The twenty-two-year-old trooper was promoted to sergeant in November 1861 and was elected lieutenant in April 1862. He was killed in action at Boonsboro, Maryland, on 15 September 1862. *Jones R. Christian* was described in his June 1861 enlistment papers as twenty-six years of age, five feet eleven inches in height, with dark hair, dark eyes, and a dark complexion. He began his service as a private but was elected to a lieutenancy in April 1862. He was mentioned in General J. E. B. Stuart's Peninsula circuit report as a scout. Christian was promoted to captain in November 1862. He was captured near Spotsylvania Court House on 8 May 1864 and was sent to Fort Delaware from May until August 1864. He was transferred to Hilton Head, South Carolina, from August through October 1864, as one of the "Immortal Six Hundred" (see J. Ogden Murray's book by the same title). Christian was paroled on 16 June 1865 from Fort Delaware. He died in Richmond on 20 May 1895 and was buried in Hollywood Cemetery. *Henry Carrington* enlisted in the Catawba Troop on 25 May 1861 as a lieutenant. Carrington, a twenty-five-year-old farmer, was elected to captain in April 1862 and was promoted to major in October 1862. He was captured at Aldie on 17 June 1863 and spent a portion of his prison time (February–March 1864) at Johnson's Island before being exchanged from Pt. Lookout on 18 March 1864. Carrington rejoined the 3rd Virginia Cavalry in time for the spring campaign of 1864 and resigned his position on 4 February 1865. He died on 11 February 1893 at Hampden-Sydney, Virginia. *Isaac J. Tynes* enlisted in the Catawba Troop on 25 May 1861 as a private. Tynes, a twenty-six-year-old farmer, was promoted to lieutenant in July 1862. Tynes resigned his commission on 14 January 1863 and returned to the ranks. He transferred to the 50th Virginia Infantry in March 1863. Tynes died in Arkansas sometime after 1894. *James V. Garner* enlisted as a sergeant at Barksdale's Store on 25 May 1861. On 25 April 1862, the twenty-five-year-old was elected to a lieutenancy in which capacity he was serving when he was wounded at Kelly's Ford, 17 March 1863. Garner believed that a promotion was due him and resigned on 10 June 1863 when one was not forthcoming. *Joel Hubbard, Jr.,* was a twenty-eight-year-old farmer when he enlisted on 25 May 1861 as a private. Hubbard was promoted to lieutenant to replace James V.

Garner on 10 June 1863. No further records exist for Hubbard's service. *William Meade Feild* left his farm to enlist as a lieutenant on 29 May 1861. The twenty-four-year-old was elected captain of Company I on 25 April 1862. Feild was wounded in the buttock at Haw's Shop on 28 May 1864 but returned to duty in time to serve in the Shenandoah Valley campaign, where he had a horse killed at Tom's Brook on 9 October 1864. He was promoted to lieutenant colonel to rank from 4 February 1865. *Edmund O. Fitzgerald,* twenty-nine years old, enlisted at Dinwiddie Court House on 29 May 1861, leaving a law practice to become a lieutenant in Company I. Fitzgerald served as a recruiting officer from January through March 1862. In March 1864 he was made regimental commissary officer, but in May 1864 Fitzgerald was placed under arrest; no reasons were listed in his records. He received his parole on 18 April 1865. Fitzgerald died on 14 April 1905 and was buried in Nottoway County. *William H. Rogerson* enlisted in Company I on 5 July 1861 as a thirty-eight-year-old private. He was elected to a lieutenancy in April 1862 but was sent to a military hospital in August 1862, suffering from paralysis. Rogerson applied for a less-strenuous position but finally resigned his commission and left the service on 14 January 1863. *Berryman J. Hill* enlisted as a sergeant in the Dinwiddie Troop on 29 May 1861. The twenty-eight-year-old was detailed as commissioner of revenue in Dinwiddie County in January 1862. Hill was promoted to junior lieutenant in the April 1862 elections and to a second lieutenant grade in January 1863. He was detailed to duty as an assistant provost marshal in the cavalry division in September 1863. Hill was killed in action at Trevilian Station on 12 June 1864. *Peyton R. Berkeley* enlisted as a lieutenant at Prince Edward Court House on 24 June 1861. At fifty-seven years of age, Berkeley was an old man in a young men's war. He was promoted to captain in company elections on 26 April 1862 but resigned his commission on 1 November 1862 due to ill health. *Richard Henry Watkins* enlisted in Company K as a thirty-six-year-old private. He was detailed to the Commissary Department during July and August 1861. Watkins was elected to a lieutenancy in April 1862 and was promoted to captain of the company in October 1862, succeeding Captain Berkeley. Wounded by a sabre blow to the head at Mountsville in November 1862, Watkins recovered and led the Prince Edward Dragoons at Kelly's Ford. He was wounded in the left hand at Tom's Brook on 9 October 1864 and spent five months in the hospital. Watkins retired from the service in March 1865 and signed a parole at Danville, Virginia, on 12 May 1865. He died in 1905 and was buried in Westview Cemetery, Farmville, Virginia. *James Bell* enlisted on 24 June 1861 as a private. He was elected to second lieutenant in April 1862 but resigned his commission on 20 October 1862 because of rheumatism. *John Hughes Knight* was thirty-one years old when he enlisted at Prince Edward Court House on 24 June 1861 as a sergeant. He was elected to a junior second lieutenancy in April 1862 and was promoted to second lieutenant in October 1862 when James Bell resigned. Knight spent nearly half of 1863 in the hospital, including five months due to general debility (October 1862–February 1863) and three more months with fever (June–August 1863). He was wounded in the thigh at Stony Creek (Ream's Station) on 28 June 1864 but was able to serve in the Shenandoah Valley campaign.

Knight was promoted to captain on Richard Watkins's resignation in March 1865 and was paroled with the Army of Northern Virginia at Appomattox Court House on 9 April 1865. He was buried in Westview Cemetery, Farmville, Virginia.

5. "A LITTLE STREAM OF LIMESTONE WATER"

1. Many authorities believed that Lee actually promoted the Maryland campaign with the hope that a move north into the border state would attract recruits to the Confederate army from among sympathetic Marylanders and would allow his army to resupply from Maryland's bountiful farms. Lee also hoped that a successful campaign might influence the Federal government, Northern voters in the 1862 congressional elections, and European governments. Emory M. Thomas, *Robert E. Lee: A Biography* (New York: W. W. Norton, 1995), 256; Douglas S. Freeman, *R. E. Lee: A Biography* (New York: Charles Scribner's Sons, 1935), 2:350–53.

2. Estimates of Lee's losses during the early days of the Maryland campaign as the result of illness, lack of shoes, straggling, and desertion run as high as ten thousand troops. According to one modern campaign history, Lee's troop strength on 3 September 1862, counting the addition of two divisions and two brigades sent from Richmond after the 2nd Manassas fight, was approximately fifty thousand men. Consequently, most sources place Confederate numbers in the range of forty thousand men at Sharpsburg on 17 September 1862. Stephen W. Sears, *Landscape Turned Red* (New Haven, Conn.: Ticknor and Fields, 1983), 69.

3. Jackson's investment and capture of Harper's Ferry occurred on 13–15 September 1862. The cavalry escape on the night of 14 September resulted in thirteen hundred Federal troopers avoiding capture the next day. The Federal cavalry also captured a Confederate reserve ammunition train and six hundred escort troops. Julius White, "The Surrender of Harper's Ferry," in *Battles and Leaders of the Civil War*, vol. 2, edited by Robert U. Johnson and Clarence C. Buel (New York: Century Co., 1887), 613; *O.R.*, ser. 1, vol. 19, pt. 1, p. 142.

4. Samuel Garland, Jr., was a highly regarded officer who led a brigade in Daniel H. Hill's division. He was mortally wounded on 14 September 1862 while supporting his troops at Fox's Gap on South Mountain. Faust, *Historical Times Illustrated*, 299.

5. Hubard's secondhand version of the confusion and chaos in the streets of Boonsboro does not do full justice to the scene. According to a participant, "A general stampede followed, our whole force rushing from the town down the pike at full gallop. . . . In the middle of the turnpike, were piles of broken stone, placed there for repairing the roadway. On these, amidst the impenetrable dust, many horses blindly rushed, and falling, piled with their riders one on another. Here and there, blinded by the dust, horses and horsemen dashed against telegraph posts and fell to the ground, to be trampled by others behind." G. W. Beale, *A Lieutenant of Cavalry in Lee's Army* (Boston: Gorham Press, 1918), 45–46.

6. Southside Virginia, much like the Tidewater, Piedmont, and Shenandoah Valley, is a region of the Old Dominion. According to one authority, it is roughly defined as all counties south of the James River to North Carolina. The eastern border of

Southside is considered the region around Petersburg. The western extent of the region is defined by a line from Lynchburg south to Danville near the North Carolina border. Landon C. Bell, *Sunlight on the Southside* (Philadelphia, Pa.: George S. Ferguson Co., 1931), 9–12.

7. Edward N. Price enlisted in Company K on 24 June 1861 as a sergeant. He was detailed to serve as an orderly at cavalry headquarters from July 1863 through July 1864. Price developed a fistula on his buttocks and spent at least five months in the hospital—from July to December 1864. There are no further records of Price's service. CSR, 3rd Va. Cav.

8. Beale notes that Fitz Lee's brigade was actually retreating from an exposed position to which it had been led after dark on 16 September "through the mistake of a blundering guide" when Federal artillery spotted the cavalry column, opened on it, and Thornton was struck. According to General Stuart's after-action report, "About this time, Lieut. Col. John T. Thornton, of the Third Virginia Cavalry, was mortally wounded at the head of his regiment. To the service he was a brave and devoted member. In him one of the brightest ornaments of the State has fallen." As well, on 7 April 1865, during his retreat from Petersburg, General Robert E. Lee stopped at Thornton's home in Farmville, Virginia, to express his condolences to Thornton's widow. Beale, *Lieutenant of Cavalry,* 48; O.R., ser. 1, vol. 19, pt. 1, pp. 819–20; Freeman, *R. E. Lee,* 3:95.

9. Longstreet and his staff did, late in the battle, serve a cannon belonging to the Washington Artillery of New Orleans. G. Moxley Sorrel, *Recollections of a Confederate Staff Officer* (New York: Neale Publishing Co., 1905), 112.

10. Federal losses at Antietam amounted to 12,401 men killed, wounded, and missing out of 75,000 engaged in the battle. Confederate casualties were calculated to have been 10,318. Sears, *Landscape Turned Red,* 296.

11. Federal cavalry under Alfred Pleasanton temporarily occupied Martinsburg on 1 October 1862, when they surprised pickets of Stuart's Confederate cavalry and drove them from the town. Stuart's men rallied and reoccupied the town as Pleasanton retreated across the Potomac River. McClellan, *Life and Campaigns,* 135; O.R., ser. 1, vol. 19, pt. 2, pp. 10–14.

12. Stuart's Chambersburg Raid, ordered as a reconnaissance by General R. E. Lee on 8 October 1862, was his second ride around the Federal army. Hubard's critical summary is misleading in that Stuart's charge was multifaceted: to gather information about the Federal army; to destroy bridges in Pennsylvania; to capture government officials in Pennsylvania, if possible; and, finally, to bring back horses to replenish artillery, wagon train, and cavalry needs. McClellan, *Life and Campaigns,* 55. See also Lieutenant Colonel William R. Carter's diary entry regarding his view of the raid in appendix B.

13. The Bower is located about eight miles from Martinsburg, West Virginia, and was the home of Mr. and Mrs. A. Stephen Dandridge and "a house full of daughters and nieces, all grown and attractive—some very handsome." Blackford, *War Years,* 154.

14. General William E. Jones, known as "Grumble," started the war as a captain in the 1st Virginia Cavalry and replaced Jeb Stuart as colonel of the same regiment. After being voted out of office by his command, Jones was appointed colonel of the 7th Virginia Cavalry. In the autumn of 1862 he was given command of a brigade of cavalry posted to the Shenandoah Valley district, where he saw most of his service until his death at Piedmont, Virginia, on 5 June 1864. Warner, *Generals in Gray*, 167.

15. In a review of probably the same action, G. W. Beale credits his 9th Virginia Cavalry with leading the charge while being supported by the 3rd Virginia Cavalry. Beale, *Lieutenant of Cavalry*, 52–54.

16. Combat strengths of the contending forces during the November 1862 cavalry fights near Union, Upperville, and Barbee's Crossroads are difficult to determine. On the basis of H. B. McClellan's memoirs and Federal reports in the *Official Records*, however, it appears that Stuart's numbers were approximately two thousand cavalry, five hundred supporting infantry under General Carnot Posey, and one battery of horse artillery under Major John Pelham. Federal forces numbered approximately five thousand: three thousand cavalry under Pleasanton and General William Averell, one thousand troopers nominally engaged under General George D. Bayard, nine hundred infantry under Lieutenant Colonel J. William Hofman, and three batteries of artillery. McClellan, *Life and Campaigns*, 169–86; O.R., ser. 1, vol. 19, pt. 2, pp. 103, 125–29, 131–33.

17. Captain George B. Jones, Company B, resigned on 10 October 1862. CSR, 3rd Va. Cav.

6. "STUART SET OUT ON A RAID"

1. John B. Hood did not succeed Samuel Garland. Hood was already in command of a division during the Sharpsburg campaign while Garland was leading a brigade in D. H. Hill's division.

2. Federal engineers began laying pontoon bridges across the Rappahannock River on the morning of 11 December despite harassing musket fire from Barksdale's Confederate troops. An amphibious assault by four Federal infantry regiments forced Barksdale's troops to withdraw from the riverfront. The bridges were completed later the same day. O.R., ser. 1, vol. 21, pp. 282–84, 578–79.

3. Federal losses are estimated to have numbered 12,653 out of approximately 114,000 troops. Confederate casualties amounted to 5,309 from the 72,500 engaged. Long, *Civil War Day by Day*, 296.

4. Pelham, promoted to a majority after 2nd Manassas, took only two guns into battle at Fredericksburg and lost one to counterbattery fire within moments of his arrival on the field. Displaying great skill and valor on the occasion, he directed his return fire only on attacking Federal infantry columns. Long, *Civil War Day by Day*, 546–47; Faust, *Historical Times Illustrated*, 568.

5. The dates of the Dumfries Raid were actually 26–31 December 1862, and troops from Fitz Lee's Brigade as well as Hampton's and W. H. F. Lee's brigades numbered about twenty-four hundred. O.R., ser. 1, vol. 21, pp. 731–35; McClellan, *Life and*

Campaigns, 197–202; William R. Carter, diary, 1 January 1863, Virginia State Library, Richmond.

6. The retreating Federal troopers were from the 2nd and 17th Pennsylvania Cavalry regiments, and the camp that was captured belonged to the 3rd Pennsylvania Cavalry. Carter, diary, 12 December 1862; McClellan, *Life and Campaigns,* 201.

7. According to H. B. McClellan, "He [Stuart] caused his operator to send a message to General M. C. Meigs, Quartermaster General, at Washington, in which he complained that the quality of the mules recently furnished to the army was so inferior as greatly to embarrass him in moving his captured wagons." McClellan, *Life and Campaigns,* 201.

8. Stuart killed or wounded about one hundred Federals, brought back nearly two hundred prisoners, and captured twenty wagons of supplies in the Dumfries Raid at the cost of one killed, thirteen wounded, and fourteen missing. *O.R.,* ser. 1, vol. 21, pp. 732, 734; McClellan, *Life and Campaigns,* 202; Carter, diary, 1 January, 1863.

CORRESPONDENCE, 1862

1. The 50th New York Engineers took the brunt of the Confederate rifle fire while they moved pontoon equipment into place on the Rappahannock River. They were supported by several infantry units, particularly the 57th and 66th New York Infantry regiments. Frederick Gilbert, *The Story of a Regiment* (n.p., 1895), 116–17; Josiah Marshall Favill, *The Diary of a Young Officer* (Chicago: R. R. Donnelley and Sons, 1909), 208–9.

7. "ONE OF THE BEST CAVALRY FIGHTS OF THE WAR"

1. Ca Ira (pronounced: "Sigh Irrah") was a small Cumberland County settlement about five miles west of Cumberland Court House. The village name means roughly "We will win!" and is probably a reference to a very popular song of the same name from the French Revolution.

2. The Hartwood Church scout occurred on 24–26 February 1863. *O.R.,* ser. 1, vol. 25, pt. 1, pp. 20–26.

3. Benjamin Watkins Lacy enlisted in Company F on 24 June 1861 as a private. Promoted to first sergeant on 14 September 1861, he was reelected to that post in April 1862. Lacy was promoted to first lieutenant on 7 January 1863. According to Hubbard's records, he was wounded at Kelly's Ford. He recovered but was wounded again at St. Mary's (Samaria) Church on 24 June 1864. Lacy appears to have been detached from service in February 1865. He was paroled in Farmville, Virginia, in April 1865. CSR, 3rd Va. Cav. George Munford Betts was a twenty-two-year-old farmer when he enlisted as a sergeant in Company C on 20 May 1861. CSR, 3rd Va. Cav.

4. Hugh French Goodman enlisted in Company G on 14 May 1861 as a private. He was detailed for courier service from November 1861 through April 1862 first for

Colonel William M. Levy and then for Fitz Lee. Goodman was wounded at Kelly's Ford on 17 March 1863 and, after serving through the end of the war, was paroled at Farmville in April 1865. CSR, 3rd Va. Cav.

5. Whether as a result of the wound to his horse or not, Hubard received an additional mount and saddle from home in mid-April 1863. Thomas, "Plantations in Transition," 137.

6. Casualties among General Fitz Lee's men at Kelly's Ford were reported to be eleven killed, eighty-eight wounded, and thirty-four lost as prisoners. Averell's losses were reported as six killed, fifty wounded, and twenty-two captured. In addition, Fitz Lee later estimated the loss in horses to be 170 killed, wounded, or lost. O.R., ser. 1, vol. 25, pt. 1, pp. 47–64; McClellan, *Life and Campaigns,* 217.

7. In Fitz Lee's report of the Kelly's Ford fight were mentioned the following 3rd Virginia troopers: "In the Third; Captain [William] Collins, Company H; Lieuts. [Bernard] Hill Carter, Jr., and John Lamb, of Company D; Lieutenant [H. W.] Stamper, of Company F; Lieutenant R. T. Hubbard, Jr., Company G, and First Lieutenant [J. W.] Hall, of Company C (was twice wounded before he desisted from the charge, and when retiring received a third and still more severe wound, and was unable to leave the field). Adjt. H. B. McClellan is also particularly commended for his gallantry; also Acting Sergt. Major E. W. Price, Company K; Private [C. A.] Keech, Company I, and Bugler Drilling. Sergeant [G. M.] Betts, of Company C; Privates [W. W.] Young, Company B; [F. S.] Fowler, Company G, and [J. T.] Wilkins, of Company C, died as became brave men—in the front of the charge at the head of the column." O.R., ser. 1, vol. 25, pt. 1, p. 62.

8. The 2nd Virginia did not include a company from Roanoke County and claimed but one company from Albemarle County, but enlisted three from Bedford County as well as one each from Appomattox and Franklin counties. The 4th Virginia also included companies from Goochland County and the city of Richmond.

9. All of the following information is from CSR, 3rd Va. Cav.; names are italicized to enhance ease of reading. *David D. Gayle* enlisted as a private in Company A at Boydton on 14 May 1861. He was elected to second lieutenant on 21 January 1863 and was captured at Gettysburg on 3 July 1863. He was held as a prisoner of war at Johnson's Island, Ohio, until exchanged in March 1865. *John P. Puryear* enlisted in Company A (Mecklenburg County) as a sergeant on 14 May 1861. He was promoted to lieutenant in January 1863, and on 9 June 1863 he was shot through both legs in the fight at Brandy Station, Virginia. Puryear was wounded again at Todd's Tavern, Virginia, on 6 May 1864, with a gunshot to the right lung. He was paroled in Richmond on 17 May 1865. Little is known of *C. Miller.* He was enlisted in Company B as a lieutenant, but except for a hospital record, there is no other information about his service. *Henry W. Stamper* enlisted in the New Kent Light Dragoons (Company F) at New Kent Court House on 28 June 1861 as a private. He was promoted to sergeant during 1862, but no month is noted in the records. He was promoted to lieutenant on 17 January 1863 but resigned on 17 August 1863 in order to join John

Hunt Morgan's cavalry nearer to his home in Woodford County, Kentucky. He died in Richmond on 11 January 1921. *Edgar M. Crump* was described at his enlistment in Company F as twenty-three years of age, five feet six inches tall, with hazel eyes, dark hair, and light complexion. He joined as a private but was promoted to lieutenant on 7 January 1863. He was wounded in the leg near Harrisonburg, Virginia, on 25 September 1864 and captured by Federal cavalry. He was held for some time at Point Lookout, Maryland, and was released at Fort Delaware on 17 June 1865. *Joseph H. Bourdon* was a twenty-eight-year-old farmer when he enlisted in Company I as a private at Dinwiddie Court House on 19 May 1861. He was promoted to sergeant in January 1862 and to a lieutenancy in January 1863. He was killed in action at Haw's Shop on 28 May 1864. *Archer Alexander Haskins* enlisted in Company K on 24 June 1861 at Prince Edward Court House. He was twenty-one years old (birth date of 4 November 1839) and was promoted to lieutenant in November 1862. Haskins was paroled in Farmville, Virginia, in April 1865. He died in Meherrin, Virginia, on 4 June 1910. *Henry T. Meredith* enlisted in Company K on 24 June 1861 at Prince Edward Court House. He was promoted from private to sergeant in July 1862. Meredith was captured at Boonsboro, Maryland, on 15 September 1862 and was exchanged on 17 October 1862. He was promoted to lieutenant in March 1864 and served until paroled at Appomattox Court House on 9 April 1865.

10. The 3rd and 5th Virginia Cavalry encountered the 6th New York Cavalry in the dark near Todd's Tavern. According to a trooper in Company B, "Great confusion prevailed. Many of the 3rd Virginia were mixed in with the 6th New York Cavalry and you could hear the cry not to shoot coming in every direction. Colonel Carter killed a sergeant, also Captain Jesse S. Jones captured one of the enemy; the confusion was caused by the thick shaded road, it being impossible to tell the color of clothing." The Federals were badly worsted in the confused fighting, leaving behind ten dead, including their commanding officer, and a dozen prisoners. Casualties in the 3rd Virginia were limited to one man wounded and several captured who later escaped. William T. Daougherty, "Reminiscences of the Late War" (unpublished manuscript, Hampton, Virginia, 1886, Robert West private collection, Poquoson, Virginia), 30; Carter, diary, 30 April 1863; *O.R.*, ser. 1, vol. 25, pt. 1, pp. 1045–48.

8. "OUR BRIGADE ADVANCED TO ALDIE"

1. Alexander Swift "Sandie" Pendleton was a graduate of Washington College in Lexington, Virginia, and left his graduate studies at the University of Virginia in 1861 to enter Confederate service as a lieutenant in the Corps of Engineers. He was almost immediately transferred to the staff of Thomas J. "Stonewall" Jackson, where he served first as Jackson's ordnance officer and then as assistant adjutant general. He was promoted to major and permanent assignment as adjutant general of Jackson's staff in December 1862. It was in this rank and position that he met Hubard at Chancellorsville. Faust, *Historical Times Illustrated*, 569–70.

2. The captured staff officer could not have been on General Burnside's staff at

Chancellorsville because Burnside's resignation from the Army of the Potomac had been accepted in January 1863. Burnside was sent to Cincinnati and had been commanding the Department of the Ohio since 25 March.

3. General Oliver O. Howard commanded the XI Corps at Chancellorsville.

4. Crutchfield was a V.M.I graduate (1855) and began the war as a major in the 9th Virginia Infantry. He rose in rank in the Confederate infantry before transferring to the artillery as Stonewall Jackson's chief of artillery in May 1862. Colonel Crutchfield lost a leg at Chancellorsville. He survived the wound but was killed in the last week of the war in Virginia at Sayler's Creek on 6 April 1865. Krick, *Lee's Colonels*, 107. Among the group who were killed were a Jackson aide, Captain James Keith Boswell, and three couriers. General A. P. Hill's chief of staff, Major William Palmer, and two lesser staff officers were wounded. James I. Robertson, Jr., *Stonewall Jackson* (New York: Macmillan, 1997), 729.

5. "Truth without fear and without reproach."

6. Dabney's American edition of *Life and Campaigns of Lieut. Gen. Thomas J. Jackson (Stonewall Jackson)* (New York: Blelock and Co.) was published in 1866. Douglas S. Freeman, *The South to Posterity* (New York: Charles Scribner's Sons, 1939), 38.

7. The twenty-six thousand Federal forces at Second Fredericksburg and, subsequently, at Salem Church were commanded by General John Sedgwick. Confederate troops, commanded by General Jubal Early, numbered about 12,700, including those reinforcing Wilcox's brigade. Stephen W. Sears, *Chancellorsville* (Boston: Houghton Mifflin, 1996), 349; Early's report: *O.R.*, ser. 1, vol. 25, pt. 1, pp. 1000–1003.

8. According to Freeman, Lafayette McLaws's reputation suffered somewhat after Chancellorsville for a lack of aggressive behavior on the battlefield. Freeman, *Lee's Lieutenants*, 2:661–62; *O.R.*, ser. 1, vol. 25, pt. 1, p. 801; Krick, "John Bankhead Magruder," *Confederate General*, 4:130.

9. Federal losses at Chancellorsville were approximately seventeen thousand, and Confederate casualties numbered about thirteen thousand. Faust, *Historical Times Illustrated*, 129.

10. A. P. Hill's Corps division commanders were Henry Heth, Richard H. Anderson, and William Dorsey Pender. Kershaw led a brigade in McLaws's division (Longstreet's Corps), and Wilcox led a brigade in Anderson's division.

11. John D. Imboden began the war as an artillery officer but organized a mounted infantry unit and attained the rank of brigadier general of cavalry in January 1863. During the Gettysburg campaign, Imboden's ill-equipped and somewhat independent-minded brigade ranged westward along the Baltimore and Ohio Railroad but subsequently performed good service guarding the retreat of the Confederate army's ambulance trains. Imboden survived the war, entered the coal mining business in western Virginia, and died on 15 August 1895. Albert G. Jenkins hailed from western Virginia and rose to command of the 8th Virginia Cavalry early in the war. Though elected to the Confederate Congress in February 1862, Jenkins left that body when he accepted a brigadier general's appointment in August 1862. His cavalry brigade

was attached to the Army of Northern Virginia for the Gettysburg campaign but was criticized by some for aggressive foraging through the Pennsylvania countryside as well as for poor combat discipline. Jenkins was seriously wounded at the Battle of Cloyd's Mountain 9 May 1864 and, after the amputation of his arm, died on 21 May. Warner, *Generals in Gray*, 147, 154–55.

12. According to H. B. McClellan, three Confederate cavalry reviews were held after Chancellorsville: 22 May, 5 June, and an unexpected review for the benefit of General R. E. Lee on 8 June, the day before Pleasanton's attack at Brandy Station. McClellan, *Life and Campaigns*, 261.

13. Federal losses at Brandy Station were reported as 936. Confederate casualties totaled 523. Because their posting on 9 June was some distance out on the Confederate left flank at Oak Church north of the Hazel River, the 3rd Virginia Cavalry took part only in the closing phase of the battle and suffered lighter casualties (one killed, eight wounded) than many of the regiments in Stuart's Cavalry Corps. Stuart's report: *O.R.*, ser. 1, vol. 27, pt. 2, pp. 679–85; Faust, *Historical Times Illustrated*, 76; Thomas P. Nanzig, *3rd Virginia Cavalry* (Lynchburg, Va.: H. E. Howard, Inc., 1989), 36.

14. Federal losses at Second Winchester exceeded even Hubard's estimates: four thousand captured or missing, four hundred killed or wounded, twenty-three cannons captured, and three hundred each of wagons and horses taken by Ewell's Corps. Faust, *Historical Times Illustrated*, 835.

15. Colonel Thomas T. Munford had taken charge of Fitz Lee's Brigade on or about 8 June when Lee was disabled by rheumatism in his knee. James L. Nichols, *General Fitzhugh Lee: A Biography* (Lynchburg, Va.: H. E. Howard, Inc., 1989), 52.

16. The Federal charge was probably made by the 1st Maine and 4th New York Cavalry regiments. Contrary to Hubard's statements, most of the fighting at Aldie was between two brigades, Munford's Confederates and Kilpatrick's Federals. The 1st Maine was from J. I. Gregg's brigade and was the only outside help that Kilpatrick received during the fight. Fitz Lee Brigade reports: *O.R.*, ser. 1, vol. 27, pt.2, pp. 737–46; Robert F. O'Neill, Jr., *The Cavalry Battles of Aldie, Middleburg, and Upperville* (Lynchburg, Va.: H. E. Howard, Inc., 1993), 57, 59–60.

17. Thomas B. Johnson enlisted in Company I on 13 March 1862. He sustained a wound at Aldie when his horse was killed. Johnson was promoted to corporal in July 1863 and then demoted to private by order of Colonel Owen in September 1863. He was last reported on company rolls in June 1864. CSR, 3rd Va. Cav.

18. Hubard is probably referring to the Furr House, which still stands along the Snickers Gap Turnpike and overlooks the point at which that road made a "blind" right angle turn to charging Federal cavalrymen.

19. Oakley, the estate of Henry G. and Ida Dulaney, is located between Middleburg and Upperville. O'Neill, *Cavalry Battles*, 145.

20. William was the second eldest of the Hubard siblings (born 24 December 1836) and was two years older than Robert, Jr. There is no evidence to indicate that he served in the military during the war. Hubard, *Hubards*, 36.

21. The Federal troops in Middleburg on 17 June were Colonel Alfred N. Duffie's 1st Rhode Island Cavalry. Although he had occupied the village and had nearly captured Jeb Stuart and his staff in the bargain, Duffie was also behind enemy lines and vastly outnumbered. An attack by the 4th and 5th North Carolina cavalry regiments after dark dislodged the Rhode Islanders. The pursuit went well into the early hours of the morning as the Tarheels captured 210 Federals. O'Neill, *Cavalry Battles*, 69–74; *O.R.*, ser. 1, vol. 27, pt.1, pp. 964–65.

22. Hubard has mistakenly condensed the cavalry actions after the Aldie and Middleburg (17 June) fights. Skirmishing occupied the cavalry forces around Middleburg on 18 June and gave way to more serious fighting outside the village on the nineteenth. Stuart's men finally withdrew from Middleburg, and both sides used 20 June to rest and reorganize. The final clash of cavalry occurred on 21 June at Upperville, with Stuart holding back Pleasanton's efforts to break through the Southern screen. Stuart's Aldie-Middleburg-Upperville report: *O.R.*, ser. 1, vol. 27, pt. 2, pp. 687–92.

23. Stuart's force actually crossed the Potomac River at Rowser's Ford. This was his third and most controversial ride around the Federal army. Although he captured horses, wagons, and supplies, his absence from Lee's main forces deprived the Southern army effective screening and intelligence. Stuart's report of his circuit of the Federal army: *O.R.*, ser. 1, vol. 27, pt. 2, pp. 692–97.

24. There has been widespread speculation that the severe wound that cost Ewell his leg in August 1862 left him a changed man in spirit and audacity. A recent biography of Ewell tackles this question: "Ewell did not perform as well under Lee. After the war, individuals surmised that the loss of his leg, his marriage to Lizinka, his formal acceptance of Christianity or some combination of the three had impaired his fighting spirit. No one would have suggested such a thing in June 1863. . . . Critics then and later accused Ewell of being indecisive, but no one has offered any credible evidence to back up such a claim." Donald C. Pfanz, *Richard S. Ewell: A Soldier's Life* (Chapel Hill: University of North Carolina Press, 1998), 501.

25. Hubard completely neglected to mention the fighting that took place during the afternoon and evening of 2 July. As for the assertion that Lee was swayed by his generals into making the 3 July attack, there does not appear in the conventional histories of the Battle of Gettysburg or the Army of Northern Virginia any evidence to sustain this claim.

26. Hubard's postwar estimates of Gettysburg casualties were not far from the mark. Federal losses totaled twenty-three thousand, including more than five thousand missing. Confederate losses were estimated to be about twenty-eight thousand. Faust, *Historical Times Illustrated*, 307.

27. Hubard's comment on "Q" as a final letter was probably a reference to the military's use of letters for company designations. Most ten-company infantry and cavalry regiments used "A" through "K" (omitting "J"). Larger regiments, however, such as heavy artillery units, sometimes contained as many as sixteen companies, thus making "Q" the final letter.

28. In his memoirs, Hubard was off by one day on his dates for the fighting near Funkstown. Those dates have been corrected as indicated by brackets. D. B. Ellyson enlisted in Company F on 21 August 1862 at Brandy Station, Virginia. He was killed at Funkstown, Maryland, on 10 July 1863. CSR, 3rd Va. Cav. John McKendree Jeffries was twenty-six years old at the time of his enlistment in Company G on 23 April 1861. He was promoted from private to corporal in March 1862 and then to sergeant some time before July 1863. He was wounded in the hand by artillery fire at Funkstown, Maryland, on 10 July 1863. Jeffries was unable to return to active duty and applied for retirement from military service on 22 March 1864. He signed his parole in Farmville, Virginia, on 28 April 1865. CSR, 3rd Va. Cav. Theophilus Foster enlisted in Company E as a private on 27 May 1861. He was promoted to sergeant in July 1863. Foster was killed in action by artillery fire at Funkstown, Maryland, on 10 July 1863. CSR, 3rd Va. Cav.

29. According to most accounts, on the night of 13 July, Longstreet's Corps and Hill's Corps crossed at Falling Waters, and Ewell's Corps, followed by the cavalry, crossed at Williamsport. At dawn on the fourteenth, only Heth's division of Hill's Corps remained on the north bank of the Potomac River at Falling Waters. John W. Schildt, *Roads From Gettysburg* (Shippensburg, Pa.: Burd Street Press, 1998), 103–8.

30. "Plunder" was a common slang term used in both armies for a soldier's personal belongings or baggage, not necessarily stolen goods.

31. According to Jeb Stuart's report of the campaign, Fitz Lee had sent two squadrons of cavalry from Williamsport to Falling Waters to follow the last infantry units across. The cavalrymen mistook the end of Longstreet's column for the last troops across, leaving Pettigrew's men without a cavalry screen and leading to the misidentification of the Federal cavalry as Confederates. *O.R.*, ser. 1, vol. 27, pt. 2, p. 705.

32. Confederate losses at Falling Waters on 14 July amounted to 719 officers and men. Edward B. Coddington, *The Gettysburg Campaign* (New York: Charles Scribner's Sons, 1968), 571.

33. Although the burning of the Shenandoah Valley did not occur until October 1864, Federal soldiers had already pillaged homes and public buildings on the Peninsula and had sacked the town of Fredericksburg in December 1862.

34. There is no evidence to indicate a Federal retreat before Lee began the Confederate withdrawal. The fact was that General George G. Meade had to ascertain Lee's intentions before he could move his own Federal army so as not to leave either Washington or Baltimore vulnerable to a Confederate strike. Coddington, *Gettysburg Campaign,* 539.

35. The cavalry fight at Shepherdstown involved the brigades of Fitz Lee, Chambliss, and Jenkins against the Second Brigade (J. I. Gregg's) of D. McM. Gregg's Third Division, Federal Cavalry. Although total casualties were not reported by either side, the wounding and resulting death of Colonel James H. Drake, 1st Virginia Cavalry, was keenly felt by Stuart and his command. *O.R.*, ser. 1, vol. 27, pt. 1, pp. 977–79; *ibid.,* pt. 2, p. 706.

36. Stuart's two brigades were pushed back on Confederate infantry supports by General John Buford's division of three brigades on 1 August 1863. *O.R.*, ser. 1, vol. 27, pt. 3, p. 827.

9. "TO GAIL KILPATRICK'S REAR AT BUCKLAND"

1. Federal cavalry had been scouting the region, and a week after Owen's foray across the river, Kilpatrick mounted a brief campaign against two Confederate gunboats that had been ferrying forage across the Rappahanock River from Port Conway south to Port Royal. In a 2 September 1863 attack on the Confederate boats, the *Satellite* was sunk, and the *Reliance* was damaged. Willard W. Glazier, *Three Years in the Federal Cavalry* (New York: R.H. Ferguson and Co., 1874), 315–18; *O.R.*, ser. 1, vol. 29, pt. 1, pp. 96–98.

2. A pungy schooner is a two-masted vessel type whose beginning is generally accepted to be the late 1840s. Pungies were oyster and fishing boats that plied the Chesapeake Bay until the late nineteenth century.

3. According to George Wilson Booth, the night ride ended in some confusion. Booth rode with the 1st Maryland Cavalry and was assigned the advance position on Colonel Owen's expedition. When gunfire broke out in the rear of his column, Booth ordered his men to ford the Rappahannock River, which was still at flood tide. Moments later the Marylanders covered Owen's crossing. According to Booth, "I have always thought that the firing that gave us away was from our own men, some of whom in the darkness had taken a road . . . which led them by a longer route than that followed by the main column, which they struck in the rear as their path reentered the main road." George Wilson Booth, *A Maryland Boy in Lee's Army* (Baltimore: Press of Fleet, McGinley and Co., 1898), 96–97.

4. Wade Hampton and Fitz Lee received their promotions to major general on 3 September 1863, effective 3 August 1863. The Cavalry Corps was officially reorganized by Stuart into two divisions on 9 September 1863. Jeffry D. Wert, "Wade Hampton," in *The Confederate General*, vol. 3, edited by William C. Davis (Harrisburg, Pa.: National Historical Society, 1991), 52; Peter S. Carmichael, "Fitzhugh Lee," in *The Confederate General*, vol. 4, edited by William C. Davis (Harrisburg, Pa.: National Historical Society, 1991), 38; Jeffrey D. Wert, "James Ewell Brown Stuart," in *The Confederate General*, vol. 6, edited by William C. Davis (Harrisburg, Pa.: National Historical Society, 1991), 23.

5. The Northern Neck is the northernmost of Virginia's three large peninsulas that extend into the Chesapeake Bay. It is comprised of Westmoreland, Richmond, Lancaster, and Northumberland counties.

6. According to Hubard plantation records, by August Robert needed to replace both his mount and saddle. This trip home may well have been to retrieve a new horse and equipment, as was the practice in the Confederate cavalry. Thomas, "Plantations in Transition," 137.

7. "Captain Newton drew his sabre, gave the word to his men, and with impetuous courage spurred his horse upon the enemy. Captain Williams rode by his side as Company A was in the lead squadron." Stiles, *4th Virginia Cavalry*, 37.

8. This incident in which Stuart's command was trapped between the II and III corps of Federal infantry occurred near Auburn, Virginia. Considering the fact that Hubard was not present to witness the predicament into which Stuart rode, his review of the circumstances is very accurate. Stuart's report: *O.R.*, ser. 1, vol. 29, pt. 1, pp. 447–48; McClellan, *Life and Campaigns,* 388–93.

9. Heth lost about thirteen hundred men in the Bristoe Station attack. Faust, *Historical Times Illustrated,* 80–81; Heth's report: *O.R.*, ser. 1, vol. 29, pt. 1, pp. 430–32.

10. Kilpatrick's forces lost about two hundred men in the Buckland fight. Stuart's Buckland reports: *O.R.*, ser. 1, vol. 29, pt. 1, pp. 438–39, 451–52; James H. Kidd, *Personal Recollections of a Cavalryman* (Ionia, Mich.: Sentinel Print Co., 1908), 212–26.

11. Davidson Bradfute Penn, a graduate of Virginia Military Institute (1856) and the University of Virginia, was colonel of the 7th Louisiana. Krick, *Lee's Colonels,* 303.

12. Confederate losses at the Rappahannock Station bridge were about sixteen hundred, most of whom were captured. *O.R.*, ser. 1, vol. 29, pt. 1, pp. 618–26.

13. John Buford's Federal troopers tried the Confederate left flank at Jack's Shop (south of Madison Court House) on 22–23 September 1863, only to be met by portions of Stuart's command. Judson Kilpatrick's Federal division encircled Stuart's position, cutting Stuart off from his route of support or retreat at Liberty Mills. At one point in the fight, Stuart's troopers and artillery were charging and firing to the front and rear simultaneously. Henry Davies's Federal brigade was finally driven back enough to allow Stuart's cavalry to retreat below the Rapidan River to safety. Stuart harassed the Federals as they withdrew north across the Robertson River on 23 September, but he never submitted a report of either action. McClellan, *Life and Campaigns,* 374–75; Edward Longacre, *General John Buford* (Conshohocken, Pa.: Combined Books, 1995), 232–33.

14. Averell had been ordered to take his column to the line of the Virginia and Tennessee Railroad at either Bonsack's Station in Botetourt County or Salem (present-day Roanoke) in Roanoke County in order to destroy as much of the rail line as possible. At Salem the Federals destroyed miles of track, five bridges, the depot filled with railroad repair supplies, food stores, and leather goods. *O.R.*, ser. 1, vol. 29, pt. 1, pp. 920, 924–25.

CORRESPONDENCE, 1863

1. Recognized for his intelligence, dedication, and valor in May 1863, Henry B. McClellan was promoted to major and appointed by General J. E. B. Stuart to be the Cavalry Corps assistant adjutant general. McClellan served with Stuart until the latter's death in 1864, after which he was assigned to staff positions under R. E. Lee and Wade Hampton. An educator at heart, McClellan served as a girls' school teacher and administrator in Lexington, Kentucky, from 1870 until his death in 1904. Trout, *They Followed the Plume,* 201–4.

2. James Alexander Seddon was a native of Goochland County, Virginia, a graduate of the University of Virginia law school, and a member of the U.S. House of Representatives from 1845 to 1847 and from 1849 to 1851. He was appointed fifth

Confederate secretary of war in November 1862 and served in that post until he resigned in February 1865. Edmund Wilcox Hubard, Robert Jr.'s uncle, was a native of Petersburg, Virginia, attended the University of Virginia law school, served in the U.S. House of Representatives from 1841 to 1847, and was a candidate for governor of Virginia in 1863. He owned a large plantation, called Saratoga, in Buckingham County and was, no doubt, on good terms with Seddon. Faust, *Historical Times Illustrated,* 664–65; Hubard, *Hubards,* 21–22.

3. Several regiments of Virginia cavalry were located in the western counties of Virginia in the spring of 1863, including Imboden's Brigade (62nd Mounted Infantry, 18th Virginia Regiment, Partisan Rangers), Jenkins' Brigade (14th, 16th, 17th, 19th Regiments, and the 34th and 36th Battalions, 37th Mounted Infantry) and William E. Jones' Brigade (6th, 7th, 11th Regiments, 35th Battalion). Coddington, *Gettysburg Campaign,* 595.

4. A raid by Federal general George Stoneman's corps of ten thousand cavalrymen from 29 April to 8 May 1862 threatened to disrupt communications, supply lines, and routes of retreat behind the Confederate lines at Chancellorsville and Fredericksburg. Although judged by some to have been a failure, the raid inflicted temporary damage to Confederate infrastructure, including the destruction of commissary stores, railroad supply trains, wagon trains, and depots stocked with wheat and corn. These depot losses may have prompted the citizen complaints to which Hubard refers in this passage. A. Wilson Greene, "*Stoneman's Raid,*" *Chancellorsville: The Battle and Its Aftermath,* edited by Gary W. Gallagher (Chapel Hill: University of North Carolina Press, 1996), 65–106.

5. Benjamin Franklin Randolph Hubard was James and Isaetta Hubard's first child. He was born 2 February 1862. Hubard, *Hubards,* 36.

6. Hubard may have been referring to a Federal cavalry force of nine hundred men from Williamsburg, Virginia, that skirmished with Confederate troops near Bottom's Bridge during a 26–29 August 1863 expedition. According to Lieutenant Colonel Carter's diary entry, the only movement that the 3rd Virginia Cavalry made was on 31 August: "Moved camp to Mr. Howison's near Hamilton's crossing." *O.R.,* ser. 1, vol. 29, pt. 1, pp. 86–89; Carter, diary, 63.

7. Roger A. Pryor, an antebellum lawyer, newspaper editor, U.S. congressman, and outspoken secessionist, rose from early war command of the 3rd Virginia Infantry to lead an infantry brigade throughout 1862. Displaced from his brigade position in March 1863, Pryor acted as a scout until enlisting in the Nottoway Troop (Company E), 3rd Virginia Cavalry, in August 1863. He was detailed as a special courier in May 1864. Pryor was captured near Petersburg in November 1864 and spent the remainder of the war as a prisoner of war in Fort Lafayette, New York. Jeffry Wert, "Roger Atkinson Pryor," in *The Confederate General,* vol. 5, edited by William C. Davis (Harrisburg, Pa.: National Historical Society, 1991), 64–65.

8. In the late 1830s Rockbridge Alum Springs was built as a summer resort by James Campbell, whose father, a country surveyor, had discovered alum water on the property in 1799. Located fifteen miles west of Lexington, Virginia, the alum

water springs were touted as a cure for many internal diseases and for external skin diseases. By the 1850s the resort boasted a hotel, several guesthouses and cottages, bath houses, bowling alleys, and a billiard room. Hubard was probably referring to Federal general William Averell's engagement with Confederate forces near White Sulphur Springs, West Virginia, 26–27 August 1863. (Edmund P. Tomkins, "Rockbridge County, Virginia: An Informal History," Whittet & Shepperson, Richmond, Va., 1952. 118–126.) *O.R.,* ser. 1, vol. 29, pt. 1, p. 32.

9. Hubard's remark about the North Carolina troops may be a reference to any of several morale issues that could have affected North Carolina troops in September 1863: the loss in the Gettysburg campaign of generals W. Dorsey Pender and J. Johnston Pettigrew; the desertion of many Confederate soldiers from infantry regiments, and particularly North Carolina units; and the rise in the summer and fall of 1863 of a significant North Carolina peace faction led by Raleigh editor and gubernatorial hopeful W. W. Holden. Confederate general James Longstreet's Corps was detached from the Army of Northern Virginia on 9 September 1863 and sent to north Georgia to reinforce General Braxton Bragg's forces near Chickamauga Creek. Freeman, *Lee's Lieutenants,* 3:217–19; John G. Barrett, *The Civil War in North Carolina* (Chapel Hill: University of North Carolina Press, 1963), 194–96.

10. Isham Swann was a slave from Chellowe who accompanied Robert to war. At war's end, he was one of the few freedmen who did not immediately leave Chellowe to test his independence. Thomas, "Plantations in Transition," 389.

11. Hubard is referring to the Jack's Shop fight that was noted earlier in his memoir.

12. The movement was in pursuit of Averell's Federal raiders in western Virginia. The two railroads mentioned by Hubard were the Orange and Alexandria, which ran north and south, and the east-west Virginia Central Railroad.

13. Martha Burke ("Patsy") Jones Eppes of Millbrook was Robert Hubard's kin through marriage. Mrs. Eppes's daughter, Sarah Ann ("Sallie") Eppes Hubard, was married to Robert's uncle, Edmund W. Hubard, one of two executors of Mrs. Eppes's estate. Thomas, "Plantations in Transition," 186; Hubard, *Hubards,* 21.

14. Uncle Philip was Philip A. Bolling, Robert's mother's brother. He married another of Martha Eppes's daughters, Mary, thus entitling that family to a portion of her estate on her death. Thomas, "Plantations in Transition," 186; Kenneth M. Stampp, *Records of Ante-Bellum Southern Plantations from the Revolution through the Civil War,* series J: Selections from the Southern Historical Collection, pt. 10: Hubard Family Papers, 1741–1865 (Frederick, Md.: University Publications of America, 1992), 14, http://www.lexisnexis.com/academic/guides/southern_hist/plantations/plantj10.asp).

15. Hubard and Captain Henry C. Lee, Fitz Lee's younger brother, had been students at the University of Virginia in 1861, Hubard as a first-year law student and Lee as an undergraduate. Henry Lee, who had served on his brother's staff since Fitz's elevation to brigade command in July 1862, may have been responsible for recommending other college mates for positions. According courier John Gill, "I sup-

pose I was indebted for this slight elevation to Capt. Henry Lee, brother of Gen. Fitz Lee, a classmate of mine at the University of Virginia prior to the war." John Gill, *Courier for Lee and Jackson: Memoirs, 1861–1865,* edited by W. D. Swank (Shippensburg, Pa.: Burd Street Press, 1993), 43; Edward G. Longacre, *Fitz Lee* (Cambridge, Mass.: Da Capo Press, 2005).

10. "BOYS, YOU HAVE MADE THE MOST GLORIOUS FIGHT"

1. General Braxton Bragg had commanded the Confederate Army of Tennessee but was replaced by General Joseph E. Johnston after Bragg's army was badly beaten at Chattanooga in November 1863. Bragg, a West Point classmate of Confederate president Jefferson Davis, was immediately called to Richmond to serve as Davis's closest military advisor.

2. The column that moved toward Charlottesville on 29 February 1864 was Custer's Michigan Cavalry Brigade acting as a diversion to allow Kilpatrick and Dahlgren to slip through the Confederate lines. Custer, with twenty-five hundred cavalry and a section of artillery, attacked the winter quarters of the Stuart Horse Artillery at Rio Hill. The Union cavalry, more intent on destroying the camp and killing horses than capturing the Confederate cannon, allowed Major Roger Preston Chew to get his guns into position and open fire. Chew and James Breathed formed a mounted squadron of the sick and other unengaged cannoneers. Having few weapons, most of the men brandished sticks to represent sabres and carbines. Chew brought his pseudo cavalry up to the Confederate flank and shouted, "Tell Colonel Dulaney to bring up the 7th Regiment." Custer did not know that Dulaney and the 7th Virginia Cavalry were miles away. Not wishing to risk an attack against cavalry and artillery, Custer retreated. *O.R.,* ser. 1, vol. 33, pp. 161–63; Jefferson County Museum, "Battle of Rio Hill," *http://jeffctywvmuseum.org/html/stuart_s_horse_artillery_flag.html*) (accessed February 2005).

3. General Henry A. Wise was, in fact, visiting his son-in-law, Plumer Hobson, at Eastwood plantation. He escaped on horseback just moments before a patrol from the 5th New York Cavalry surrounded Eastwood. Although Wise may well have ridden to Richmond with news of the raiders, there is also ample evidence that General Wade Hampton's scouts had been following the Federal column since shortly after its departure near Stevensburg. Virgil Carrington Jones, *Eight Hours before Richmond* (New York: Henry Holt and Co., 1957), 72–73; Duane Schultz, *The Dahlgren Affair* (New York: W. W. Norton, 1998), 105–6.

4. Ulric Dahlgren's body was returned to his father, Admiral John Dahlgren, in June 1865. A memorial service attended by President Johnson and a host of dignitaries was held in Washington, D.C., later that year, and Dahlgren's body was subsequently laid to rest in the family plot in Philadelphia. Schultz, *Dahlgren Affair,* 259–60.

5. General James Longstreet's Corps had spent the autumn and winter of 1863–

1864 in Georgia and Tennessee. They participated in the Confederate victory at Chickamauga Creek, Georgia, and unsuccessfully laid siege to Federal armies in Chattanooga and Knoxville, Tennessee, before returning to Virginia in May 1864.

6. John Wesley Garrett enlisted in Company G on 14 May 1861 as a private and was promoted to sergeant in October 1861. He was wounded on 29 May 1864 at Haw's Shop but returned to service and was paroled in Farmville, Virginia, in April 1865. CSR, 3rd Va. Cav.

7. Contrary to Hubard's recollection, John W. Fitzgerald was not killed at Spotsylvania Court House. According to his military records, Fitzgerald was twenty-three years old at the time of his enlistment in Company E on 27 May 1861. He was nearly six feet tall and had blue eyes, dark hair, and a dark complexion. He was captured at Williamsburg on 4 May 1862 and was exchanged on 5 August 1862. Fitzgerald was promoted to corporal in July 1863. He was captured at Spotsylvania Court House on 8 May 1864 and was held at Elmira, New York, from July 1864 through his parole on 16 July 1865. CSR, 3rd Va. Cav. James D. Vaughan was an eighteen-year-old farmer, six feet tall, with blue eyes, light hair, and a sallow complexion. He enlisted in Company E at Nottoway Court House on 27 May 1861. Private Vaughan was discharged in 18 August 1861 on a certificate of disability. He reenlisted on 5 January 1863 and served until killed in action at Spotsylvania Court House on 8 May 1864. CSR, 3rd Va. Cav. Thomas A. Pride enlisted in Company G on 14 May 1861 as a twenty-one-year-old private. He served throughout the regiment's campaigns until he was killed in action on 8 May 1864 at Spotsylvania Court House. CSR, 3rd Va. Cav.

8. Hubard's narrative jumps again moving from action at Spotsylvania Court House on 8 May to Stuart's pursuit of Sheridan's Federal cavalry on 9 May near Mitchell's Shop.

9. Edmund Wilcox Hubard's enlistment in the 4th Virginia Cavalry was delayed by eighteen months when his father paid a Richmond man $900 in July 1862 to enter the army in Edmund's place. Thomas, "Plantations in Transition," 130.

10. All of the following information is from CSR, 3rd Va. Cav.; names are italicized to enhance ease of reading. *Archer T. McLaurine* enlisted in Company G on 14 May 1861 as an eighteen-year-old private. He was promoted to corporal in July 1863 and was killed at Mitchell's Shop on 9 May 1864. *Rodophil Jeter* was drafted into the cavalry on 15 April 1864. Three weeks later, on 9 May, he was killed at Mitchell's Shop. *Benjamin Branch Overton* enlisted on the Peninsula for service in Company G on 14 March 1862. He served in the regiment until killed in action at Mitchell's Shop on 9 May 1864. *John Vincent Ryals* enlisted in Company G at Richmond on 15 May 1862. He served as a private until he was severely wounded at Mitchell's Shop on 9 May 1864. He was sent to Chimborazo Hospital in Richmond for care. *George B. Mayo* enlisted in the Cumberland Troop (Company G) on 19 February 1862 at Richmond. Mayo served through the war without incident until he was wounded on 9 May 1864 at Mitchell's Shop. He was paroled at Farmville, Virginia, in April 1865. *Powhatan Jones Ayers* enlisted in the Cumberland Troop on 29 March 1862 at

Richmond. He served as a private soldier until detailed as a flag bearer in April 1864. Ayers was wounded in the face at Mitchell's Shop on 9 May 1864. After recovering, he was detailed as a courier to General Williams C. Wickham. No parole records are included in Ayers's military file.

11. The James City Troop had started the war assigned to the 3rd Virginia Cavalry as Company I. They were transferred to the 5th Virginia Cavalry in May 1862.

12. William C. Meredith enlisted in the 4th Virginia Cavalry on 27 April 1862 and was appointed regimental chaplain on 14 August 1862. He was paroled in April 1865. Stiles, *4th Virginia Cavalry*, 125.

13. "It is a sweet and glorious thing to die for one's country" is taken from the Roman poet Horace's "Odes."

14. Sheridan had ten thousand cavalry troopers and six batteries of artillery with him on the Yellow Tavern raid, whereas Stuart commanded approximately forty-five hundred men with whom to oppose the Federals. In addition, Hubard misrepresented Sheridan's troopers as mounted infantry. Several Federal cavalry units were equipped with seven-shot Spencer repeating rifles, giving them a tremendous advantage in weaponry over the Confederate horsemen. Philip H. Sheridan, *Personal Memoirs of P. H. Sheridan* (New York: Charles L. Webster and Co., 1888), 1:357; Starr, *Union Cavalry*, 2:97; McClellan, *Life and Campaigns*, 410; Gordon C. Rhea, *The Battles for Spotsylvania Court House and the Road to Yellow Tavern, May 7–12, 1864* (Baton Rouge: Louisiana State University Press, 1997), 99.

15. Stuart graduated from West Point in 1854, thirteenth out of a class of forty-six. His distinction may have been his appointment as a cadet "cavalry officer" in recognition of superior horsemanship. He was first assigned to the Mounted Rifles and then transferred to the 1st United States Cavalry. Emory M. Thomas, *Bold Dragoon* (New York: Harper and Row, 1986), 30–40.

11. "A FURIOUS CHARGE WAS MADE UPON OUR LINE"

1. "Stuart's force was so much reduced and he was in need of artillery, having broken down his own batteries in the rapid march he had been making to overtake Sheridan. Stopping for a few moments [at Hanover Junction] he asked Colonel [Bradley T.] Johnson to lend him one of our batteries, the Baltimore Light, promising to take good care of it and to return it in a few days." In the Battle of Yellow Tavern, the Baltimore Light lost two of four guns to Federal charges. Booth, *Maryland Boy*, 107–8.

2. James Breathed was, indeed, wounded in the battle. He was known for his courage in the heat of combat, and according to one account, he had only three days earlier at Spotsylvania Court House displayed that same spirit of derring-do when he rescued one of his battalion artillery pieces from advancing Federal infantry: "Before the gun could be moved the drivers and horses . . . were killed or wounded and Ryan, the driver of the wheel team, had his arm shattered by a bullet. As if unconscious of the presence of the enemy, Breathed jumped from his horse,

cut loose the teams that were struggling on the ground, mounted a wheel horse and brought off the gun almost by a miracle." Robert J. Trout, *Galloping Thunder* (Mechanicsburg, Pa.: Stackpole Books, 2002), 470; McClellan, *Life and Campaigns,* 408.

3. Lieutenant Colonel Robert Lee Randolph had been ordered to withdraw his men at once. Before leaving Meadow Bridge, he stood to have his line give the Federals one more volley and was killed instantly by a bullet in the head. Stiles, *4th Virginia Cavalry,* 49.

4. According to a map of the region, a ford across the Chickahominy River was available to Federal troopers a few miles north, or upriver, of Meadow Bridge. The ford road east of the river ran up and past the residence of a Mrs. Crenshaw, located on the Virginia Central Railroad halfway between Meadow Bridge and Atlee's Station. George B. Davis, *The Official Military Atlas of the Civil War* (New York: Arno Press, 1978), plate C, number 2.

5. Fort Kennon was also referred to by its local designation, Wilson's Wharf, and was referred to by the Federals as Fort Pocahontas. Fitz Lee was directed by General Braxton Bragg, President Jefferson Davis's military advisor, to break up the fort and the U.S. Colored Troops at the location "and [to] stop their uncivilized proceedings in the neighborhood." Nichols, *General Fitzhugh Lee,* 70.

6. Hubard's qualifying statement, "though Negroes, they fell back firing," indicates the belief by many soldiers, North and South, that African American soldiers would not fight with discipline and coolness. According to one authority, "Many whites argued that because blacks lacked the character to sustain themselves in battle, attempts to convert them into soldiers were preposterous." Joseph T. Glatthaar, *"Forged in Battle: The Civil War Alliance of Black Soldiers and White Officers* (New York: Free Press, 1990), 121.

7. According to John Gill, one of Fitz Lee's couriers, "I carried a message from General Lee, under flag of truce, to the commander of the fort to surrender. This was refused by Brigadier-General [E. A.] Wild, in command, and I was told to say to General Lee, 'Take the fort if you can.' This garrison consisted of three regiments of colored troops, and a number of transports and gunboats were in the river in reserve. On my return I was asked if the fort could be taken, and I replied that it could not. I had been so close to it, surrounded as it was by a moat, that my mind was quickly made up that any attempt, even to attack, would prove disastrous." Gill, *Courier for Lee and Jackson,* 49.

8. Fort Kennon/Fort Pocahontas was garrisoned during the fight by about 1,300 United States Colored Troops with white officers and 150 white reinforcements, who were hailed ashore from a passing transport. They were supported by the gunboat USS *Dawn* and the armed tug USS *Young America. O.R.,* ser. 1, vol. 36, pt. 3, pp. 269–72; Edward Besch, "More Information: Historical Report on the Battle of Fort Pocahontas," http://www.fortpocahontas.org (accessed July 2006).

9. H. Emory Coleman had enlisted in Company C (Black Walnut Dragoons) on 9 August 1863 at Fredericksburg as a private. Coleman was wounded in the right leg

on 28 May 1864 at Haw's Shop. Coleman returned to duty after a short stay in a hospital in Richmond. He was paroled at Appomattox Court House on 9 April 1865 and was noted as "courier with Lt. Gen'l Anderson." CSR, 3rd Va. Cav.

10. Francis Wortham Guy was a twenty-one-year-old private when he enlisted in Company E on 27 May 1861 but was elected sergeant in April 1862. He was wounded at Brandy Station on 9 June 1863 and was mortally wounded in the lungs at Haw's Shop on 28 May 1864. Guy died in transit to the hospital the same day. CSR, 3rd Va. Cav.

11. As noted on a period map, Mrs. Newton's house is about two and one-half miles east of Haw's Shop at Hanovertown. Davis, *Official Military Atlas*, plate XIX, map number 1.

12. Thomas Stanhope Flournoy (1811–1883) had served as a congressman from Halifax, Virginia, from 1847 to 1849. He helped raise Company G (Flournoy Troop) of the 6th Virginia Cavalry in May 1861. He was elected captain of that company and was later promoted to colonel of the regiment. He resigned his position in October 1862 in an unsuccessful campaign for governor of Virginia. "Biographical Directory of the United States Congress," http://www.bioguide.congress.gov. (accessed 2002); Krick, *Lee's Colonels*, 142. Cabell Edward Flournoy was the second of five children, and the eldest son, of Thomas Stanhope Flournoy. He organized Company E (Pittsylvania Dragoons), 6th Virginia Cavalry in May 1861. He was elected captain of same, was promoted to major of the 6th Virginia in July 1862, and functioned as its colonel at the time of death. Krick, *Lee's Colonels*, 142; Wallace, *Guide*, 47.

13. On 31 May the Confederate cavalry was driven back after initial success in holding Grant's advancing forces. Their stand, however, bought time for Confederate engineers to build breastworks in the rear. Infantry reinforcements from Breckinridge's Division arrived to solidify the line.

14. The following incidents involving Breathed and his horse artillery, as well as those involving Echols Brigade, occurred on 2 June 1864 when Breckinridge's Division occupied Turkey Hill on the right flank of the Confederate line.

15. McClellan's Bridge was more commonly called Grapevine Bridge. Major James Breathed's Confederate horse artillery units near Turkey Hill were Johnston's Battery and Moorman's section of Shoemaker's Battery. Trout, *Galloping Thunder*, 490.

16. The assault described here occurred at about 4:30 a.m. on 3 June 1864 when elements of the Federal II Corps broke through the Confederate line after several attacks. A Southern counterattack drove the Federals back, and the fighting was over by 5:30 a.m. *O.R.*, ser. 1, vol. 51, pt. 2, p. 437; William C. Davis, *Breckinridge* (Baton Rouge: Louisiana State University Press, 1974), 437.

17. Dates have been moved forward one day in each bracketed note. Hubard was off by one day in his memoirs when compared to other brigade evidence. Driver, *First Virginia Cavalry*, 88.

18. General William Jones was killed at the Battle of Piedmont on 5 June 1864. General John McCausland led a Confederate cavalry brigade of western Virginians

who harassed Federal columns in the Shenandoah Valley from 1 June until the Federal withdrawal from Lynchburg on 18–19 June 1864. *O.R.,* ser. 1, vol. 37, pt. 1, p. 160; Richard R. Duncan, *Lee's Endangered Left* (Baton Rouge: Louisiana State University Press, 1998), 205, 297–98.

19. A recent work on the Trevilian Station fight shows that Sheridan probably mounted 9,600 troopers and artillerists. Wade Hampton's force numbered about 6,400. Eric J. Wittenberg, *Glory Enough for All : Sheridan's Second Raid, the Battle of Trevilian Station* (Washington, D.C.: Brassey's Inc., 2001), 25, 44.

20. Mellborne Arvin enlisted in Company K on 24 June 1861 as a private. He was captured in the Shenandoah Valley near Nineveh, Virginia, on 12 November 1864. Arvin was exchanged on 10 February 1865. CSR, 3rd Va. Cav.

21. John Blanton Phillips was twenty-four years old when he enlisted in the Cumberland Troop on 14 May 1861. He served in the regiment's campaigns through the loss of a horse at Tom's Brook of 9 October 1864. No further records are in his file. CSR, 3rd Va. Cav.

22. John Edward Young enlisted in the Dinwiddie Company on 29 May 1861. According to his enlistment papers, he was a thirty-six-year-old farmer, five feet ten inches in height, with blue eyes, light hair, and a light complexion. Young's file contains a September 1862 discharge form on account of his age, but he evidently stayed in the cavalry and was promoted to corporal on 1 September 1863. He was wounded at Trevilian Station on 12 June 1864 and lost an arm as a result. CSR, 3rd Va. Cav. James H. Ware enlisted at Charles City Court House on 9 May 1861 as a private. He served through the war until he lost his right hand caused by a wound received at Trevilian Station on 12 June 1864. Ware was detailed from the hospital in Richmond to work on his father's farm in Charles City County. He was paroled in Richmond on 26 April 1865. CSR, 3rd Va. Cav.

23. Hubard's opinion of the importance of Lynchburg was not without foundation. Lynchburg was a transportation and communication hub with six turnpikes, three railroads lines, and a major canal connecting residents and merchants to eastern and western Virginia. As such, its loss as a supply depot, hospital complex, foundry, manufactory and textile center, and connector to the western theater of military operations could well have shortened the war by many months. Duncan, *Lee's Endangered Left,* 258–60.

24. The attack on the Federal right took place on 2 June at Bethesda Church. General Jubal Early sent three Confederate divisions against Burnside's IX Corps and portions of General Warren's V Corps. *O.R.,* ser. 1, vol. 36, pt. 3, pp. 491–92; see also Gordon C. Rhea, *Cold Harbor: Grant and Lee, May 26–June 3, 1864* (Baton Rouge: Louisiana State University Press, 2002), 296–306. Wyatt's Battery suffered not in the Bethesda Church fight but from an ill-advised maneuver at daybreak on 3 June. They were directed with another battery to take position on the flank of Cooke's (infantry) Brigade but were decimated by Federal skirmish fire when they completed the move. William T. Poague, *Gunner with Stonewall* (Jackson, Tenn.: McCowat-Mercer Press, 1957), 96–98.

25. Grant's Cold Harbor assault took place on 3 June when he lost approximately six thousand men killed, wounded, and captured. The Cold Harbor campaign (26 May–15 June) cost the Federal forces approximately eleven thousand casualties. Confederate casualties are estimated to have been less than fifteen hundred on 3 June and six thousand for the entire campaign. Rhea, *Cold Harbor*, 382.

26. The Federal forces that failed to take Petersburg were not Burnside's but rather the XVIII Army Corps under General W. F. "Baldy" Smith.

27. With General Stuart's death in May, command of the cavalry passed to the three division commanders, Generals Wade Hampton, Fitz Lee, and W. H. F. "Rooney" Lee. General R. E. Lee directed that the three divisions would constitute separate commands and take orders from army headquarters. Hampton was senior to the Lees in date of brigadier rank as well as on the promotion list for major generals, however. In combined cavalry operations, then, Hampton led the corps, with Fitz Lee second in command. Manly Wade Wellman, *Giant in Gray* (New York: Charles Scribner's Sons, 1949), 140.

28. Major Henry Carrington, Jr., assumed command of the regiment on the fall of Lieutenant Colonel W. R. Carter at Trevilian Station. Nanzig, *3rd Virginia Cavalry*, 54.

29. The Nance's Shop, or Samaria Church, fight was not nearly as one-sided as Hubard describes it. The Federal troopers and artillerists of Gregg's Division were unsupported and outnumbered but showed plenty of fight. They repulsed several determined Confederate charges before being driven toward Charles City Court House late in the evening of 24 June. The Federal casualties tallied 357 killed, wounded, or captured. Confederate killed and wounded totaled about two hundred. Wittenberg, *Glory Enough for All*, 284–85; Hampton's report: *O.R.*, ser. 1, vol. 36, pt. 1, pp. 1096–98; Gregg's report: *O.R.*, ser. 1, vol. 36, pt. 1, pp. 855–856.

30. It is possible that Hubard, not being intimately familiar with this region of Virginia, mistook the waterways across which the 3rd Virginia Cavalry pursued Wilson's raiders. Stony Creek was some miles farther south from the initial point of contact with Wilson's force, so this first stream may have been a branch of Rowanty Creek.

31. The word *pandemonium* was coined by John Milton in *Paradise Lost* (1667), from Greek elements *pan*, "all," and *daímon*, "demon." In Milton the word referred to the capitol of Hell.

32. This action probably took place at Stony Creek on the evening of 29 June where a single bridge over the watercourse created a traffic jam of mounted and dismounted Federal cavalry, artillery, and more than one thousand runaway slaves. Although another source cites the bottleneck to have taken place at the Nottoway River double-bridges crossing, General James H. Wilson is quite clear in his campaign report that the single bridge at Stony Creek was the location of the incident. *O.R.*, ser. 1, vol. 40, pt. 1, p. 629; Starr, *Union Cavalry*, 2:202; G. G. Benedict, *Vermont in the Civil War* (Burlington, Vt.: Free Press Association, 1886–1888), 2:654.

33. Captain Benjamin L. Farinholt, 53rd Virginia Infantry, was the officer credited with organizing the defense of the Staunton River bridge on 24 June 1864.

12. "WE'RE OFF FOR THE VALLEY"

1. Another 3rd Virginian noted: "The dust is everywhere from six inches to knee deep and the slightest breeze blows it about in clouds reminding one of the descriptions given by travelers of a storm upon the desert of Sahara. . . . Not a drop of rain for six weeks and vegetation dying rapidly. Corson, *My Dear Jennie,* 119–20.

2. Hubard is probably describing scabies, a fairly common infectious disease of the skin caused by a mite. Scabies mites burrow into the skin, producing pimplelike irritations or burrows.

3. The picket force, armed with Spencer repeating rifles, was from the 6th Michigan Cavalry, Major Harvey H. Vinton commanding. Kidd, *Personal Recollections,* 375; Donald F. Kigar, *Small Arms Used by Michigan Troops in the Civil War* (Lansing, Mich.: Michigan Civil War Centennial Observance Commission, 1966), 58–59.

4. Breathed's guns, Johnston's Battery, were under the immediate command of Captain Philip P. Johnston. Captain Dunbar R. Ransom commanded the Federal horse battery, Company C, 3rd U.S. Artillery. Trout, *Galloping Thunder,* 580–81; Edward G. Longacre, *Custer and His Wolverines: The Michigan Cavalry Brigade, 1861– 1865* (Conshohocken, Pa.: Combined Publishing, 1997), 243.

5. George A. Custer did, indeed, lose a lock of hair from a near shot during the fighting at Guard Hill. Kidd, *Personal Recollections,* 377.

6. The 3rd Virginia Cavalry was charged by the 5th and 6th Michigan cavalry regiments as well as by the 4th and 6th New York regiments from Devin's Cavalry Brigade. Kidd, *Personal Recollections,* 376; *O.R.,* ser. 1, vol. 43, pt. 1, pp. 472–73.

7. Federal participants in the battle also noted Custer's demeanor in battle, riding calmly along his line "to encourage the men." Jeffry D. Wert, *Custer* (New York: Simon and Schuster, 1996), 173.

8. James A. Baker enlisted in the Prince Edward Dragoons on 24 June 1861. He received a promotion to corporal in July 1863 and was wounded twice in 1864, the first time at Spotsylvania Court House (8 May) and the second time at Front Royal (16 August). He was paroled on 23 April 1865. CSR, 3rd Va. Cav.

9. At the Guard Hill battle, Custer was not yet a division leader but commanded the Michigan Cavalry Brigade. Torbert was his division commander.

10. Thomas H. Hall enlisted as a private in the Black Walnut Dragoons on 20 May 1861. The twenty-five-year-old farmer was six feet tall and had gray eyes, dark hair, and a ruddy complexion. Hall was detailed as a courier to Colonel Robert Johnston from September 1861 through March 1862. Promoted to lieutenant 18 April 1863, Hall was wounded at Aldie on 17 June 1863. He was captured at Front Royal in 16 August 1864 and was a prisoner of war at Fort Delaware from 27 August 1864 until he was paroled at that prison on 5 June 1865. Hall was not released from Fort Delaware until

4 July 1865. He returned to Halifax County, Virginia, and died in January 1902 at Black Walnut. CSR, 3rd Va. Cav. In addition to the losses noted by Hubard, the 3rd Virginia Cavalry also lost its regimental colors to two 4th New York Cavalry troopers, Frank Leslie and Henry J. Mandy, each of whom received a Medal of Honor for the exploit. That flag now rests in the collection of the Museum of the Confederacy in Richmond, Virginia. U.S. Senate, Subcommittee on Veterans' Affairs of the Committee on Labor and Public Welfare, *Medal of Honor Recipients: 1863–1963* (Washington, D.C.: Government Printing Office, 1964), 496, 503.

11. These were but the first burnings committed by Sheridan's troops as they sought to destroy everything of use to Confederate forces in Virginia. The most notorious incidents of the burning of the Shenandoah Valley occurred in September and October 1864, after Federal victories at Winchester and Fisher's Hill left the lower valley in Sheridan's control.

12. The 1860 census in Buckingham County, Virginia, lists a boardinghouse resident as Joseph K. Irving, Virginian, twenty-three, law student. U.S. Bureau of the Census, *United States Census, 1860, Buckingham County, Virginia*, schedule 1, page 68 (Washington, D.C.: Government Printing Office, 1864).

13. "TATTERED FLAGS SPORTING IN THE BREEZE"

1. Shoemaker's and Johnston's batteries supported Munford's Brigade during the early part of the Winchester fight. Trout, *Galloping Thunder*, 591.

2. Fitz Lee's favored mount since First Manassas, "Nellie Gray," went down in the Winchester action with what appeared to be a broken leg. On a borrowed mount, Lee returned to the fight, only to be shot in the thigh, the bullet continuing through his saddle and killing the second mount. Nichols, *General Fitzhugh Lee*, 78.

3. Shoemaker's battery sent a section of two guns to the top of Fort Hill to support Munford's Brigade. Shoemaker reported, "My battery went to the top of Fort Hill at an angle of nearly 45 degrees—a most extraordinary feat—and one, I believe, which could not have been accomplished under less exciting circumstances." The 3rd Virginia held horses while the 1st, 2nd, and 4th cavalry regiments dismounted and manned the fort. Trout, *Galloping Thunder*, 593.

4. It is unknown on what facts "from both sides" Hubard relied, but Sheridan's 40,000 Federal troops lost about 5,000 casualties in the Battle of the Opequon (or Third Battle of Winchester), and Early's 12,500 men lost about 1,700, with an additional 1,800 scattered, straggled, or demoralized. Jeffry D. Wert, *From Winchester to Cedar Creek* (Carlisle, Pa.: South Mountain Press, 1987), 103.

5. Alfred T. A. Torbert had been promoted to command of the Federal Cavalry Corps in August 1864. Custer, however, did not command a division but was still serving as a brigadier under Wesley Merritt.

6. According to Colonel Munford, Breathed was fully prepared to dispute a Federal advance: "If Billy (Colonel Payne) can hold that bridge—and it looks like he is going to do it—I'll put a pile of canister near my guns and all h——l will never move me from this position." Trout, *Galloping Thunder*, 595.

7. The "adjutant general having lost a leg" may be a reference to William H. H. Emmons, General Wesley Merritt's assistant adjutant-general. According to Merritt's campaign report, Emmons was "dangerously wounded during the day by one of the enemy's sharpshooters." *O.R.*, ser. 1, vol. 43, pt. 1, p. 441.

8. Three days after their defeat at Winchester, Early's retreating Confederate army was completely routed again by Sheridan's force at the Battle of Fisher's Hill on 22 September 1864. Only nightfall saved Early's troops from total destruction. Faust, *Historical Times Illustrated*, 260–61.

9. According to General Merritt's report of 24 September, "Wickham's cavalry was met near Luray and routed by the First and Reserve Brigades, with a loss of nearly 100 prisoners and one battle-flag belonging to the Sixth Virginia Cavalry [of Lomax's Brigade]." *O.R.*, ser. 1, vol. 43, pt. 1, p. 441.

10. Merritt and Devin reported of this 26 September morning action, "The Second Brigade [Devin's] in the advance, [drove] the enemy's cavalry before it across Middle River into Brown's Gap, where the enemy's army was found in force. . . . The artillery of the division [Lieutenant Frank Taylor's 1st U. S. batteries K and L] was placed in an advantageous position and shelled Kershaw's trains with great effect. An attack was ordered on the train at the same time but it was found that they were too strongly guarded to be taken, and the attack had no other effect than to scare the enemy mightily." Artillery fire and skirmishing continued through the afternoon, after which Merritt withdrew his force toward Weyer's Cave. *O.R.*, ser. 1, vol. 43, pt. 1, pp. 441–42, 447.

11. According to one source, "General Wickham arrived and ordered the guns to commence firing. This alerted the enemy to the Confederate presence and in the subsequent fighting, Powell [the Federal commander] was able to retreat with little damage." Trout, *Galloping Thunder*, 600.

12. Gildersleeve, professor of Greek at the University of Virginia, was delivering orders to the front when gunfire shattered his leg. Gildersleeve's own comment on this incident summed it up: "I lost my pocket Homer, I lost my pistol, I lost one of my horses and, finally, I came very near losing my life." Gildersleeve survived, returned to teaching, retired in 1915 after a professorial career spanning nearly sixty years, and passed away quietly on 9 January 1924. James Stimpert, "Hopkins History: First Greek Prof, Basil Gildersleeve," *Gazette Online*, September 18, 2000, http://www.jhu.edu/~gazette/2000/sep1800/.

13. The Federal troops at Waynesboro on 28–29 September were under General Torbert's immediate command and included Wilson's 3rd Division accompanied by Lowell's Reserve Brigade of the 1st Division. Several of the Confederate casualties were inflicted during an unsupported charge by one Federal officer as the Confederates entered Waynesboro. Captain George N. Bliss, 1st Rhode Island Cavalry, who was awarded the Medal of Honor for his actions, wounded at least four 4th Virginia troopers with his sabre before being wounded, unhorsed, and captured. *O.R.*, ser. 1, vol. 43, pt. 1, p. 519; Stiles, *4th Virginia Cavalry*, 68.

14. The *Official Records* and the regimental history of the 4th Virginia Cavalry

have the skirmish dated on 2 October with "Wooldridge's 4th and the 3rd formed on the road as the 1st and 2nd Cavalry covered the flanks. Crossing the river and charging through the town, Wickham's Brigade rushed into the unwary Federal camp driving the Federal soldiers down the road with little trouble." *O.R.,* ser. 1, vol. 43, pt. 1, p. 612; Stiles, *4th Virginia Cavalry,* 68.

15. Hubard went to the Charlottesville Confederate hospital for immediate attention and was then allowed to recover at Chellowe until returning to duty in November. Thomas, "Plantations in Transition," 145.

16. The rout of Confederate cavalry at Tom's Brook on 9 October 1864 resulted in the loss of more supplies than men: forty-two wagons, three ambulances, five artillery pieces, four caissons, five forges, sixty-eight horses and mules, fifty-two prisoners, and one Confederate battalion flag for which a Medal of Honor was awarded. *O.R.,* ser. 1, vol. 43, pt. 1, pp. 446–48, 550.

17. Rosser's arrival allowed General Williams C. Wickham to depart the army to claim a seat in the Confederate Congress. As the new commander of the cavalry division, Rosser was hardly welcomed by all of his subordinates. Colonel Thomas T. Munford, who had assumed Fitz Lee's old brigade command on Wickham's departure, held Rosser in particularly low esteem. He believed that he had been snubbed in past promotions by J. E. B. Stuart in favor of Rosser and that Rosser lacked certain qualities essential to a commander. Anne Trice Thompson Akers, "Colonel Thomas T. Munford and the Last Cavalry Operations of the Civil War in Virginia" (master's thesis, Virginia Polytechnic and State University, 1981), 25.

18. Although General Jubal Early's infantry was chased from the Cedar Creek battlefield by Sheridan's army, Rosser's Cavalry Division routed an infantry and cavalry camp on the Federal right flank, covered the retreat, and repulsed several tentative Federal thrusts in the wake of the Confederate disaster. Corson, *My Dear Jennie,* 131–32; Thomas L. Rosser, *Riding with Rosser,* edited by S. Roger Keller (Shippensburg, Pa.: Burd Street Press, 1997), 51.

19. The action described in this passage actually took place on 22 November, not 18 November as Hubard remembered it.

20. Earlier, from 26 November until 2 December, Rosser had made a raid to Moorefield and New Creek, West Virginia. He brought back seven hundred to eight hundred prisoners and a large herd of sheep, cattle, and horses. The 7 December raid into Hardy and Pendleton counties was led by Colonel Munford and succeeded only in gathering a modest supply of forage. *O.R.,* ser. 1. vol. 43, pt. 1, pp. 669–70; Millard K. Bushong and Dean M. Bushong, *Fightin' Tom Rosser, C.S.A.* (Shippensburg, Pa.: Beidel Printing House, 1983), 151–54.

21. Hubard's summary of activities in the first months of 1865 neglected to note an acrimonious dispute between his brigadier, Thomas T. Munford, and the division commander, Thomas L. Rosser. Ill will that had surfaced after the Tom's Brook debacle intensified in January 1865 when Rosser called for volunteers to accompany him on yet another raid into West Virginia. According to Munford, "I told him that my men, as he knew, had lost everything, but that my quartermaster was expected

from Richmond the next day . . . and I could shoe up my horses [and] I would be glad to second him in his wishes." Rosser had no time for Munford, and when Munford's subordinates could not get volunteers for the mission, Rosser had Munford placed under arrest. The subsequent court-martial acquitted Munford of all charges and chastised Rosser for bringing them in the first place. Akers, "Colonel Thomas T. Munford," 27–28.

CORRESPONDENCE, 1864

1. To review, after severe fights at Spotsylvania Court House (8 May), Jerrel's Mill and Mitchell's Shop (9 May), Yellow Tavern (11 May), and Meadow Bridge (12 May), the Confederate Cavalry Corps withdrew to rest and refit. The Federal cavalry column under Sheridan took itself out of the campaign by retreating to Yorktown on the Virginia Peninsula.

2. Dr. Lewis Carter Randolph, Isaetta Randolph Hubard's younger brother by two years, attended Virginia Military Institute and the University of Virginia and was surgeon of the 9th Virginia Cavalry. He married Louisa Hubard, Robert, Jr.'s, only sister, at Chellowe in 1867. Hubard, *Hubards*, 40; Robert K. Krick, *9th Virginia Cavalry* (Lynchburg, Va.: H. E. Howard, Inc., 1982), 94.

3. On 16 May 1864, General P. G. T. Beauregard, with twenty thousand Confederate troops, attacked two Federal corps of thirty-nine thousand men at Drewry's Bluff, north of Petersburg. The Federals were under the overall command of General Benjamin F. Butler and were driven back, losing hundreds of prisoners, including General Charles Heckman and many of his brigade. Faust, *Historical Times Illustrated*, 227–28.

4. General Leonidas Polk never moved any of his troops from Georgia to Virginia. Hubard may have mistaken Polk's name for that of General Robert F. Hoke, whose division had arrived in Petersburg from North Carolina on 10 May 1864. General John C. Breckinridge was able to concentrate scattered Confederate forces to meet Federal general Franz Sigel's army near New Market. Breckinridge defeated Sigel on 15 May 1864.

5. Hubard was making reference to his 29 June Reams' Station booty, a set of photographs from a Federal cavalry officer's baggage. He also claimed an overcoat and cape.

6. Ursula and "aunt" Sarah were Hubard family slaves. Ursula Jones, as she was known after the war, was a house servant who held the special affection and trust of the Hubard family. Aunt Sarah was evidently a member of Edmund W. Hubard's Saratoga household staff. Thomas, "Plantations in Transition," 389, 401.

14. "A SPECTACLE OF MONSTROUS ABSURDITY!"

1. The Confederate Congress did allow blacks to enlist in February 1865, two months before the Southern surrender.

2. According to a 27 February 1865 report from Colonel Thomas T. Munford commanding the brigade:

I beg leave to respectfully report that the bad condition of this brigade arises from two causes:

1st We have been actively engaged since the 4th of May, 1864, have been marching and countermarching, [have been subjected] to stormy and rough weather, and the inadequate amount of forage for the horses has depleted their strength, that until now no opportunity has been afforded to reorganize and the heavy loss in officers, sick and wounded in battle, and by sickness from exposure is the prime cause.

2nd We have been compelled to send the sick and wounded "back to the rear" and the surgeon has scattered the men to the four winds. I respectfully suggest that an imperative [erased] order be issued making it "imperative" upon the Brigade Surgeon to send the men to some specified hospital, that he be required to record at Brigade Hd. Quarters the name, time, and cause of the absence of each man sent off and that an ambulance corps of light-duty men be formed from the brigade to act as guards who will in all cases bring back receipts for men taken off by them. Men sent off to hospital in their own counties rarely ever report and when once off are beyond the control of the Colonel.

Another great difficulty arises from the fact that we rarely ever stay long enough at any one point to carry into affect the "sentence of court martial" and the difficulty of getting and keeping regimental courts together is beyond, the scarcity of officers and demand for them in the field is so great.

The want of transportation is another serious [concern]. It is almost impossible for a wounded cavalryman to retain his arms and it is not infrequent that they are left on the field. We have no possible way of carrying them and the difficulty of stopping their pay for the loss of arms is insuperable in the fact they have been . . . so far behind [unreadable] in paying the troops and the men so constantly engaged, it frequently happens that we can have no "regular muster" at the time required by law, and the number of men who are on "horse details" at the time that their companies are paid off renders it a difficult matter to settle.

Another serious difficulty is the want of "tactics" and books, many of the new officers have never seen a work on tactics and they cannot be had, and the scanty allowance of forage will not admit the horses to be used much at drills.

Notwithstanding these manifold difficulties, I am happy to say that the spirit of the men [is good] and when the time comes to take the field, they will be as ready as ever to uphold our glorious old state flag as the emblem of her majesty and glory.

Inspection Reports and Related Records Received by the Inspection Branch in the Confederate Adjutant and Inspector General's Office, microfilm publication M935, roll 16, inspection reports group P-64-5-S-12, National Archives and Records Administration, Washington, D.C.

3. Although not covered in Hubard's memoirs, the 3rd Virginia Cavalry spent the first half of March shadowing Sheridan's Federal cavalry force as it descended the James River from their late winter bivouac near Charlottesville. Lieutenant Samuel E. Garrett, Company G, left the following account from camp near Mechanicsville: "As we had heard that Sheridan was at Charlottesville, we concluded at once that we were bound up river. . . . On Friday morning [March 10], General [Fitz] Lee ordered me to report with my Company to Major Mason of his staff, who was at Columbia watching the movements of the enemy. I left at sunrise and reached Columbia at three o'clock p.m., a distance of 38 miles. Here I found the enemy in and around Columbia. We made arrangements to give them a warm reception if they had attempted to cross the river. Eight of them had crossed a few days earlier and had frightened the citizens very much who magnified them into Sheridan's whole force. Sunday morning they began to leave and we went down to Cartersville and crossed and followed in their rear, annoying them all we could, and sending dispatches to Richmond of their progress. We succeeded in getting ahead of them and skirmished with their advance guard. But, of course, our force was too small to frighten them and we continued to fall back before them. Their intentions, no doubt, was to cross at or near Hardwicksville but the high water prevented it after the bridge of that place was burnt. It was [Fitz] Lee's intention, no doubt, to permit them to cross as he felt confident of being able to thrash them, in which event they would have been entirely destroyed. I must confess that however anxious I was to use them up, I did not wish them to cross at all. . . . Yesterday [19 March] we returned to this camp being gone nearly a fortnight. Samuel E. Garrett to Emily Frances Guerrant Garrett, 20 March 1865, Lucy and Nabil Dubraque, private collection.

4. Fitz Lee was sidelined with his Winchester wound from September 1864 until January 1865, at which time he returned to duty as senior to his two fellow cavalry division commanders, Thomas Rosser and W. H. F. "Rooney" Lee.

5. Charles C. Croxton, Company K, 4th Virginia Cavalry, had transferred from the 1st Company, Richmond Howitzers, in September 1861. He was one of sixteen troopers captured as the Federals crossed at Kelly's Ford on 17 March 1863. He spent time in Old Capitol Prison and was then exchanged and subsequently injured in the fight at Bridgewater, Virginia, on 2 October 1864. Stiles, *4th Virginia Cavalry*, 106. Garrett was buried in the family cemetery in Cumberland County. Nanzig, *3rd Virginia Cavalry*, 108. Feild was wounded on 31 March 1865 at Dinwiddie Court House and signed a parole in Richmond on 22 May 1865. He died in Richmond on 17 July 1895 and was buried at Concord Presbyterian Church in Dinwiddie County. CSR, 3rd Va. Cav.

6. The Battle of Dinwiddie Court House on 31 March was a Confederate tactical victory. Sheridan's secure position in and around Dinwiddie Court House at the

close of battle and the nocturnal arrival of the Federal V Corps to support Sheridan left the way open for a renewed Federal attack the next day, however.

7. According a postwar letter attributed to Rosser, "The day I spent on Nottoway River [on the way to Five Forks] I caught quite a lot of very fine shad by dragging a borrowed seine and, having them along with me in my ambulance, I invited Fitz Lee and Picket back to a shad bake. While we were thus enjoying a delightful meal two pickets reported the advance of the enemy on all roads I was picketing." Akers, "Colonel Thomas T. Munford," 77.

8. James L. Hubard, formerly lieutenant colonel in the 44th Virginia Infantry, was turned out by his men in the regimental elections of April 1862. It appears from family correspondence that James was next offered a position in Selma, Alabama, by his wife's uncle, George Wythe Randolph, the Confederate secretary of war. Hubard turned it down. In November 1862 he accepted a commission as major and quartermaster with General Beverly H. Robertson, who was training cavalry near Garysburg, North Carolina. Claiming his health was not equal to the demands of the position, James Hubard resigned his commission in January 1863. Subject to Confederate conscription laws, Hubard was assigned to military service in the 21st Virginia Infantry in October 1864, but only after applying for an exemption and appealing to his uncle Edmund for assistance. He finally paid an acquaintance $700 to exchange unit assignments, and he joined his brother Edmund in Company K, 4th Virginia Cavalry, as a private. Thomas, "Plantations in Transition," 69–72, 80–81.

9. According to Munford's recollections, "A portion of the 3rd Virginia Cavalry under Adjutant Hubard crossed a little higher up [Hatcher's Run] and joined [J. Risque] Hutter of the 11th Virginia Infantry. A moment later, the Federal General Joshua Chamberlain . . . attacked Ransom's left with great dash and spirit, brilliantly captured Hutter and the entire 11th regiment, but Hubard and his men managed to escape." Akers, "Colonel Thomas T. Munford," 67.

10. There is neither a trooper named Brown in Company A, nor does any Sergeant Brown appear on the 3rd Virginia Cavalry regimental roll.

11. Pickett's infantry division numbered about five thousand men at the beginning of the campaign, reinforced by about thirty-six hundred cavalry under Fitz Lee. Sheridan's mounted force numbered about nine thousand troopers, and Warren's V Corps added approximately twelve thousand infantry troops. Federal losses were about eleven hundred. Casualties among the Confederates in two days of fighting were about one thousand killed or wounded and forty-five hundred captured; also, six guns were lost, and thirteen colors were taken. Among the colors lost was the regimental flag of the 3rd Virginia Cavalry, which was taken by Private Charles N. Gardner, 32nd Massachusetts Infantry. Edwin C. Bearss and Christopher M. Calkins, *The Battle of Five Forks* (Lynchburg, Va.: H. E. Howard, Inc., 1985), 10, 14, 46, 89, 113; Museum of the Confederacy, *Report on 3rd Virginia Cavalry Flags* (Richmond, Va.: Museum of the Confederacy, 2004).

12. According to the 1860 Census, A. Bruce was a fifty-five-year-old Scotsman by

birth and a tobacconist by trade. Dr. James Lyle was listed in the same census as a sixty-year-old physician married to Ann, age fifty, and parent of two children, Annie C., age fourteen, and James A., age nine. The surgeon referred to in the passage may have been called from the Confederate military hospital in Farmville, a facility with twelve hundred beds intended for chronic cases and convalescent patients. U.S. Bureau of the Census, *United States Census, 1860, Prince Edward County, Virginia*, Schedule 1 (Washington, D.C.: Government Printing Office, 1864), 35, 38; Christopher M. Calkins, *The Appomattox Campaign* (Conshohocken, Pa.: Combined Books, 1997), 123.

13. Henry B. Nicholas enlisted in the Cumberland Troop at White House plantation, New Kent County, on 17 July 1862. He suffered a gunshot wound to the left arm at Cold Harbor on 1 June 1864, was hospitalized, and left no further military records. CSR, 3rd Va. Cav.

FINIS

1. Unlike the Appomattox Court House parolees who were allowed to go directly home, thousands of Confederates who were captured along the retreat route prior to General R. E. Lee's surrender on 9 April 1865 were subject to temporary imprisonment in the North. The prison camp at Point Lookout, Maryland, held nineteen thousand of the approximately sixty-four thousand prisoners of war held in twenty-two northern locations. In the wake of the Lincoln assassination, prisoners were held even longer as parole lists were prepared and sent to Secretary of War Edwin M. Stanton for review and approval. After the oath of allegiance was administered, prisoners were released in a variety of priorities: by alphabetical order, by time of imprisonment, and, at one facility, in reverse order of how the respective prisoners' states seceded from the Union, South Carolinians waiting until all others had departed. Lonnie R. Speer, *Portals to Hell: Military Prisons in the Civil War* (Mechanicsburg, Pa.: Stackpole Books, 1997), 288–89.

POSTWAR CORRESPONDENCE

1. George Jefferson Hundley was a Confederate veteran, having served in the 19th Virginia Infantry and the 5th Virginia Cavalry. In 1910 Hundley was a judge in the 5th Judicial District of Virginia. Charles Edward Burrell, *History of Prince Edward County, Virginia, from Its Formation in 1753 to the Present* (Richmond, Va.: Williams Printing Co., 1922), 360.

AFTERWORD

1. Burrell, *History of Prince Edward County, Virginia*, 390.

2. Burdick, "From Virtue to Fitness," 29–30.

3. "Sketch of the Life of Robert T. Hubard, Jr.," Hubard Papers, Box 21, No. 8039, University of Virginia Special Collections, Charlottesville.

4. Burdick, "From Virtue to Fitness," 32.

5. Ibid., 30.

6. William Shepherd, "Robert Thruston Hubard," *Today and Yesterday in the Heart of Virginia, Farmville (Va.) Herald,* reprint, March 29, 1935, 385.

7. Obituary of Colonel Robert Thruston Hubard, *Farmville (Va.) Herald,* 30 September 1921, 1.

APPENDIX A

1. Mills Lane, ed., *"Dear Mother: Don't Grieve about Me. If I Get Killed, I'll Only Be Dead." Letters from Georgia Soldiers in the Civil War* (Savannah, Ga.: Beehive Press, 1990), 86–87.

Bibliography

PUBLISHED MATERIALS

Barrett, John G. *The Civil War in North Carolina.* Chapel Hill: University of North Carolina Press, 1963.

Beale, G. W. *A Lieutenant of Cavalry in Lee's Army.* Boston: Gorham Press, 1918.

Bearss, Edwin C., and Christopher M. Calkins. *The Battle of Five Forks.* Lynchburg, Va.: H. E. Howard, 1985.

Bell, Landon C. *Sunlight on the Southside.* Philadelphia: George S. Ferguson Co., 1931.

Benedict, G. G. *Vermont in the Civil War.* 2 vols. Burlington, Vt.: Free Press Association, 1886–1888.

Bergeron, Arthur W., Jr. "John Randolph Chambliss, Jr." In *The Confederate General,* vol. 1, edited by William C. Davis. Harrisburg, Pa.: National Historical Society, 1991.

Blackford, William W. *War Years with Jeb Stuart.* New York: Charles Scribner's Sons, 1946.

Booth, George Wilson. *A Maryland Boy in Lee's Army.* Baltimore: Press of Fleet, McGinley and Co., 1898.

Burdick, John. "From Virtue to Fitness: The Accommodation of a Planter Family to Postbellum Virginia." *Virginia Magazine of History and Biography* 93, no. 1 (January 1985): 14–35.

Burrell, Charles Edward. *History of Prince Edward County, Virginia, from Its Formation in 1753 to the Present.* Richmond, Va.: Williams Printing Co., 1922.

Bushong, Millard K., and Dean M. Bushong. *Fightin' Tom Rosser, C.S.A.* Shippensburg, Pa.: Beidel Printing House, 1983.

Calkins, Christopher M. *The Appomattox Campaign.* Conshohocken, Pa.: Combined Books, 1997.

Carmichael, Peter S. "Fitzhugh Lee." In *The Confederate General,* vol. 4, edited by William C. Davis. Harrisburg, Pa.: National Historical Society, 1991.

Carter, William R. *Sabres, Saddles, and Spurs.* Edited by Walbrook D. Swank. Shippensburg, Pa.: Burd Street Press, 1998.

Casdorph, Paul D. *Prince John Magruder: His Life and Campaigns.* New York: John Wiley and Sons, 1996.

Coddington, Edward B. *The Gettysburg Campaign.* New York: Charles Scribner's Sons, 1968.

Corson, William Clark. *My Dear Jennie.* Edited by Blake W. Corson, Jr. Richmond, Va.: Dietz Press, 1982.

Dabney, Robert L. *A Memorial of Lieut. Colonel John C. Thornton, of the Third Virginia Cavalry, C.S.A.* Richmond, Va.: Presbyterian Committee of Publication, 1864.

Daly, R. W. *How the Merrimac Won.* New York: Thomas Y. Crowell Co., 1957.

Davis, George B. *The Official Military Atlas of the Civil War.* New York: Arno Press, 1978.

Davis, William C. *Breckinridge.* Baton Rouge: Louisiana State University Press, 1974.

———. *Duel between the First Ironclads.* Garden City, N.Y.: Doubleday, 1975.

———. *First Blood: Fort Sumter to Bull Run.* Alexandria, Va.: Time-Life Books, 1983.

———. "James Monroe Goggin." In *The Confederate General,* vol. 2, edited by William C. Davis. Harrisburg, Pa.: National Historical Society, 1991.

———, ed. *The Confederate General.* 6 vols. Harrisburg, Pa.: National Historical Society, 1991.

Driver, Robert J. *First Virginia Cavalry.* Lynchburg, Va.: H. E. Howard, Inc., 1991.

Driver, Robert J., and H. E. Howard. *Second Virginia Cavalry.* Lynchburg, Va.: H. E. Howard, Inc., 1995.

Duncan, Richard R. *Lee's Endangered Left.* Baton Rouge: Louisiana State University Press, 1998.

Farmville (Va.) Herald, 30 September 1921.

Farrar, Emmie Ferguson. *Old Virginia Houses.* New York: Bonanza Books, 1957.

Faust, Patricia L., ed. *Historical Times Illustrated Encyclopedia of the Civil War.* New York: Harper and Row, 1986.

Favill, Josiah Marshall. *The Diary of a Young Officer.* Chicago: R. R. Donnelley and Sons, 1909.

Freeman, Douglas S. *R. E. Lee: A Biography.* 3 vols. New York: Charles Scribner's Sons, 1935.

———. *The South to Posterity.* New York: Charles Scribner's Sons, 1939.

———. *Lee's Lieutenants: A Study in Command.* 3 vols. New York: Charles Scribner's Sons, 1942.

Garnett, Theodore Stanford. *Riding with Stuart: Reminiscences of an Aide-de-Camp.* Edited by Robert J. Trout. Shippensburg, Pa.: White Mane Publishing, 1994.

Gilbert, Frederick. *The Story of a Regiment.* N.p., 1895.

Gill, John. *Courier for Lee and Jackson: Memoirs, 1861–1865.* Edited by W. D. Swank. Shippensburg, Pa.: Burd Street Press, 1993.

Glatthaar, Joseph T. *Forged in Battle: The Civil War Alliance of Black Soldiers and White Officers.* New York: Free Press, 1990.

Glazier, Willard W. *Three Years in the Federal Cavalry.* New York: R. H. Ferguson and Co., 1874.

Gordon, Armistead C. *Memories and Memorials of William Gordon McCabe.* Richmond, Va.: Old Dominion Press, 1925.

Grant, Ulysses S. *Personal Memoirs of U.S. Grant.* 2 vols. New York: Charles L. Webster and Co., 1885.

Greene, A. Wilson. "*Stoneman's Raid,*" *Chancellorsville: The Battle and Its Aftermath.* Edited by Gary W. Gallagher. Chapel Hill: University of North Carolina Press, 1996.

Haskell, John Cheves. *The Haskell Memoirs.* Edited by G. E. Govan and J. W. Livingood. New York: G. P. Putnam's Sons, 1960.

Hastings, Earl C., Jr., and David Hastings. *A Pitiless Rain: The Battle of Williamsburg.* Shippensburg, Pa.: White Mane Publishing Co., 1997.

Hennessy, John J. *Return to Bull Run.* New York: Simon and Schuster, 1993.

Hewitt, Lawrence L. "John Buchanan Floyd." In *The Confederate General,* vol. 2, edited by William C. Davis. Harrisburg, Pa.: National Historical Society, 1991.

Hood, John B. *Advance and Retreat.* New Orleans: Hood Orphan Memorial Fund, 1880.

Hotchkiss, Jedediah. *Virginia.* Vol. 3, pt. 2, *Confederate Military History.* Edited by Clement Anselm Evans. Atlanta: Confederate Publishing Co., 1899.

Howard, Wiley C. *Sketch of Cobb Legion Cavalry and Some Incidents and Scenes Remembered.* Atlanta, Ga., 1901.

Hubard, William Stebbins. *Hubards of North America.* Roanoke, Va.: William Stebbins Hubard, 1998.

Hudgins, Robert S., II. *Recollections of an Old Dominion Dragoon.* Edited by Garland C. Hudgins and Richard B. Kleese. Orange, Va.: Publisher's Press, 1993.

Jones, Virgil Carrington. *Eight Hours before Richmond.* New York: Henry Holt and Co., 1957.

Kennedy, Frances H., ed. *The Civil War Battlefield Guide.* 2nd ed. Boston: Houghton Mifflin Co., 1998.

Kidd, James H. *Personal Recollections of a Cavalryman.* Ionia, Mich.: Sentinel Print Co., 1908.

Kigar, Donald F. *Small Arms Used by Michigan Troops in the Civil War.* Lansing, Mich.: Michigan Civil War Centennial Observance Commission, 1966.

Krick, Robert K. *9th Virginia Cavalry.* Lynchburg, Va.: H. E. Howard, Inc., 1982.

———. "John Bankhead Magruder." In *The Confederate General,* vol. 4, edited by William C. Davis. Harrisburg, Pa.: National Historical Society, 1991.

———. *Lee's Colonels.* Dayton, Ohio: Morningside House, 1992.

Lamb, John. *Malvern Hill (July 1st, 1862): An Address Delivered before Picket* [sic] *Camp Confederate Veterans, Richmond, on March 8, 1897.* Richmond, Va.: James E. Goode Printing Co., 1897.

———. "The Confederate Cavalry, Its Wants, Trials, and Heroism: An Address." *Southern Historical Society Papers* 26 (1898): 359–65.

———. "The Battle of Fredericksburg: Details of the Mighty Conflict." *Southern Historical Society Papers* 27 (1899): 231–40.

———. "The Character and Services of the Confederate Soldier." *Southern Historical Society Papers* 40 (1915): 230–39.

Lane, Mills, ed. *"Dear Mother: Don't Grieve about Me. If I Get Killed, I'll Only Be Dead." Letters from Georgia Soldiers in the Civil War.* Savannah, Ga.: Beehive Press, 1990.

Lee, Robert E., Jr. *Recollections and Letters of General Lee.* Garden City, N.Y.: Garden City Publishing, 1924.

Long, E. B. *The Civil War Day by Day: An Almanac, 1861–1865.* Garden City, N.Y.: Doubleday and Co., 1971.

Longacre, Edward G. *General John Buford.* Conshohocken, Pa.: Combined Books, 1995.

———. *Custer and His Wolverines: The Michigan Cavalry Brigade, 1861–1865.* Conshohocken, Pa.: Combined Publishing, 1997.

———. *Lee's Cavalrymen.* Mechanicsburg, Pa.: Stackpole Books, 2002.

———. *Fitz Lee.* Cambridge, Mass.: Da Capo Press, 2005.

Mahon, Michael G. *The Shenandoah Valley: 1861–1865.* Mechanicsburg, Pa.: Stackpole Books, 1999.

Martin, Samuel J. *Kill-Cavalry.* Mechanicsburg, Pa.: Stackpole Books, 2000.

McClellan, Henry B. *The Life and Campaigns of Major-General J. E. B. Stuart.* Boston: Houghton Mifflin, 1885.

Museum of the Confederacy. *Report on 3rd Virginia Cavalry Flags.* Richmond, Va.: Museum of the Confederacy, 2004.

Nanzig, Thomas P. *3rd Virginia Cavalry.* Lynchburg, Va.: H. E. Howard, Inc., 1989.

Nevins, Allan. *The War for the Union: The Improvised War, 1861–1862.* New York: Charles Scribner's Sons, 1959.

———. *The War for the Union: War Becomes Revolution, 1821–1863.* New York: Charles Scribner's Sons, 1960.

Newton, Steven H. *Joseph E. Johnston and the Defense of Richmond.* Lawrence: University Press of Kansas, 1998.

Nichols, James L. *General Fitzhugh Lee: A Biography.* Lynchburg, Va.: H. E. Howard, Inc., 1989.

"Old Dominion Dragoons: The Muster Roll of this Hampton Organization." *Southern Historical Society Papers* 24 (1896): 187–89.

O'Neill, Robert F., Jr. *The Cavalry Battles of Aldie, Middleburg, and Upperville.* Lynchburg, Va.: H. E. Howard, Inc., 1993.

Pfanz, Donald C. *Richard S. Ewell: A Soldier's Life.* Chapel Hill: University of North Carolina Press, 1998.

Poague, William T. *Gunner with Stonewall.* Jackson, Tenn.: McCowat-Mercer Press, 1957.

Rhea, Gordon C. *The Battles for Spotsylvania Court House and the Road to Yellow Tavern, May 7–12, 1864.* Baton Rouge: Louisiana State University Press, 1997.

———. *Cold Harbor: Grant and Lee, May 26–June 3, 1864.* Baton Rouge: Louisiana State University Press, 2002.

Robertson, James I., Jr. *Stonewall Jackson.* New York: Macmillan, 1997.

Rosser, Thomas L. *Riding with Rosser.* Edited by S. Roger Keller. Shippensburg, Pa.: Burd Street Press, 1997.

Schildt, John W. *Roads from Gettysburg.* Shippensburg, Pa.: Burd Street Press, 1998.

Schultz, Duane. *The Dahlgren Affair.* New York: W. W. Norton, 1998.

Sears, Stephen W. *Landscape Turned Red: The Battle of Antietam.* New Haven, Conn.: Ticknor and Fields, 1983.

———. *To the Gates of Richmond: The Peninsula Campaign.* New York: Ticknor and Fields, 1992.

———. *Chancellorsville.* Boston: Houghton Mifflin, 1996.

Shepherd, William. "Robert Thruston Hubard." *Today and Yesterday in the Heart of Virginia, Farmville (Va.) Herald.* Reprint, March 29, 1935.

Sheridan, Philip H. *Personal Memoirs of P. H. Sheridan.* 2 vols. New York: Charles L. Webster and Co., 1888.

Sommers, Richard J. "George Thomas Anderson." In *The Confederate General,* vol. 1, edited by William C. Davis. Harrisburg, Pa.: National Historical Society, 1991.

Sorrel, G. Moxley. *Recollections of a Confederate Staff Officer.* New York: Neale Publishing Co., 1905.

Speer, Lonnie R. *Portals to Hell: Military Prisons in the Civil War.* Mechanicsburg, Pa.: Stackpole Books, 1997.

Stampp, Kenneth M. *Records of Ante-Bellum Southern Plantations from the Revolution through the Civil War.* Series J: Selections from the Southern Historical Collection. Part 10: Hubard Family Papers, 1741–1865. Frederick, Md.: University Publications of America, 1992. http://www.lexisnexis.com/academic/guides/southern_hist/plantations/plantj10.asp.

———. *Records of Ante-Bellum Southern Plantations from the Revolution through the Civil War.* Series L: Selections from the Earl Gregg Swem Library, College of William and Mary. Part 3: Skipwith Family Papers, 1760–1977. Frederick, Md.: University Publications of America, 1992. http://www.lexisnexis.com/academic/guides/southern_hist/plantations/plantl3.asp.

Starr, Stephen Z. *The Union Cavalry in the Civil War.* 3 vols. Baton Rouge: Louisiana State University Press, 1979–1985.

Stiles, Kenneth L. *4th Virginia Cavalry.* Lynchburg, Va.: H. E. Howard, Inc., 1985.

Stimpert, James. "Hopkins History: First Greek Prof, Basil Gildersleeve." *Gazette Online,* September 18, 2000. http://www.jhu.edu/~gazette/2000/sep1800/ (accessed February 2006).

Thomas, Emory M. *Bold Dragoon.* New York: Harper and Row, 1986.

———. *Robert E. Lee: A Biography.* New York: W. W. Norton, 1995.

Thomason, John W., Jr. *Jeb Stuart.* New York: Charles Scribner's Sons, 1930.

Tomkins, Edmund P. *Rockbridge County, Virginia: An Informal History.* Richmond, Va.: Whittet and Shepperson, 1952.

Trout, Robert J. *They Followed the Plume*. Mechanicsburg, Pa.: Stackpole Books, 1993.

———. *Galloping Thunder*. Mechanicsburg, Pa.: Stackpole Books, 2002.

U.S. Bureau of the Census. *United States Census, 1860, Buckingham County, Virginia*. Schedule 1, page 68. Washington, D.C.: Government Printing Office, 1864.

———. *United States Census, 1860, Prince Edward County, Virginia*. Schedule 1. Washington, D.C.: Government Printing Office, 1864.

U.S. Senate. Subcommittee on Veterans' Affairs of the Committee on Labor and Public Welfare. *Medal of Honor Recipients: 1863–1963*. Washington, D.C.: Government Printing Office, 1964.

U.S. War Department. *The War of the Rebellion: A Compilation of the Official Records of the War of the Union and Confederate Armies*. 128 volumes. Washington, D.C.: Government Printing Office, 1880–1901.

Virginia Work Projects Administration, Writers' Program. *Virginia: A Guide to the Old Dominion*. New York: Oxford University Press, 1940.

Wallace, Lee. *A Guide to Virginia Military Organizations: 1861–1865*. Lynchburg, Va.: H. E. Howard, Inc., 1986.

Ware, W. H. *The Battle of Kelley's Ford, Fought March 17, 1863*. Newport News, Va.: Warwick Print Co., 1922.

Warner, Ezra J. *Generals in Gray*. Baton Rouge: Louisiana State University Press, 1959.

Wellman, Manly Wade. *Giant in Gray*. New York: Charles Scribner's Sons, 1949.

Wert, Jeffry D. *From Winchester to Cedar Creek*. Carlisle, Pa.: South Mountain Press, 1987.

——— "James Ewell Brown Stuart." In *The Confederate General*, vol. 6, edited by William C. Davis. Harrisburg, Pa.: National Historical Society, 1991.

———. "Roger Atkinson Pryor." In *The Confederate General*, vol. 5, edited by William C. Davis. Harrisburg, Pa.: National Historical Society, 1991.

———. "Wade Hampton." In *The Confederate General*, vol. 3, edited by William C. Davis. Harrisburg, Pa.: National Historical Society, 1991.

———. *Custer*. New York: Simon and Schuster, 1996.

White, Julius. "The Surrender of Harper's Ferry." In *Battles and Leaders of the Civil War*, vol. 2, edited by Robert U. Johnson and Clarence C. Buel. New York: Century Co., 1887.

Wise, Stephen R. *Lifeline of the Confederacy*. Columbia: University of South Carolina Press, 1988.

Wittenberg, Eric J. *Glory Enough for All: Sheridan's Second Raid, the Battle of Trevilian Station*. Washington, D.C.: Brassey's, Inc., 2001.

UNPUBLISHED MATERIALS

Akers, Anne Trice Thompson. "Colonel Thomas T. Munford and the Last Cavalry Operations of the Civil War in Virginia." Master's thesis, Virginia Polytechnic and State University, 1981.

Besch, Edward, "More Information: Historical Report on the Battle of Fort Poca-
    hontas." http://www.fortpocahontas.org (accessed 2002).
"Biographical Directory of the United States Congress." http://www.bioguide.
    congress.gov (accessed 2002).
Carter, William R. Diary. Virginia State Library, Richmond.
Cook, Kenneth, Scrapbook Collection. "Stories Are Part of County's History, Heri-
    tage." News clippings. 24 vols. South Boston, Virginia, Public Library, South Bos-
    ton.
Daougherty, William T. "Reminiscences of the Late War." Unpublished manuscript,
    Hampton, Virginia, 1886. Robert West private collection, Poquoson, Virginia.
Garrett, Samuel E. Correspondence. Lucy and Nabil Dubraque private collection.
Hubard Papers. University of Virginia Special Collections. Charlottesville.
Jefferson County Museum. "Battle of Rio Hill." http://jeffctywvmuseum.org/html/
    stuart_s_horse_artillery_ flag.html (accessed February 2005).
National Archives and Record Administration. "Compiled Service Records of Con-
    federate Soldiers Who Served in Organizations from the State of Virginia, Rolls
    1–200." Record group 109 (microfilm collection no. 324A, Virginia), 1961. 3rd Vir-
    ginia Cavalry (previously 2nd Virginia Cavalry), rolls 25–37. Washington, D.C.
———. Inspection Reports and Related Records Received by the Inspection Branch
    in the Confederate Adjutant and Inspector General's Office. Microfilm publica-
    tion M935, roll 16, inspections reports group P-64-5-S-12. Washington, D.C.
Randolph-Hubard Papers. University of Virginia Special Collections. Charlottes-
    ville.
Thomas, Percial Moses. "Plantations in Transition: A Study of Four Virginia Plan-
    tations, 1860–1870." PhD diss., University of Virginia, 1979.

Index